The Second Birth of Theatre

INTERDISCIPLINARY STUDIES IN PERFORMANCE
HISTORICAL NARRATIVES. THEATER. PUBLIC LIFE

Edited by Mirosław Kocur

VOL. 8

Zu Qualitätssicherung und Peer Review der vorliegenden Publikation

Die Qualität der in dieser Reihe erscheinenden Arbeiten wird vor der Publikation durch einen externen, von der Herausgeberschaft benannten Gutachter geprüft.

Notes on the quality assurance and peer review of this publication

Prior to publication, the quality of the work published in this series is reviewed by an external referee appointed by the editorship.

Mirosław Kocur

The Second Birth of Theatre

Performances of Anglo-Saxon Monks

Translated by Grzegorz Czemiel

Bibliographic Information published by the Deutsche Nationalbibliothek
The Deutsche Nationalbibliothek lists this publication in the Deutsche Nationalbibliografie; detailed bibliographic data is available in the internet at http://dnb.d-nb.de.

Library of Congress Cataloging-in-Publication Data
Names: Kocur, Mirosław, 1955- author.
Title: The second birth of theatre : performances of Anglo-Saxon monks / Mirosław Kocur.
Description: Frankfurt am Main ; New York : Peter Lang Edition, 2017. | Series: Interdisciplinary studies in performance ; vol. 8 | Includes bibliographical references.
Identifiers: LCCN 2016054389 | ISBN 9783631679128
Subjects: LCSH: Catholic Church—England—Liturgy—History--To 1500. | Ritual—England—History—To 1500. | Liturgy and drama—History—To 1500. | Liturgical drama—England. | Performance—Religious aspects—Christianity—History—To 1500. | England—Church history—Middle Ages, 600-1500. | Monasticism and religious orders—History—Middle Ages, 600-1500.
Classification: LCC BX1973 .K63 2017 | DDC 271.00942/09021—dc23 LC record available at https://lccn.loc.gov/2016054389

Cover Image:
The Expulsion from Paradise. St Albans Psalter, p. 18. Dombibliothek Hildesheim, Hs St God. 1.
Courtesy of the Basilika of St Godehard, Hildesheim

This publication was financially supported by the University of Wrocław.

ISSN 2364-3919
ISBN 978-3-631-67912-8 (Print)
E-ISBN 978-3-653-07127-6 (E-PDF)
E-ISBN 978-3-631-70959-7 (EPUB)
E-ISBN 978-3-631-70960-3 (MOBI)
DOI 10.3726/978-3-653-07127-6

© Peter Lang GmbH
Internationaler Verlag der Wissenschaften
Frankfurt am Main 2017
All rights reserved.
Peter Lang Edition is an Imprint of Peter Lang GmbH.

Peter Lang – Frankfurt am Main · Bern · Bruxelles · New York ·
Oxford · Warszawa · Wien

All parts of this publication are protected by copyright. Any utilisation outside the strict limits of the copyright law, without the permission of the publisher, is forbidden and liable to prosecution. This applies in particular to reproductions, translations, microfilming, and storage and processing in electronic retrieval systems.

This publication has been peer reviewed.

www.peterlang.com

Table of Contents

Abbreviations 7

List of Illustrations 11

Prologue: Cædmon 13

Part one: Monk as Performer 25
  Monasticism 26
  The Rule 32
  Evangelization 36
  Mynster 40
  Regularis Concordia 43
  Everyday Performances 47
  Bodily Performances 56

Part two: Liturgical Performances 63
  Christmas 64
  Feast of the Purification of the Virgin 67
  Lent 73
  Palm Sunday 75
  Holy Thursday 79
  Good Friday 82
  Easter Eve 87
  Easter 92
  Quem Quaeritis 97
  The Second Birth of Theatre 111

5

Liturgical Performances after the 10th Century 120

Performance Art of Anglo-Saxon Monks 142

Part three: Church and Theatre 147

The Clergy 148

Mass 152

Transubstantiation 160

Ordo Representacionis Ade 166

Towards Christian Performativity 193

A personal epilogue: Performer as Monk 197

Bibliography 201

Index 219

Abbreviations

- *ASE: Anglo-Saxon England*
- Bede, *HE*: Bede, *Historia ecclesiastica gentis Anglorum*, ed. C. Plummer, 2 vols. (Oxford, 1896)
- *CCSL*: Corpus Christianorum. Series Latina (Turnhout)
- *CED*: *Councils and Ecclesiastical Documents Relating to Great Britain and Ireland*, eds. A.W. Haddan and W. Stubbs, 3 vols. (Oxford, 1869–1871)
- *CHBT*: *The Cambridge History of British Theatre*, ed. P. Thomson, 3 vols. (Cambridge, 2004)
- *CHC*: *The Cambridge History of Christianity* (Cambridge):
  - 1: *Origins to Constantine*, eds. M.M. Mitchell and F.M. Young (2006)
  - 2: *Constantine to c. 600*, eds. A. Casiday and F.W. Norris (2007)
  - 3: *Early Medieval Christianities, c. 600 – c. 1100*, eds. T.F.X. Noble, J.M.H. Smith and R.A. Baranowski (2008)
  - 4: *Christianity in Western Europe c. 1100 – c. 1500*, eds. M. Rubin and W. Simons (2009)
- *CIC*: *Corpus iuris canonici*, edition Lipsiensis secunda post Aemili Ludouici Richteri curas ad librorum manu scriptorium et editionis Romanae fidem recognouit et adnotatione critica instruxit Aemilius Friedberg, vol. 1: *Decretum Magistri Gratiani* (Leipzig, 1879)
- CNRS : Centre National de la Recherche Scientifique
- CS : Cystercian Studies Series
- *CT 3.2*: *Corpus troporum*, vol. 3: *Corpus du propre de la messe*, part 2: *Cycle de Pâques* (Acta Universitatis Stokholmiensis 25), eds. G. Björkvall, G. Ivesren and R. Jonsson (Stockholm, 1982)
- CSASE: Cambridge studies in Anglo-Saxon England
- CSEL: Corpus scriptorium ecclesiasticorum latinorum
- CUA: The Catholic University of America
- *The Digby Plays*: *The Late Medieval Religious Plays of Bodleian Mss. Digby 133 and E Museo 160* (EETS ES 238), eds. D.C. Baker, J.L. Murphy and L.B. Hall (London, 1982)
- *DNP*: *Der neue Pauly. Enzyklopädie der Antike*, eds. H. Cancik and H. Schneider, 16 vols. (Stuttgart, 1996–2003)
- *DTRB*: Ian Lancashire, *Dramatic Texts and Records of Britain. A Chronological Topography to 1558* (SEED 1) (Toronto and Buffalo, 1984)
- EDAM: Early Drama, Art and Music

- EETS OS, ES, SS: Early English Text Society, Original Series, Extra Series, Supplementary Series
- *Ep.*: *Epistolae*
- *ETJ*: *Education Theatre Journal*
- fol.: *folio*
- GCS: Die griechische christliche Schriftsteller der ersten drei Jahrhundert (Berlin)
- HBS: Henry Bradshaw Society
- *HE*: *Historia ecclesiastica*
- *HL*: *Historia Lausiaca*
- *HR*: *Historia religiosa*
- *JAC*: *Jahrbuch für Antike und Christentum*
- *JEH*: *Journal of Ecclesiastical History*
- *JTS*: *Journal of Theological Studies*
- Lipphardt: W. Lipphardt (ed.), *Lateinische Osterfeiern und Osterspiele*, 9 vols. (Berlin and New York, 1975–1990)
- *Ludus MERTD*: *"Ludus". Medieval and Early Renaissance Theatre and Drama*
- MES: *The Medieval European Stage 500–1550* (Theatre in Europe. A documentary history), ed. W. Tydeman (Cambridge, 2001)
- MGH: Monumenta Germaniae historica
- *Missale Sarum*: *Missale ad usum insignis et praeclarae Ecclesiae Sarum* (Salisbury Marian Missal), ed. F.H. Dickinson (Burntisland, 1861–1883)
- MS: Manuscript
- *OED*: Oxford English Dictionary
- *PG*: *Patrologiae Graeca*
- *PL*: *Patrologiae Latina*
- *PRIA Section C*: Proceedings of the Royal Irish Academy. Section C: Archaeology, Celtic studies, history, linguistics, literature
- r: *recto*
- RB: *The Rule of St. Benedict in English*, ed. T. Fry (Collegeville, Minnesota, 1981)
- RC: *Regularis concordia anglicae nationis monachorum santcimonialiumque / The Monastic Agreement of the Monks and Nuns of the English Nation* (Nelson's Medieval Classics), ed. T. Symons OSB (London, 1953)
- *REED*: *Records of Early English Drama* (Toronto):
  - *Devon*, ed. J. Wasson (1986)
  - *Kent: Diocese of Canterbury*, ed. J.M. Gibson, 3 vols. (2002)
  - *Somerset, including Bath*, eds. J. Stokes and R.J. Alexander, 2 vols. (1996)
  - *York*, eds. A.F. Johnston, M. Rogerson, 2 vols. (1979)
- *REEDN*: *Records of Early English Drama Newsletter*

- SEED: Studies in Early English Drama
- SPCK: Society for Promoting Christian Knowledge (Great Britain)
- v: *verso*

Unless stated otherwise, all quotations from the Bible are provided following the New Revised Standard Version (NRSV).

List of Illustrations

1. Bede, *Historia ecclesiastica* (VIII Century), one of two earliest copies of the Latin text. Old English recension of *Cædmon's Hymn* has been copied in the bottom margin of the page. St. Petersburg, National Library of Russia, MS lat.Qv.1.18, fol. 107r 19
2. The Prologue to St. Benedict's Rule (late X Century). Oxford, Corpus Christi College, MS 197, fol. 1r. © Corpus Christi College, Oxford, UK / The Bridgeman Art Library 32
3. The Presentation of Christ to Simeon. Benedictional of Æthelwold. MS Additional 49598, fol. 34v © British Library board. All Rights Reserved 2016 69
4. The Entry into Jerusalem. Benedictional of Æthelwold. MS Additional 49598, fol. 34v © British Library board. All Rights Reserved 2016 75
5. *Visitatio Sepulchri*. Benedictional of Æthelwold. MS Additional 49598, fol. 51v © British Library board. All Rights Reserved 2016 95
6. The simplest version of the trope *Quem quaeritis*, MS Cod. Sang. 484, p. 111. St. Gallen, Stiftsbibliothek 100
7. The transcription into modern notation of the trope *Quem quaeritis* from St Gallen 101
8. *Quem quaeritis*, Winchester troper, MS 775, fol. 17r. The Bodleian Libraries, University of Oxford 104
9. *Quem quaeritis*, Winchester troper, MS 775, fol.17v. The Bodleian Libraries, University of Oxford 105
10. The transcription into modern notation of the trope *Quem quaeritis* from Winchester troper 106
11. The Expulsion from Paradise, on the left the cherub with the flaming sword. *St Albans Psalter*, p. 18. Dombibliothek Hildesheim, Hs St God. 1 (Property of the Basilika of St Godehard, Hildesheim) 167
12. The Fall. *Cædmon Manuscript*, MS Junius 11, p. 20, The Bodleian Libraries, University of Oxford 175
13. The Fall, *St Albans Psalter*, p. 17. Dombibliothek Hildesheim, Hs St God. 1 (Property of the Basilika of St Godehard, Hildesheim) 176

11

Prologue: Cædmon

The history of English literature begins in the second half of the 7th century with a performance by a simple, illiterate shepherd. However, this event is mentioned only by one author, known for his penchant for miracles. There is no text or other archaeological proof which would confirm the performer's existence. Perhaps he was a figment of the learned man's imagination. Nevertheless, the story about the miraculous metamorphosis of the shepherd into a poet – still widely read and commented – contains a coherent and radical description of a revolution in the art practiced by the performer. Many elements of this story would resurface later in theatrical practices, not only those of the Middle Ages. The shepherd miraculously transformed into a poet was not aware that he had become an artist. This is how the Christian art of performance was born. Those who practiced it – the monks – also did not know what it was that they actually invented. Monks are perfect performers, because they have to submit to the detailed provisions of monastic rule, which order them to ceaselessly engage in a strictly regulated performance. It was in monasteries, among performers practicing obedience and religious acts, that the seeds of theatre were sown. They have bloomed many times since this inception, recently towards the end of the 20th century in Poland.

1. "Hence sometimes at a feast, when for the sake of providing entertainment, it had been decided that they should all sing in turn, when he saw the harp approaching him, he would rise up in the middle of the feasting, go out, and return home."[1] Cædmon was a simple cattle shepherd, who could neither read nor write. He knew no songs either. An old man, he worked for many years at the Whitby Abbey, which was built ca. 657 in Yorkshire, at the north-eastern shores of England.[2] It was called a "double monastery," because Hild (ca. 614–680), the royal-born prioress, ruled over both monks and nuns. Hild was the first princess christened in Northumbria, and a vocal proponent of the monastic movement. During her lifetime, the Whitby Abbey became an important centre of religious life. It hosted the famous Synod in 664, during which Northumbria adopted the

---

1   Bede, *HE* 4.24, pp. 414–417 (page numbers from translation by Colgrave and Myrons): "Vnde nonnumquam in conuiuio, cum esset laetitiae causa decretum ut omnes per ordinem cantare deberent, ille, ubi adpropinquare sibi citharam cernebat, surgebat a media caena et egressus ad suam domum repetabat."
2   In the earliest sources from before Viking invasion the monastery is referred to as Streanæshalch.

Roman liturgy, rejecting the Celtic method of calculating the Easter date used by monks from Ireland. Without hesitating, Hild supported the illiterate shepherd when he revealed his poetic talent. As a result, the abbey founded by the princess became the place where the first religious lines were composed in Old English.

It all began with a miraculous vision. Cædmon fled the feast to avoid singing, but instead of going home he went to the barn, since it was his turn to mind the cattle at night. When he finally stretched out comfortably and went to sleep, he saw in a dream a figure standing over him and calling him by his name:

> "Cædmon, sing me something!"
> "I cannot sing; that is why I left the feast and came here because I could not sing."
> "Nevertheless you must sing to me."
> "What must I sing?"
> "Sing about the beginning of created things."[3]
> And so Cædmon sang.

The Old Testament God had similar difficulties when he was appointing his prophets. Moses, for example, was tending sheep and initially rejected to become the chosen one, claiming that he is not "articulate" enough and that God should find someone more fitting.[4] *Elijah*, the only play written by Martin Buber (1878–1965), begins with a dialogue between a Voice and Elijah:

> "Elijah!"
> "No! No! No!"
> "Elijah!"
> "No!"
> "Elijah! Go!"
> "I resist you. You cannot compel me."
> "I cannot compel you."
> "Cruel driver, leave off! My Lord, where shall I go?"[5]

---

3   Bede, *HE* 4.24, pp. 416–417: "'Cædmon,' inquit, 'canta mihi aliquid.' At ille respondens 'Nescio' inquit 'cantare; nam et ideo de conuiuio egressus huc secessi, quia cantare non poteram.' Rursum ille qui cum eo loquebatur 'At tamen' ait 'mihi cantare habes.' 'Quid' inquit 'debeo cantare?' Et ille 'Canta' inquit 'principium creaturarum.'"
4   Exodus 4:10 and 13. Cf. Thundy (1989); O'Donnell (2005, 29–59, 191–202), and (2007) for a critical analysis of the forty-five literary and historical analogies to stories about Cædmon.
5   Trans. Friedman (1970, 114–115). M. Buber, *Elija. Ein Mysterienspiel* (erste Szene): "DIE STIMME: Elija! ELIJA: Nein! nein! nein! DIE STIMME: Elija! ELIJA: Nein! DIE STIMME: Elija! Geh! ELIJA: Ich widerstehe dir. Du kannst mich nicht zwingen. DIE STIMME: Ich kann dich nicht zwingen. ELIJA: Grausamer Treiber, lass ab! Mein Herr, wohin soll ich gehen?"

Elijah, also an illiterate shepherd, was supposed to go to the city and report what he saw. "I know nothing," he said, but the voice reassured him: "You will know it."[6] It is the man who acts, but the initiative belongs elsewhere.

When Hesiod, another illiterate shepherd, was minding sheep "under holy Helicon," the Muses came down to him; however, they did not present him with the "gift of singing," but rather taught him this art.[7] Nevertheless, they began from reprimanding Hesiod:

> "Field-dwelling shepherds, ignoble disgraces, mere bellies:
> we know how to say many false things similar to genuine ones,
> but we know, when we wish, how to proclaim true things."[8]

Greek Gods taught poets not only to speak the truth, but also to lie effectively. The art of singing was about seducing and deceiving. Greek artists would be skilled deceivers, capable of creating beguiling illusions. Christian artists, on the other hand, were meant to testify to the truth without interfering with it, at least as far as it is possible, lest they distort or deform the ideal message. Ultimately, the illiterate Cædmon becomes himself, i.e. a poet, through a "total act" – one that consists in trusting the inspiration that one does not comprehend. Thus, Cædmon is not singing but rather being sung.

2. All known information about Cædmon is preserved in the *Ecclesiastical History of the English People* (*Historia ecclesiastica gentis Anglorum*) completed by Venerable Bede in 731. Had this text been lost, we would not have even known the name of the said shepherd. Fortunately, the *Ecclasistical History* is among the most popular historical treatises in Europe, surviving in one hundred and sixty manuscripts despite wars and Reformation.

Bede saw Cædmon's poem on the "beginnings of creation" as a performance, always referring to it with the noun *carmen*, i.e. "song." The historian deployed his verbs with similar consistency. In his magnum opus, it is only the act of composing that is described with the word *facere*. In all cases of dream visions and artworks inspired by them the only verbs to recur are *cantare* and *canare*, which both mean "to sing."[9] These words foreground the performative character of Cædmon's composition, and accentuate the miraculous character of the shepherd's metamorphosis into a poet. Paraphrasing the beginning of St. Paul's Epistle to the Galatians (1:1), Bede writes:

---

6   "ELIJA: Ich weiß nichts. DIE STIMME: Du wirst es wissen."
7   Hesiod, *Theogony* 22. For commentary on this line see: West (1966, 161).
8   Hesiod, *Theogony* 26–28, trans. G.W. Most (Loeb).
9   Jones (1929), entries "caneo" and "canto." For commentary see: Hines (2007, 192–193).

| Namque ipse non ab hominibus neque per hominem institutus canendi artem didicit, sed diuinitus adiutus gratis canendi donum accepit.[10] | For he did not learn the art of poetry from men nor through a man but he received the gift of song freely by the grace of God. |

The "gift of song" is juxtaposed here with "the art of song." Cædmon, an illiterate old shepherd of low social status (probably not a free person; therefore, subordinate to the reeve, or *uilicus*), would be precluded from obtaining education in a strictly hierarchic society, so he had to be endowed with "song."

Bede emphasizes the radical or even absolute illiteracy of Cædmon, who is described as an utter ignoramus: not only was he unable to sing or play an instrument, but also could not learn anything, not even memorize a simple ballad or a trivial song. Thus, the message of this story becomes clear: a Christian poet owes his art solely to God, and this is why his song may testify to the truth.

3. The fourth book of Bede's *Ecclesiastical History* – the one containing the story of Cædmon – abounds in dramatized descriptions of astounding events. Accounts of visions or miracles can be found in eighteen out of thirty-two chapters. In the Christian world, miracles would be considered real, for they constituted an effective and fully acceptable means of communication, allowing God to speak to humankind. To the mediaeval mind, *miracula* were proofs of God's care over people and His presence in the world. Miraculous events witnessed by saints strengthened Christians. Average people would even regard any doubts about miracles as proof of utter lack of faith.[11]

The meeting of God and man is an extraordinary event. Biblical descriptions of Elijah's journeys abound in divine interventions. Epiphanies legitimize the prophet's missions. Did Cædmon meet God in his dream? The mysterious figure is identified by Bede only with an indefinite pronoun *quidam*, meaning "somebody." He refers to this entity as neither God nor even an angel. However, the miraculous nature of this event recedes into the background as the story focuses on revealing the new competences acquired by the shepherd. After all, we learn about Cædmon only because he became a poet overnight.[12] And when he started singing, he would not do anything else, at least according to Bede's account. We only learn that he was extremely devout and that he piously observed the monastic rule. Finally,

---

10 Bede, *HE* 4.23, pp. 414–415.
11 Colgrave and Myrons (1969, xxxv).
12 O'Donnell (2007, 15); (2005, 16–17).

Cædmon is a unique artist, the antithesis of a shaman.[13] With his calling, as well as his later performances and monastic career, he questioned the entire tradition of secular performances – the same he would walk out on during feasts. Singing religious songs not only defined Cædmon's new identity, but also came to embody his way of life. He would become "himself whole" only while singing sacred texts.

4. In his famous dream, Cædmon praised the Creator in verse he had never heard before. It was the only instance of his being an autonomous artist, because later on he would only rework holy texts written by others. Cædmon's poem – which came to be called a "hymn"[14] – acquired a unique status probably quite early on. Although Bede claims Cædmon's output to be prolific, it is only this one inspired song that survived to this day. In the *Ecclesiastical History*, Bede gives a Latin translation of the *Hymn*[15]:

| Nunc laudare debemus auctorem regni caelestis, potentiam Creatoris et consilium illius, facta Patris gloriae: quomodo ille, cum sit aeternus Deus, omnium miraculorum auctor extitit, qui primo filiis hominum caelum pro culmine tecti, dehinc terram Custos humani generis omnipotens creauit. | Now we must praise the Maker of the heavenly kingdom, the power of the Creator and His counsel, the deeds of the father of glory and how He, since He is the eternal God, was the Author of all marvels and first created the heavens as a roof for the children of men and then, the almighty Guardian of the human race, created the earth. |

As Bede, himself an accomplished stylist, declares with regret, "[t]his is the sense but not the order of the words which he sang as he slept. For it is not possible to translate verse, however well composed, literally from one language to another without some loss of beauty and dignity."[16]

Bede's choice not to include the Old English original in the Latin text of the *Ecclesiastical History* was probably deliberate. Perhaps it did not even cross his mind. Latin – backed by the authority of great ancient writers – was inseparable from written culture, and also constituted the official language of church liturgy. Therefore,

---

13 O'Donnell (2007, 33); (2005, 23).
14 The poem was called a "hymn" only in the 19th century, for the first time in J.J. Conybear's *Illustration of Anglo-Saxon Poety* (London, 1826): "Hymn of Cædmon" (3–8). See Hines (2007, 191). Bede, however, uses only the term *carmen*.
15 Bede, *HE* 4.24, pp. 416–417.
16 Bede, *HE* 4.24, pp. 416–417: "Hic est sensus, non autem ordo ipse uerborum, quae dormiens ille canebat; neque enim possunt carmina, quamuis optime conposita, ex alia in aliam linguam ad uerbum sine detrimento sui decoris ac dignitatis transferri." For commentary on proper interpretation of Latin terms *decor* and *dignitas* see: Wallace-Hadrill (1988, 166–167).

Cædmon's song was born under dramatic circumstances: at the border between oral and written culture.[17] In the first half of the 8th century, a hymn phrased in Old English could acquire the status of literature only in Latin translation.

5. Nevertheless, Cædmon's *Hymn* survived in two early Old English dialects. It was added to the Latin manuscripts of Bede's *Ecclesiastical History* as a glossa on the margin, sometimes next to Bede's Latin paraphrase, or as part of the main text. Out of sixteen known manuscripts containing Old English versions of the *Hymn*, fourteen have survived. They were made in England in the period between the 8th and 12th century. Since the times of King Alfred (871–899), when the entire *Historia ecclesiastica* was translated into West Saxon, Cædmon's *Hymn* became an integral part of the Old English translations of Bede's work (preserved in five manuscripts).[18]

Interesting conclusions may also be drawn from an analysis of the form in which the poem was recorded. In all manuscripts, the text of the *Hymn* is provided in continuous script, without line breaks. This seems particularly intriguing in the case of Latin manuscripts, because since the 8th century Latin poetry was rendered in England in verse form. Latin manuscripts of Bede's *Ecclesiastical History* also contain hexametres and elegiac distichs, which are clearly different from prose.[19] Would it be possible that mediaeval copyists considered Cædmon's *Hymn* as a performative work and not a literary text? Oral cultures, like the one in ancient Greece, recorded poetry using continuous script. After all, when reading aloud or singing the grammatical and metric divisions become obsolete. Ancient Greeks did not even use word breaks. Greek poetry preserved in writing survived in the form of strings of capital letters. Old English variants of Cædmon's *Hymn* can be thus seen as the earliest attempts at preserving oral performance in England.[20]

6. Twenty-one different versions of the poem have been preserved to this day. After a meticulous and painstaking analysis of all these sources, Daniel O'Donnell proposed a hypothetical reconstruction of Cædmon's song in the Northumbrian original, a language that the poet must have used insofar as he lived in Whitby.[21] O'Donnell claims that although Cædmon was illiterate, he must have been a competent poet. Four out of five main types of Old English rhythm variants can be discerned in the *Hymn* if we adopt the classification formulated towards the end

---

17 Hines (2007, 217); O'Keeffe (1987).
18 For facsimiles, transcriptions and notes on all five sources see: O'Donnell (2005). Cf. also Dobbie (1937), Smith (1968), and commentary by O'Keeffe (1990, 23–46).
19 O'Keeffe (1987, 4–9).
20 Fry (1974). Cf. the entry on "oral-formulaic theory" (by A. Orchard), in Lepidge (1999, 345).
21 O'Donnell (2005, 205).

1. Bede, Historia ecclesiastica *(VIII Century), one of two earliest copies of the Latin text. Old English recension of* Cædmon's Hymn *has been copied in the bottom margin of the page. St. Petersburg, National Library of Russia, MS lat.Qv.1.18, fol. 107r*

of the 19th century by Eduard Sievers (types A, B, D and E).[22] These measures are related to half-lines. The entire nomenclature is contemporary, because not a single Old English treatise on metre has been preserved. A half-line must comprise at least four syllables. In each line, it is at least the first (or more) accented syllable in the left-hand half-line that alliterate (usually designated as "a") with the first accented syllable of the right-hand half-line ("b"). Cædmon's poem meets all of these criteria. In the scansion beneath, the symbol "/" refers to a strongly accented syllable, while "\" – to a weakly accented one. The symbol "x" stands for unaccented syllables, and "(x)" – for ignored syllables. Bold font denotes alliteration[23]:

	Nu scylun hergan A3: x x x / x	hefaenricaes uard, E: / x \ x /	Now let us praise	the Keeper of heavenly Kingdom,
	metudæs maecti, A1: / x x / x	end his modgidanc, B: x x / x \	The might of the Creator,	and His thought,
	uerc uuldurfadur - D2: / / (x) \ x	sue he uundra gihaes, B2: x x / x x /	the works of the glorious Father,	how He of each of wonders,
	eci dryctin, A1: / x / x	or astelidæ! A1: / x / x x	eternal lord,	established the beginning.
5	He aerist scop B1: x / x /	eordu barnum A1: / x / x	He first created	for the sons of men
	heben til hrofe, A1: / x x / x	haleg sceppend; A1: / x / x	heaven as a roof,	the holy Shaper;
	tha middungeard, B1: x / x /	moncynnæs uard, E: / \ x /	then middle-earth,	the Keeper of mankind,
	eci dryctin, A1: / x / x	æfter triadæ A1: / x / x	eternal Lord,	afterwards made
	firum foldu, A1: / x / x	frea allmectig. A1: / x / x	for men the earth,	the Lord almighty.

At least nine out of eighteen half-lines have been indicated by scholars to have close parallels in later works, while some even claim that Old English texts contain analogies to all phrases found in this poem.[24]

Moreover, the *Hymn* has a clear structure and an explicit message. God is invoked in every line, always with a different epithet: *uard* ("keeper"), *metud* ("the measuring one"; "creator"), *uuldurfadur* ("glorious father"), *dryctin* ("lord"; "leader"), *he* ("He"), *haleg sceppend* ("holy shaper"), *moncynnæs uard* ("keeper of mankind"), *eci dryctin* ("eternal lord"), and *frea allmectig* ("lord almighty").

The poem can be divided into two main parts, each comprising two segments. The first part, spanning lines 1–4, initially declares the main subject of the song,

---

22 O'Donnell (2005, 61–65).
23 Trans. Greenfield and Calder (1986, 229; translation modified).
24 Fry (1974). For a contrary argument see: O'Donnell (2005, 68).

i.e. the need to praise the Creator, and then explains why "the measurer" should be worshipped: He has, after all, initiated every miracle. The second part (lines 5–9) develops the subject and contains a masterful display of poetic variation. Miracles materialized in a specific order: first God created heaven, and then earth for people. This two-part structure echoes the mediaeval concept of the dual nature of creation. The "first" creation gave life to the ideal, eternal, spiritual world, whereas the "second" one lent the original ideas a temporal and spatial dimension.[25]

7. After waking up, the shepherd still remembered the song, and even added several similar God-praising lines of his own design. In the morning, the reeve brought him to the prioress. Hild submitted Cædmon to a strict test. He was supposed to recount his dream and recite the song in the presence "of a number of the more learned men."[26] They unanimously ruled that the shepherd had been blessed with divine grace. To achieve maximum certainty, however, he was asked to compose a song on the basis of a sacred story. Cædmon returned the next morning and delivered the entire passage in rhythmic verse. Hild considered it as ultimate proof of divine presence in the man. She ordered Cædmon to shed his secular attire and take oaths. Thus, he was admitted to the monastic community.

Chapter twenty of book four in Bede's *Ecclesiastical History*, devoted in its entirety to Cædmon, is mysteriously structured. The infinitive form of the verb *suscipere*, used by Hild to order the shepherd to take monastic oaths, occurs almost right in the middle of the account: it is the 450th word in a 820-word-long chapter.[27] This may be mere coincidence, but even if it is so, this symmetry holds quite a significance: becoming a monk was a defining moment in Cædmon's life. His transformation entailed a radical change of social status as he turned from an illiterate shepherd into a member of an elite monastic community.

The internal metamorphosis was supposed to be confirmed by outer change, too. Cædmon assumed the habit, a symbol of monastic vocation and discipline. His humble attire distinguished him from everyone else and defined as a performer of the monastic rule. In all probability, he was also tonsured, which was a sign of radical humiliation. It was criminals and slaves who had their hair cut obligatorily. Monks, on the other hand, willingly imposed this humiliation on themselves. Tonsures came in different varieties. In the Roman Catholic Church, a ring of hair, shaped like the crown of thorns, was left on the head. The Celtic tradition, on the other hand, demanded long hair to be preserved at the back, and

---

25 O'Donnell (2005, 65–66); Huppé (1968, 129–131).
26 Bede, *HE* 4.24, p. 416: "multis doctioribus uiris."
27 O'Donnell (2005, 4).

the front to be completely shaved. The tonsure not only denoted spiritual obligation, but also visibly demonstrated the rejection of the world and one's sexuality.[28] The monk's image was an identity-forming performance.

8. Bede emphasizes that Cædmon never composed a frivolous or trivial piece, because his talent originated in a "gift" from God. He could only sing religious songs, and would not add anything from himself. Monks would read passages from sacred texts aloud to him, probably in the Northumbrian dialect, and Cædmon would meditate on them and adapt into metrical poems. A master of transformation, he converted Christian learning into powerful performances. According to Bede, Cædmon's compositions were so magnificent that they turned his teachers into listeners.[29] Although many tried to imitate him, he remained unmatched.[30]

Meditation constituted Cædmon's creative method. "He ruminated," Bede writes in vivid language, "like an animal," on every word he heard from the Scriptures or liturgy and "transformed" it "in the most melodious song."[31] This original composition-cum-performance imitated one of the chief monastic practices: *lectio divina*, or spiritual reading, i.e. attentive and deepened reading of the sacred text. In this sense, monastic practices lay at the root of Cædmon's competence. The poet's creativity, which stemmed from being a monk, became a way of life and the foundation of his identity.

9. Music played an immensely important role in the monastery. One crucial aspect of monastic life was the obligation to all-night vigils. In order to prevent sleep and intensify their meditation, the monks would read and recite passages from the Bible, usually psalms. With the course of time, reciting the psalter turned into endless, mantra-like cycles of repetition. "Christian psalmody emphasized [...] metaphors of community and discipline, both symbolized at once by unaccompanied singing in unison."[32] Singing in unison also embodied the Gregorian concept of the unity of the Church.

---

28 Foot (2006, 157).
29 Bede, *HE* 4.24, p. 418: "doctores suos uicissim auditores sui faciebat."
30 Bede, *HE* 4.24, p. 414: "nullus eum aequiperare potuit."
31 Bede, *HE* 4.24, p. 418: "At ipse cuncta, quae audiendo discere poterat, rememorando secum et quasi mundum animal ruminando, in carmen dulcissimum conuertebat." ("He learned all he could by listening to them and then, memorizing it and ruminating over it, like some clean animal chewing the cud, he turned it into the most melodious song."). Cf. Leviticus 11:3 and Deuteronomy 14:6.
32 Taruskin (2005, 1.10).

Bede's *Historia ecclesiastica* is full of music. In the fourth book, references to singing are almost as frequent as those made to miracles. The arrival of Theodore of Tarsus in England in 667, as well as his becoming the new Archbishop of Canterbury, are described by Bede in the first chapter. This event heralded reforms in the Church, which was exhausted by arguments between supporters of Celtic and Roman liturgy. Music would embody the unity of the Church, and became the driving force of reform.

In the second chapter, Bede describes the visit paid to Northumbria by Eddius Stephanus, a great singing master, and Theodore's ordaining of Putta as the Bishop of Rochester. "He was especially skilled in liturgical chanting after the Roman manner, which he had learned from the disciples of the blessed Pope Gregory."[33] In chapter eighteen we learn that Benedict Biscop (d. 689), founder of monasteries in Monkwearmouth and Jarrow (the latter being the place where Bede spent most of his life and wrote the *Ecclesiastical History*), visited Rome and brought back with him in 674/5 a certain John, the arch-cantor at St. Peter's. John taught the English monks to sing in a one-year cycle, according to Roman practice, and "taught the cantors of the monastery the order and manner of singing and reading aloud" (4.18: "canendi ac legendi uiua uoce"). He also recorded everything that was necessary to celebrate holidays all year long (however, without using any musical notation, because it was invented a hundred years later). Bede emphasizes that John's teaching met with great interest from the monastic communities. In this learned milieu, Cædmon, an illiterate shepherd, was able to bring about a revolution. He expressed the teachings of the Catholic Church in the language of regular people, providing new momentum to the renewed effort to evangelize Great Britain.

Hild ordered the brothers to acquaint Cædmon with the entirety of the sacred history (*seriem sacrae historiae*). As a result, the rich programme of his songs preceded the great biblical cycles of the late Middle Ages. As Bede notes, Cædmon praised the beginning of the world, the origins of humankind, the entire Genesis, Israel's flight from Egypt and entry into promised land, Incarnation, Passion and Resurrection, the Descent of the Holy Spirit, the teachings of the Apostles, and the horrors of the Last Judgement. In his songs he attempted to draw people away from their fascination with sin, to inspire love and rekindle a desire to do good.[34]

---

33 Bede, *HE* 4.2, pp. 336–337: "maxime autem modulandi in ecclesia more Romanorum, quem a discipulis beati papae Gregorii didicerat, peritum."
34 Bede, *HE* 4.24, p. 418.

10. Bede describes two miracles occurring in Cædmon's lifetime, both of which reveal the true nature of the poet. The first miracle consisted in transforming the shepherd into an artist. In his famous dream, Cædmon praised God as Creator of the World. This world, however, was quite special, for it had a roof (6a: *hrōf*), just like the monastery in Whitby. Thus, the *Hymn* contains a monastic vision of the cosmos.[35] The miraculous metamorphosis had revealed his true identity: Cædmon is a monk! The model Christian performer is a "poet by gift" and "monk by nature."[36]

The second miracle occurred at the end of Cædmon's life: he predicted the time of his own death. One night, he asked his assistants to prepare a place where he could rest. He did not look like a person who is about to die. The assistants were taken aback, but obeyed the order. Around midnight, when they conversed merrily, Cædmon suddenly asked whether the Eucharist was in the house.

> They answered, "What need have you of the Eucharist? You are not likely to die, since you are talking so cheerfully with us as if you were in perfect health."
> "Nevertheless," he repeated, "bring me the Eucharist."[37]

Before taking it, he kept asking everyone if they held no grudge against him.

> Thereupon he asked them how near it was to the time when the brothers had to awake to sing their nightly praises of God. They answered, "It will not be long." And he answered, "Good, let us wait until then."[38]

He made the sign of the cross, put his head on a pillow and departed at the moment when the monks from the monastery began singing the psalm that begins the matins.

The scene of Cædmon's death unveils like "a perfect liturgical ritual."[39] He takes the Eucharist at his own demand and dies at the moment when his brothers begin praising God. The final transformation is accompanied by singing – the act from which the whole story began. Cædmon, God's servant, dies praising and imitating Christ in the act of final metamorphosis. The master of transformations ceases his performance.

---

35 Wallis (2007, 109).
36 Wallis (2007, 83).
37 Bede, *HE* 4.24, p. 420: "Respondebant: 'Quid opus est eucharistia? neque enim mori adhuc habes, qui tam hilariter nobiscum uelut sospes loqueris.' Rursus ille 'Et tamen' ait 'afferte mihi eucharistiam.'"
38 Bede, *HE* 4.24, p. 420: "Et interrogauit, quam prope esset hora, qua fratres ad dicendas Domino laudes nocturnas excitari deberent. Respondebant: 'Non longe est.' At ille: 'Bene; ergo exspectemus horam illam.'"
39 Hines (2007, 196).

Part one: Monk as Performer

Around AD 973, the south-eastern city of Winchester hosted a gathering of the priors of monasteries, who met in order to homogenize and thoroughly reform monastic life in Great Britain. At the same time, the meeting was supposed to finalize the introduction of the Rule developed by St. Benedict of Nursia (ca. 480–550) to England. Monks and nuns proved to be surprisingly attentive to the performative dimension of the liturgy. Their decisions in this matter brought about a revolution. Although members of the monastic community were staunch opponents of pagan entertainment – including the theatre of the antiquity, however understood – they have indeed given rise to Christian theatre without knowing it. All they did was reform religious life.

Latest studies on monasticism question many previous theories on the subject, attempting to consider more fully than before and reconstruct the performative aspects of life in the monastery. Its original "theatrical quality" has set many activities of monks apart from the very beginning. Particularly favourable circumstances for the development of monastic performances emerged in the re-evangelized England of the 7th century, when monks began their centuries-long domination in religious and political life of the island. The Anglo-Saxon state – isolated from Europe by sea and deprived of firm ties to the Roman cultural heritage – was able to easily assimilate the monastic reforms developed in the continent, thus becoming a true laboratory of religious practice. The Anglo-Saxon monks' creative explosion led to the creation of a comprehensive model of monastic life at the end of the 10th century. Monks received detailed scripts of performances, which were supposed to be delivered from dawn till dusk, every day, in specific cycles: weekly, monthly and yearly. After becoming a performer, the average monk was virtually forced to invent "theatre."

Monasticism

1. Isidorus – citizen of Karanis, a Greek settlement at the edge of the Fayum Oasis in Egypt – was ambushed by two people: Pamounis and Harpalus. He survived the attack and decided to file a complaint on papyrus to the local official (*praepositus*). The document dated June 324 has survived to this day. Isidorus writes in it that he would have died if it had not been for the help of "the deacon Antoninus and the monk Isaac."[40] It is the first known occurrence of the Greek term *monachós* ("single") in the meaning of "monk." However, Isaac was no desert ascetic, nor a member of the monastic community. He was a "loner" who lived in a village, and is referred to in other sources as one of those who "have renounced the world" (*apotaktikoí* in Greek)[41] yet do not shy away from other people. Traditionally, theories on the origins of monasticism traced its rise to the emergence of eastern anchorites in the 4th century (from Greek *anachōréō*, meaning "to go away" or "to retreat") and cenobites (from Greek *koinós* and *bíos*, meaning "living together"). Monasticism has been usually regarded as a form of severing all ties with the world. However, new research undermines this view. According to early sources, monks would live in villages and cities, retaining strong economic ties with the local communities. Moreover, they emerged surprisingly early, with certain groups of ascetics existing probably already in the 2nd century. Although the earliest accounts of specifically Christian monks can be only found in Eusebius (ca. 260–340) and Athanasius (ca. 296–373)[42], the Greek term *monachós* appears as many as three times in the Coptic *Gospel of Thomas* (sayings 16, 49 and 75).[43]

"The great recorded variety of monastic lifestyles makes it difficult to specify formal criteria for monasticism other than a celibate life, an emphasis on ascetic practice and a strong sense of independence in relation to society."[44] Monks rejected traditional forms of everyday life, suppressing bodily needs and focusing entirely on spiritual goals. They aimed for full unity with God through Christ. They propagated radical freedom, which encompassed not only liberation from biological and social limitations, but also freeing from oneself. Union with God would be made possible

---

40 *P.Coll. Youtie* 77. Cf. Judge (1977, 73); Pearson (2006, 350); Rubenson (2007, 638). English translation of the papyrus is provided in Harmless (2004, 459).
41 Judge (1977, 79); Goehring (1999, 53–72); Harmless (2004, 418–421).
42 According to Eusebius (*HE* 6.9.6), Narcissus, the Bishop of Jerusalem (ca. 200), was so disillusioned with the policy of the local Church that he "hid himself in desert and secret places, and remained there many years" (trans. A.C. McGiffert). Cf. Harmless (2004, 432–433); Rubenson (2007, 638); Choat (2002), Judge (1977).
43 Dorival (1999); Pearson (2006, 350).
44 Rubenson (2007, 639).

only after one is made "pure," i.e. empty, devoid of oneself and all earthly matters. In performative categories monks are ideal performers, because they acquire identity only by performing and utterly transforming themselves, with the body, which is subjected to special practices, acting as the vehicle of this metamorphosis.

2. The main inspiration for monastic Christianity, which stimulated such practices in other cultural contexts too, was the description of the original church in Jerusalem, contained in Acts 4:32: "no one claimed private ownership of any possessions, but everything they owned was held in common." Moreover, a strong influence was exerted by dualistic notions, especially the call for liberating the spirit from the body. These ideas were adopted not only by Manicheans, but also by Gnostics among Jews and Christians. Another model eagerly adopted by ascetics originated in ideas developed by Greek thinkers, who identified philosophy with the practice of a perfect life. The first Egyptian hermits imitated the model of Pythagoras and followed writings by the Stoics.[45]

New research also reveals local conditions of early monasticism. *Apophthegmata patrum*, a collection of adages attributed to hermits who lived ascetic and secluded lives in the 4th and 5th century, continued the tradition of Egyptian wisdom. Traces of old practices can be also found in the drive towards a life in isolation, often in tombs, which was characteristic for Egyptian hermits.[46] The agrarian tradition favoured patterns related to settled life. In the 320s, Pachomius organized and supervised monastic communities in Upper Egypt, both male and female. He developed rules of monastic life, which eliminated illiterate people from these circles (*Praecepta* 49 and 139–140).[47] Syrian merchants, on the other hand, had a more mercantile attitude and favoured the concept of monk as a travelling preacher, or "Saint Walker." Among Syrians there were also some very original "performers." The most famous one, Symeon the Elder, the first stylite (ca. 390–459), lived for over forty years on an increasingly high pillar located in the mountains near Antioch, which finally reached the height of over eighteen metres.[48] In Palestine, monasticism had a multi-national and multi-cultural dimension from the very beginning. Since 326 – when Helen, mother to Emperor Constantine, found "the real cross" and Christ's tomb[49] – crowds of pilgrims flocked to the Holy Land. In

---

45 Rubenson (2007, 640).
46 Lichtheim (1983); Rubenson (2007, 657–658); Harmless (2004, 417–474).
47 *Pachomian Koinonia*, vol. 2, p. 166: "even if unwilling he shall be compelled to read."
48 Evagrius Scholasticus, *HE* 1.13 (40 ells); Theodoret, *A History of the Monks of Syria* 26.12 (36 ells). Sources vary on the subject of the highest pillar's size. For more information see: Doran (1992, 16–17).
49 Rufinus, *HE* 10.7–8; Socrates, *HE* 1.17; Sozomen, *HE* 2.1; Theodoret, *HE* 1.17.

mid-century, monasteries, prayer houses and night shelters flourished around sacred sites. In Constantinople, Maratonios, a wealthy deacon of Bishop Macedonius, founded the first monastery and created a network of shelters for the sick and poor, run by monks.[50] Further east, the tendency was to create monastic communities. However, with the exception of Pachomian monasteries, monk life was never regulated by codices in the way it has been in the West.

3. Performances delivered by eccentrics transformed Christianity into a mass religion.[51] The faith of a small community of initiated people who focused on spirituality became a show. The very act of retreating into the desert had symbolic meaning: it demonstrated that one dies to the world in order to live alone with God. The greatest hermits were simple people, who taught not by delivering lectures but rather through sayings. The most important element, however, was performance, i.e. offering a living example. When he was eighteen or twenty, Anthony the Great gave away his huge property, which he inherited from wealthy parents. Soon after, he moved into a tomb far away from his home village. With the course of time, he moved further into the desert, finally settling with two students at the foot of the mountain Qolzum at the Red Sea. *The Life of Antony*, written by Athanasius shortly after the hermit died in 356, quickly became a classic of Christian literature. The author gives a particularly vivid description of Anthony's struggle with daemons. The humble son of a prosperous Egyptian, who avoided school, came to be considered "the father of monks," and transformed Church for ever.

Performances by hermits stimulated people's imagination because hardly anyone could repeat them. Abba Macarius of Alexandria ate only raw vegetables for seven years, and never went under a roof for twenty. He atoned for having accidently killed a mosquito by living at a marsh for six months, naked.[52] Abba Agathon learned to remain silent by holding a stone in his mouth for three years.[53] Abba Benjamin healed others even when he himself lay struck down by disease. Abba Dioscorus would assign himself each year a different strict exercise. Abba John the Dwarf watered dry sticks stuck in the ground and prayed for temptations. Abba Mios, a former slave, washed the feet of his previous masters every year. The Egyptian Mark did not leave his cell for thirty years. Abba Sisoes hung

---

50 Sozomen, *HE* 4.27.
51 Brown (1989, 107).
52 Palladius, *HL* 18.1–4.
53 English editions of the apophtegmata include: *The Sayings of the Desert Fathers* (trans. B. Ward) and *The Anonymous Sayings of the Desert Fathers* (trans. J. Wortley). Cf. Harmless (2004, 167–310).

over a precipice in order to overcome sleepiness. Amma Sara lived on the Nile for sixty years, but not once looked at the river. Abba Bessarion did not lay on his side for forty years, always remaining seated or standing; moreover, he once prayed for fourteen days, extending his arms towards heaven. Abba Tithoes would become ecstatic while praying if he did not keep his hands down. Finally, Abba Ammonathas could remain immobile during fervent prayer yet simultaneously visit the Caesar and secure a tax relief for his monks.

Many performances served a didactic purpose. Abba Anub kept throwing rocks at a statue's face for seven days, and then begged it for forgiveness in order to instruct his brothers that a monk ought to be as imperturbable as a stone figure. When a prostitute tempted Abba Ephrem, he offered her to have sex right in the middle of a thick crowd so that she would grasp the meaning of shame. Abba Serapion converted a hetaera with prayer. Abba Euphrenius would help the thieves who stole from him and was honestly upset when he discovered they had not taken his staff. Abba Paul taught obedience to his disciple John as if he were a Buddhist Zen master: he would order John to go to the vault and bring back the faeces of a hyena that lived there. When John asked what he was supposed to do if the hyena attacked him, Paul jokingly remarked that the student should tie it up and bring it to him. Accordingly, when John went to the vault and the hyena attacked him, he caught it, leashed it and brought before his master. Seeing this, Paul struck John and freed the animal. Abba Moue was equally radical in instilling obedience in his brother Saius, ordering him to go and steal. Saius would obey and steal from his brothers. When a certain old man questioned the presence of Christ in the Eucharist, two others decided to convince him by resorting to a specific "theatre of cruelty." First, a baby would appear over the bread during Mass. When the priest reached out to break bread, a sword-wielding angel descended and killed the baby, spilling its blood into the chalice. As the priest was breaking bread, the angel cut the baby. Finally, the doubtful old man received a piece of bloody flesh instead of crumb.

Departing spectacularly into the desert, however, undermined the show. Some hermits also expressed this performatively. Abba Joseph would sing psalms and pray with his disciples in hiding. When Abba Isaac was to be made a priest, he fled to Egypt and hid in hay. The black Abba Moses attempted to escape into the marshes when he heard that a certain dignitary was planning to visit Sekitis with his retinue in order to see him. When he accidentally stumbled upon the visitors, he did not admit who he was and only advised them to turn back because Moses "was a fool." Moreover, when Abba Simon received news that guests were arriving, he climbed a palm tree to trim it and told the official who wanted to see him that "the hermit was not there." On another occasion, he greeted the stranger covered in a thick coat, holding bread and cheese. On the sight of such luxury the official scorned him and departed immediately.

4. Monasticism was a uniquely dynamic phenomenon. According to early historians of the Church, in 373 there were three thousand monks in the vicinity of Nitria, near Alexandria, but fifteen years later there were five thousand: "the desert had become a city."[54] News of the novel, alternative lifestyle quickly reached the West. In the 340s, upon his return from the East, Bishop Eusebius from Vercella ordered his clergyman to take vows of chastity and form a commune. Monastic ideas were also developed by Christian intellectuals like Hieronymus, or Augustine of Hippo. However, upper-class Romans would remain indifferent to this trend for a long time. Asceticism and renouncement stood in opposition to the ideology of *populus bellicosus*, "the warrior people."[55] Roman women, on the other hand, were more eager to embrace monasticism, which is proven by the fact that some of its most fervent followers emerged among them at that time. As early as in the 370s, Ambrosius, Bishop of Milan, led the public ceremony of taking the veil by women who decided to retain their virginity.[56]

Towards the end of the 4th century, rich Roman widows would transform their households into seats of religious communities, where the gathered could pray, fast and meditate, but primarily study sacred writings. Religious life offered women autonomy and educational possibilities. In the light of Roman law, it was the husband, usually much older, who wielded absolute power over the household. After his death, the widow would be encouraged to remarry in order to secure the family's interest or avoid gossip. Asceticism allowed to break the vicious circle of male domination. By choosing monastic life, women would regain control over their own bodies. It was equally important that this move entailed a chance to study, because cultures of antiquity neglected the education of women. After her husband died, Melania the Elder – a wealthy twenty-two-year-old widow – left her son in the custody of the Rome prefect and took all her moveable belongings with her. She travelled to Egypt to meet in person the holy ascetics, and then visited the Holy Land, finally settling in Jerusalem, where she founded a convent on the Olive Mountain. It was believed that this was the place where Christ would descend during the Second Coming.

---

54 Rubenson (2007, 649). Cf. Athanasius, *Life of Antony* 14; Rufinus, *HE* 2.3; Palladius, *HL* 7.2. These figures cannot be taken literally, but they nevertheless reflect the dynamics of monasticism's growth.
55 Kocur (2005, 59–62).
56 Dunn (2007, 669–670). The anonymous author of *Historia monachorum in Aegypto* (5.1), who was prone to exaggeration, claimed that ca. 393 there were as many as 20,000 "virgins" in Oxyrhynchus.

For twenty-seven years she was in charge of fifty nuns. Her teacher and spiritual advisor in Jerusalem was Rufinus of Aquileia, a strong proponent of monasticism and an outstanding intellectual, who was also accused of heresy.[57]

5. In the 5th century, monasticism came to dominate Western Christianity. At the beginning of that century, two aristocrats – Honoratus and Eucherius – founded a monastery on the island of Lérins, opposite Cannes. It quickly became a famous centre of learning and spirituality, also beyond the Gaul. Many members of that community became bishops. In the affluent and aristocratic Lérins the monks would not occupy themselves with physical work. Other monasteries, however, had to find a way to support themselves. Living alongside a local community demanded regulations, just like life in the monastery itself. Already in the 390s Augustine developed the Rules *Praeceptum* and *Regula tertio*, which became very influential later on. In the 12th century, these writings inspired a revival of canonical life, culminating in the rise of the Dominican order in the 13th century.[58] However, Augustine, who was a profound thinker, did not waste his time on settling details and building hierarchy in monastic life. He believed that members of the community would watch and correct each other on their own. It was only Caesarius of Arles (502–542) who first proposed an institutional structure to be adopted in his convent in Arles. *Rule for Virgins*, developed in 512 for two hundred virgins gathered by Caesaria, sister to Caesarius, had severe limitations and provoked rebellion.

In the 6th century, monastic communities became a natural part of social life. They also served functions unrelated to religion. The practice of putting seven-year-olds in monasteries often led to abuse, especially in case of girls. They were usually ditched by families who could not or would not pay their dowry. Many of those girls had difficulty with accepting the strict way of life. Another problem was the lack of vocations. Thus, Caesarius made his *Rule* stipulate that a nun who once entered the convent could not ever leave it. Around 589–590 two princesses from the Merovingian dynasty, who were put in the prestigious convent of Holy Cross in Poitiers against their will, incited forty nuns to rebel and flee. The princesses did not agree to obey the new prioress, who was of low birth.[59] A successful attempt at solving many issues related to monastic everyday life was made in mid-6th-century by St. Benedict of Nursia. His *Rule* quickly became famous and was adopted by monks in Lérins towards the end of the 7th century, inspiring further monastic reforms in 10th-century England.

---

57 Palladius, *HL* 46. Brown (1988, 281 and 379–386).
58 Dunn (2007, 678); Lawless (1987).
59 Gregory of Tours, *Historia Francorum* 9.38–43 and 10.14–17, 20. See also: Dunn (2007, 680).

The Rule

2. The Prologue to St. Benedict's Rule (late X Century). Oxford, Corpus Christi College, MS 197, fol. 1r. © Corpus Christi College, Oxford, UK / The Bridgeman Art Library

1. Benedict would call on monks to completely renounce their own will and arm their souls with "the strong and noble weapons of obedience" in order to achieve "the loftier summits of the teaching and virtues."[60] Chapter 33 of the Rule dictated absolute sacrifice. Monks were deprived of the right to independently decide about their bodies; nor could anyone "retain anything as his own, nothing at all – not a book, writing tablets or stylus, in short not a single item" (33.3). Everything was supposed to be shared. Benedict emphasized the importance of communal life, favouring cenobites, i.e. monks living in monasteries "under a rule and an abbot" (1.2). He decidedly condemned sarabaits and wandering monks. In reference to the former he said that, "two or three together, or even alone, without a shepherd, they pen themselves up in their own sheepfolds, not the Lord's" (1.8). The latter – also called *gyrovagi* – wandered from one monastery to another, "always on the move, […] slaves to their own wills and gross appetites" (1.11).

According to Benedict, a monk living in a community had to preserve three virtues: humility, silence and most of all – obedience. The highest authority in a Benedictine monastery was God, then the Rule (the inviolable "master" meant to be absolutely obeyed), and finally the abbot, or – to put it more properly – "the abbot's office." Benedict, who was aware that not everyone can be a charismatic leader, strengthened the office itself by ordering absolute obedience. The abbot could listen to the community's opinion, but did not have to pay heed to it (3.2). "In the monastery no one is to follow his own heart's desire," Benedict recommended (3.7–8), "nor shall anyone presume to contend his abbot defiantly." The office's charisma was reinforced by a strict hierarchy of the lower offices. Direct control over groups of ten monks was held by the deacons, "chosen for virtuous living and wise teaching, not for their rank" (21.4). Competences supported the authority.

2. The monastic community was supposed to be self-sufficient. As Benedict wrote, "[t]he monastery should be so constructed that within it all necessities, such as water, mill and garden are contained, and the various crafts are practiced" (66.6). The Rule regulated in detail all kinds of contacts with the secular world. A monk could not become a priest or serve any pastoral functions. Only one of the brothers, the most "worthy" one, could be ordained a priest so that he could celebrate Mass in the monastery. Only the abbot, or a person appointed by him, could speak to guests. All those who were allowed to temporarily leave the monastery had to file a detailed report to the abbot after return, containing

---

60 Prologue 3 and 73.9. English translations of the Rule quoted after: *RB 1980* (ed. Fry).

everything they saw or heard. Even if a brother were to return to the monastery, as long as he ate outside, he would be excommunicated the same day and excluded from the community.

Benedict demanded from monks that they fully renounce themselves and break all ties with the world. Only one who is "emptied" of his personality can identify with Jesus. Following Christ, understood as imitating him, was supposed to be realized through clearly outlined practices. Benedict demanded performative acts from monks, ones that would culminate in complete internal transformation. These performative strategies were both simple and radical, encompassing change of appearance, active participation in the liturgy, meditative reading or prayer, fasting, eating humbly and infrequently, self-mortification, as well as remaining silent and staying alert, even at night. As Benedict prescribes, "[t]hey sleep clothed, and girded with belts or cords. Thus the monks will always be ready to arise without a delay when the signal is given" (22.5–6). The new way of life was supposed to facilitate the birth of a new man.

3. In the last chapter, Benedict calls his Rule "a little rule for beginners" (73.8). Dom David Knowles (1896–1974) – a Benedictine monk in the Downside Abbey and professor of history at the University of Cambridge, one of the greatest experts in mediaeval monasticism – has drawn attention to the fact that contrary to most earlier and later codices, St. Benedict's Rule was not addressed to people who distinguished themselves with a readiness to embrace asceticism, or displayed clear signs of vocation to some way of life or another.[61] Knowles calls Benedict "a legislator of great originality and creative genius," because he formulated such principles of religious life that were most suitable to the temperament and needs of Western people.

Benedict wrote his codex in mid-6th-century, having in mind a provincial, or even rural monastery he founded himself on the Monte Cassino hill in Campania, far away from any great urban centres that used to be culturally significant in antiquity. The Rule contains concise indications regarding clothing, diet and everyday activities (liturgical instructions, however, seem to be later additions since they are far too much like the officia performed in Rome's main basilicas[62]). The logical and lucid text has become the cornerstone of monasticism in Western Europe. Its copies circulated in England and northern France as early as in the

---

61 Knowles (1963, 15).
62 Dunn (2007, 682).

7th century.[63] One hundred years later, Venerable Bede of Northumbria had to know the text by heart, because many of his writings, especially sermons, are peppered with allusions to the Rule.[64] The earliest known Anglo-Saxon manuscript of St. Benedict's Rule dates back to the first half of the 8th century.[65] However, there is no preserved evidence that any of the Anglo-Saxon monasteries followed closely Benedict's orders before mid-10th-century.

---

63 Foot (2006, 1); Dunn (2000, 192–194).
64 Van der Walt (1986). Cf. Wormald (1976, 142–144).
65 MS *Hatton 48*, stored in Oxford's Bodleian Library.

Evangelization

1. In the 4th century, Britain was officially part of the Christian Roman Empire. However, Christianity, which was enforced on Celtic polytheism of late Stone Age Britons, was the religion of minorities concentrated mainly in cities, villas and forts in the south-eastern part of the island. After the year 400, Christian communities underwent a thorough transformation. Following the departure of the Romans, cities and villas were abandoned and fell into ruin, because the social and economic system that supported them collapsed. Legionaries not only built roads and cities, but also laid the foundations for a money economy. The army was paid in Roman coins made from gold, silver and copper, which revolutionized trade in Britain. Until the 4th century many households became dependent on producers of vases, vessels, building materials, as well as food and goods that were not made locally. All such wares were paid for with money obtained from sale of surplus production.[66]

The departure of the legions marked the end of an influx of cash. Coins that were in circulation quickly became worn out. After 430, Britons reverted to barter economy. In 450, most cities ceased to function. The weakened Britain became easy target for the invasion of pagan tribes from northern Germania and southern Scandinavia. Anglo-Saxon raiders and settlers pushed local Britons into the westernmost corners of the island, with only traces of British Christianity preserved in the eastern parts.[67] Even if some former centres of Romanization and Christianization survived, they fell under pagan control. Thus, Britain differed fundamentally from the continental Gaul, where urban centres survived the raids and, as seats of bishops, could undertake the evangelization of rural areas.[68] According to Bede, England was converted by monks from Rome and Ireland!

2. Roman missionaries arrived in England in the spring of 597. They were sent by Pope Gregory the Great (590–604) and led by Augustine (d. 604–609), prior of the St. Andrew monastery in Rome. Æthelberht, the King of Kent (580–616), was initially distrustful (or pretended to be so to avoid losing the support of his superstitious people). The first official meeting with Roman monks took place outdoors. Kent people believed that if the missionaries practiced magic, they could easily deceive their king in a roofed building. However, the monks arrived – as Bede puts it – "endowed with divine not devilish power"; they carried a silver

---

66 Niblett (1995, 213).
67 Wood (2000, 31–34); (2008, 233).
68 Blair (2005, 10).

cross and the image of the Saviour, sang litanies and prayed for all attendees.[69] Their performances turned out to be effective. The king "granted his teachers a place to settle in, suitable to their rank, in Canterbury, his chief city, and gave them possessions of various kinds for their needs."[70] Donations allowed Augustine to set up a bishop seat in Canterbury, making it the centre of missionary activities. In December 597, some thousand pagans were baptized there, perhaps including King Æthelberht himself.[71]

The King of Kent knew the new religion very well. Fifteen years earlier he married Bertha, a Christian princess from the Merovingian dynasty, daughter of the former King of Paris, and granddaughter of Clovis I (ca. 466–511), the most famous Merovingian ruler, who united the Franks and converted them to Catholicism. Æthelberht allowed Bertha to practice her religion freely, but remained a pagan himself. Accepting baptism from the Franks would mean submitting spiritually to alien and equally ambitious rulers. Accepting baptism from the hands of a papal legate was an entirely different matter. Æthelberht could have been certain that his rule in Northumbria would be thus consolidated by obtaining legitimization from the Latin capital of Christianity and winning the acceptance of the Roman Emperor, world's greatest ruler, among whose subjects was the Pope.[72]

3. Neither Augustine nor the papal monks that accompanied him were Benedictines, although they surely have followed some kind of a rule in Rome.[73] Gregory I often touches upon monastic issues in his ample correspondence, but he never mentions Benedict or his codex.[74] Roman missionaries brought books, relics and ecclesiastical clothing to England. As soon as the king granted them a temporary seat (*mansio*), "they began to imitate the way of life of the Apostles and of the primitive church. They were constantly engaged in prayers, in vigils and fasts."[75]

---

69 Bede, *HE* 1.25, p. 74: "illi non daemonica sed diuina uirtute praediti ueniebant, crucem pro uexillo ferentes argenteam, et imaginem Domini Saluatoris in tabula depictam, laetaniasque canentes pro sua simul et eorum, propter quos et ad quos uenerant, salute aeterna Domino supplicabant."
70 Bede, *HE* 1.26, p. 78: "doctoribus suis locum sedis eorum gradui congruum in Doruuerni metropoli sua donaret, simul et necessarias in diuersis speciebus possessiones conferret."
71 Bede, *HE* 1.26, p. 76.
72 Brown (2003, 342–347).
73 Wallace-Hadril (1988, 36); Foot (2006, 63).
74 Dunn (2007, 684). Cf. Ferrari (1957).
75 Bede, *HE* 1.26, p. 76: "coeperunt apostolicam primitiuae ecclesiae uitam imitari, orationibus uidelicet assiduis uigiliis ac ieiuniis seruiendo."

Moreover, they delivered fiery sermons, renounced the world, and accepted only those gifts from the faithful that were absolutely necessary to live a life in accordance with Christian teachings.

The evangelization of the Anglo-Saxons proceeded slowly but efficiently. Gregory I, who was a realist and an outstanding strategist, would write to King Æthelberht, urging him to "suppress the worship of idols; overthrow their buildings and shrines."[76] However, he instructed his own missionaries to destroy only the images of idols, preserving the buildings themselves. "Take holy water and sprinkle it in these shrines," the Pope recommended, "built altars and place relics in them." Animals that were previously offered to the devil should now be killed in the name of the true God, during holidays celebrating martyrs. "It is doubtless impossible to cut out everything at once from their stubborn minds: just as the man who is attempting to climb the highest place, rises by steps and degrees and not by leaps."[77] The assimilationist politics adopted with regard to the old religion also left traces in the language. The word "Easter" comes from the pagan goddess Eostre whose name also denoted the month of April, which is considered by Christians as the "paschal month." Thus, the merry celebration of spring gave its name to the most important Christian holiday.[78]

4. In the 7th century, Britain was also reached by monks from Ireland, among them Aidan (d. 651) known for his strict habits. In 635, Oswald, the King of Northumbria (d. 642), gave Aidan the "holy island" of Lindisfarne. The monastery established there by Aidan was for thirty years the main church in Northumbria and the centre of missionary activities in England. Celtic monks were not only very active in this field, but also imposed their own monastic practices. However, the triumph of those supporting the Roman Rite at the Synod of Withby in 664 ended the dominance of Lindisfarne and greatly diminished the influence of the Irish, without terminating it, however.

In that century many Anglo-Saxon travellers visited the continent and were able to personally witness the monastic life in Europe. Bede writes, for example, that a wealthy aristocrat Biscop Baducing (d. 689) – who took the name Benedict

---

76 Bede, *HE* 1.32, p. 112: "idolorum cultus insequere; fanorum aedificia euerte."
77 Bede, *HE* 1.30, p. 108: "Nam duris mentibus simul omnia abscidere inpossibile esse non dubium est, quia et is, qui summum locum ascendere nititur, gradibus uel passibus, non autem saltibus eleuatur."
78 Bede, *De temporum ratione* 15 (*De mensibus Anglorum*): "Eostur-monath, qui nunc paschalis mensis interpretetur, quondam a dea illorum quae Eostre uocabatur, et cui in illo festa celebrabant, nomen habuit, a cuius nomine nunc paschale tempus cognominant; consueto antiquae obseruationis uocabulo gaudia nouae solemnitatis uocantes."

upon becoming a monk out of his fascination with the author of the Rule – organized monastic life in Monkwearmouth (674) and Jarrow (680–1) in Northumbria by following the customs of the seventeen monasteries he visited during his twenty-year-long journey to the Gaul and Italy.[79] The former was erected at the mouth of the River Wear, "in a Roman fashion," with the help of stonemasons and glaziers brought from continental Europe. During his travels, Baducing acquired an impressive library, which could have been used by Bede many years later. He also collected paintings and relics, and brought back with himself John, abbot in the St. Martin monastery and head cantor in St. Paul's in Rome. John was supposed to ensure the proper level of liturgical singing and reading. Soon, Monkwearmouth and Jarrow became the greatest centres of learning in the northern world, while abbot Benedict Biscop and his successors were considered saints.[80]

---

79 Bede, *Historia abbatum* 11, ed. Plummer, vol. 1, pp. 374–375.
80 Blair (2005, 89).

Mynster

1. A mediaeval abbey is the perfect example of a performative space that regulates and directs everything that a monk does. Even names of places suggested performances.[81] In the 10th century, the most important parts of an Anglo-Saxon monastic complex were:

- *oratorium*, or the church, where everyone would meet at specific times of the day in order to perform the daily cycle of prayers and songs;
- *refectorium*, or refectory, the room where everyone would gather to eat;
- *dormitorium*, or the room where everyone slept;
- *claustrum*, literally "enclosed space" (hence "cloister"), which stands for a part of the monastic complex where monks would spend the day while they were not praying, eating or resting; usually, it was a place for reading or studying together;
- a special hall where the entire community would meet, especially the guilt chapter when sins were publically confessed;
- *locus aptus*, "the proper place" which featured a chimney, where everyone could hide from bad weather during winter;
- *coquina*, kitchen;
- *pistrinum*, bakery;
- *hospitium*, guesthouse;
- *infirmarium*, hospital;
- *auditorium*, a special space where it was allowed to break silence.

All of these spaces were differently arranged and each reinforced the communal identity, inclining the monks to realize certain performative tasks as a group.

Performances by members of the community also produced space. Every action, be it spiritual or physical, was supposed to be preceded by a blessing.[82] This gesture would make the space for the performance of that task sacred. Monks were allowed to pray in private in "the secret places of the oratory."[83] A monk engrossed in prayer would call God or a dead brother as witness, and created, in a moment of rapture, an immaterial space that extended far beyond the walls and the present, leading to spiritual union with transcendental forces. Private prayer would almost invariably

---

81 Flint (2000, 149); Foot (2006, 46).
82 *RC* 14, p. 11 and footnote no. 4. The beginning of Psalm 70 would be repeated thrice: *Deus in adiutorium meum intende* ("Hasten, O God, to save me"). The Rule (*Proem* 4) recommended prayer "to bring [a good work] to perfection."
83 *RC* 6, p. 4 and 67, p. 66: "secretis oratorii locis."

consist of reciting psalms, whose monotonous rhythm of recitation facilitated falling into a trance. Psalms were also recited while working, or during other activities. When travelling, brothers would celebrate the hours prescribed by the Rule on their knees, thus producing a temporary sanctified space on a dirt road.[84]

2. The Latin word *monasterium* and its Old English cognate *mynster* have a surprisingly wide usage in England before the 10th century. These terms were used to describe all kinds of religious institutions associated with the Church. The world "cloister" frequently distorts the Anglo-Saxon contexts. In texts from the said period, the terms *monasterium* or *mynster* could have been used to denote a monastic community, but they could also refer to the house of a widow who lived in seclusion with her unmarried daughters, or even to a group of like-minded people.[85] In the 7th and 8th century, mixed communities were quite commonplace, e.g. ones in Whitby and Barking, where monks and nuns were strictly separated but all adhered to strict monastic rules. The experiment carried out in Coldingham was rather unsuccessful. Brothers and sisters living there would not care for the "well-being of their souls" and – as Bede recounts with outrage in *Historia ecclesiastica* (4.25) – divine flames had to cleanse the community by devouring all buildings. On that occasion, Bede also provides a description of daily life in an Anglo-Saxon monastery. Members of the community hailed from England and Ireland. They lived in a monastic complex comprised of public and private buildings, which towered over the surroundings. "And the cells that were built for praying and for reading have become haunts of feasting, drinking, gossip, and other delights; even the virgins who are dedicated to God […] spend their time weaving elaborate garments with which to adorn themselves as if they were brides."

Other sources confirm that there were musical instruments in monasteries. Cuthbert, abbot at Wearmouth and Jarrow, wrote to Germany in 764 requesting a musician, because the abbey was in possession of an instrument that no one could play.[86] Alcuin (ca. 735–804) advised monks in his letters to avoid "pagan songs" as well as "spectacles and diabolical fictions"; moreover, he accused artists of favouring vulgar entertainment over inspirational stories.[87]

3. It was the private monasteries that sparked the greatest controversy. They were founded by affluent aristocrats, who built them on their private lands, often for

---

84 *RC* 11, p. 7.
85 Foot (2006, 5); Blair (2005, 3). Cf. Foot (1992).
86 Boniface, *Ep.* 116 (ed. Tangl, p. 251).
87 Alcuin, *Ep.* 281, 175 ("spectacula et diabolica figmenta") and 124 (ed. Dümmler, p. 439, 290 and 183).

noble reasons. However, monasteries were exempt from taxes, which invited misappropriation. Disillusioned by the decay he saw in aristocratic monasteries, Bede felt deep resentment for them just before his death, which he expressed in a 734 letter to his former friend and student, Bishop Ecgberht of York, accusing the magnates of embezzlement. They would use the construction of monasteries as a cover – Bede claims – and in reality used them to pass bribes to the king, retaining the right to inherit the land on the basis of royal edicts. In practice, this led to the situation in which monks would be completely subordinated to lay people. Bede argues that after 705 almost every aristocrat (*praefectus*) in Northumbria received royal permission to found a monastery. Their wives as well as "ministers and royal servants" supposedly followed suit.[88] Several such edicts have been preserved, but none of them are from Northumbria.[89] Towards the end of the 10th century reformers of English monasticism stated that *saecularium prioratus* – the "secular domination" – was the reason behind the decline of monasteries in the previous century. Therefore, they strictly forbade, under threat of anathema, to recognize the authority of non-clericals by "sacred communities."[90]

During the life of Bede (ca. 672–735) monastic culture came to dominate England. It was the first time since Romans left that stone constructions were erected. The permanence of these edifices gave them a central significance in religious, economic and political life. Huge monastic complexes served the function of ancient "cities." Stone statues and crosses reinforced their status and expressed the identity of those new sites. Until 800 almost everyone in England, except for mountain-dwellers, lived next to one of the hundreds of monasteries.

In 793 the Vikings ravaged Lindisfarne. Subsequent raids almost obliterated monastic life in England for the second time in the country's history. King Alfred complained in the preface to his translation of a bishop's manual by Gregory the Great (*Regula pastoralis*) that when he took the throne in 871 most centres where spiritual life had formerly flourished deteriorated to such an extent that south of the Thames there was no one who could say Mass or understand a word of Latin.[91] During Alfred's reign (871–899) monasteries had little significance in religious and political life. Their revival began only in the 960s and 970s, spurred by a reform-oriented, educated court.

---

88 Bede, *Epistola ad Ecgbertum Episcopum* 12–13 (ed. Plummer, vol. 1, pp. 415–417).
89 Blair (2005, 100–108).
90 *RC, Proem* 10, p. 7. The ban on electing lay abbots – probably inefficient – was introduced already at the Council of Clofesho in 803 (*CED* 3.545–546).
91 M. Lapidge, *Monasticism*, in: Lapidge (1999, 320–322); Knowles (1963, 32–33).

Regularis Concordia

1. The key proponents of monastic reform were three church officials: Dunstan, Archbishop of Canterbury (959–988); Æthelwold, Bishop of Winchester (963–984); Oswald, Bishop of Worcester in the years 961–992 and from 971 the Archbishop of York. The success of reforms, however, was decided in 959 upon the enthronement of Eadgar, an enlightened monarch who grasped the urgency of change. In February 964, Eadgar and his troops helped Æthelwold to expel lay canons from the Old Minster monastery in Winchester, thus cutting off their source of sumptuous benefits. They were replaced by Benedictines brought from Abingdon, where Æthelwold was abbot from 955.

Æthelwold played a key role in introducing Benedictine monasticism to England. He translated into Old English the Rule by St. Benedict, and edited – or perhaps wrote himself – a document that expanded on Benedictine principles, clearly defining and homogenizing rules of life in English monasteries: *Regularis concordia Anglicae nationis monachorum sanctimonialiumque* (*The Monastic Agreement of the Monks and Nuns of the English Nation*).[92]

The impulse to change came from the continent, primarily from the Fleury abbey, where St. Benedict's relics were deposited, transferred there in the 8th century from the ruined monastery in Monte Cassino. Reforms in Fleury, introduced by Odon of Cluny in the 930s, inspired deep changes in monastic life, also beyond France. Pilgrims from all over Europe, including guests from England, flocked to Fleury. Oda, future Archbishop of Canterbury, was a monk there, along with his cousin Oswald. Dunstan, on the other hand, would borrow books from Fleury (a reminder to return them has been preserved). Oswald in particular was impressed by his stay in France. An heir of an affluent and influential family of Danish roots, he came back to England aflame with missionary zeal and began founding Benedictine monasteries.

2. The driving force behind reforms was Archbishop Dunstan, an outstanding politician and statesman.[93] In the 940s and 950s, he thoroughly reorganized the abbey in Glastonbury, making it into one of the principal sites of Anglo-Saxon monasticism. Æthelwold studied with him there, both of them researching

---

92 The text of *Regularis concordia* was published in 1953 by Thomas Symons. This edition, which is still considered to be classic, shall be hereinafter referred to in contracted form as *RC*. In 1993 Lucia Kornexl prepared a new edition, restoring in some places the orthography of the original.
93 Preserved biographies of Dunstan are collected in *Memorials* (ed. Stubbs).

St. Benedict's Rule. Dunstan soon became influential at court, which he nevertheless paid for in banishment due to the many intrigues he was involved with. In 956 he was forced to flee to Flanders, where he would visit St. Peter's monastery in Ghent, seeing with his own eyes the practical implementation of monastic reforms in the Benedictine spirit. In 960 King Eadgar, who was enthroned as the ruler of all England the previous year, appointed Dunstan the Archbishop of Canterbury. According to his biography, penned by a writer known as B., Dunstan was supposed to experience divine inspiration, just like Cædmon before him. A young man clad in white revealed himself to him, and taught him to sing the antiphon *O rex gentium* (*O, the King of nations*). Dunstan must have repeated the song many times over, because when he woke up he could write it down.[94]

The main goal of the reform camp was to establish and spread high standards in celebrating liturgy, tending spiritual life and conducting pastoral work.[95] The three protagonists of the movement have been traditionally presented as a harmonious team, but they in fact differed. Æthelwold radically rejected all ways of life beyond the monastic ones, and although he allowed beer, cheese or even meat from time to time in Abingdon, he nevertheless subjected his monks to strict discipline. One monk named Ælfstan had to prove his obedience by putting his hand in a pot of boiling water when the abbot asked him to reach for a piece of food lying at the very bottom.[96] Oswald, on the other hand, erected a new church for monks in Worcester right next to one serving the clergy, acknowledging both groups as members of a broader family of the Bishop. Unlike the ones gathered around Æthelwold, Oswald's monks did not mind being called priests (*clerici*[97]). Finally, Dunstan himself was primarily a politician. Although he had his reservations, he did carefully introduce Benedictine reforms at Canterbury, achieving success. It was probably him who made the king so keenly interested in reforms. *Regularis concordia* begins and ends by recalling Eadgar. Royal authority was supposed to help protect the property of monasteries from any designs on the part of secular powers. Reformers presented Eadgar's reign as the golden age of Church in England. The geographic range of the movement, however, was surprisingly modest, as it was able to reach some ten per cent of all communities, mostly ones in former Wessex as well as in western and eastern parts of the

---

94 *Memorials*, ed. Stubbs, p. 41.
95 Blair (2005, 351).
96 Wulfstan, *Vita S. Æthelwoldi* 14. Cf. Kobialka (1999, 244–245).
97 Barrow (1996). The term *clerici* defined all clergymen, both of lesser and greater vows.

Midlands, where the estates of Oswald and Æthelwold were located. Women houses were practically limited to the central part of Wessex.[98]

Recognition of king and queen as patrons and guardians of monasticism as institution, as well as the introduction of prayers in the intention of king and court into the daily schedule, make English monasticism unique in the Middle Ages due to its specific, national character. This is also reflected by the remarkably high degree of participation of monasteries in the life of Anglo-Saxon people, which was exceptional on a European scale. In the 10th century, most bishops hailed from a monastic background. Together with the abbots they would take part in the "meetings of wise men" (*witenagemot*), i.e. the highest advisory and legislative body dealing with both secular and religious matters. This meant that monastic institutions had a dominant role also beyond Church.[99]

3. *Regularis concordia* has been preserved in complete editions only in two loosely related manuscripts connected with the Christ Cathedral in Canterbury. Both are currently deposited in London, in the British Library. The *Cotton Tiberius A.iii* manuscript, created in the first half of the 11th century, contains the Latin text of *Regularis concordia* with an interlinear Anglo-Saxon glossa (fol. 3r-27v), a large selection of Benedictine writings, along with the Rule, as well as numerous other documents (altogether ninety-four texts and two illustrations). The earlier manuscript, *Cotton Faustina B.iii* (fol. 159-198), which comes from the end of the 10th century, contains an erroneous copy of the Latin text, where the epilogue had been replaced by three obituaries.[100]

Both manuscripts come from the famous library of Sir Robert Cotton (1586-1631), the most important collection of manuscripts gathered in England by a private person. Individual works were placed in bookcases, on top of which stood fourteen busts of Roman emperors[101]; hence the names of the documents: *Cotton Tiberius* or *Cotton Faustina*. Cotton was also an active politician and scholar, sometimes interfering with the composition of the works he possessed. In the manuscript of *Cotton Tiberius A.iii*, which he came to own in 1621, the librarian changed the order of texts, putting *Regularis concordia* at the opening of the volume, instead of St. Benedict's Rule.[102] It probably testifies to the deep respect enjoyed in the 17th century by the work of Anglo-Saxon monks.

---

98 Blair (2005, 351).
99 Knowles (1963, 45).
100 Die "Regularis Concordia", ed. Kornexl; REED Kent: Diocese of Canterbury, p. cviii.
101 Reconstruction of the library in: Sharpe (1979, 71-72).
102 Ker (1957, 248); Gnuess (1997).

Regularis concordia was written in the so-called "hermeneutic style," typical for the 10th century, and practiced by Æthelwold.[103] It consists of twelve chapters as well as a longer prologue and a shorter epilogue. The former states unambiguously that the reformers wished to both preserve the good traditions of their country and take inspiration from the best monastic practices of their time, often travelling themselves and inviting to Winchester monks from Fleury and Ghent. *Regularis concordia* is a mosaic filled with borrowings from numerous, diverse sources, sometimes difficult to identify today. St. Benedict's Rule is invoked most frequently, through direct quotations, but references are also made to other documents of the period regulating the life of monastic communities. The text is somewhat chaotically structured, with some threads abruptly lost and others randomly intertwined, while certain important subjects are left untouched. Repetition and Latinized forms of Greek terms also make the work difficult to understand on first contact.[104]

---

103 M. Lapidge (1975, 67) defined the "hermeneutic style" as "the ostentatious parade of unusual, often very arcane and apparently learned vocabulary," featuring archaisms, "neologisms or coinages" and loan-words, mostly from Greek. For more information on Æthelwold's language see: Gretsch (1999).
104 Knowles (1963, 43).

Everyday Performances

1. *Regularis concordia* organizes monk's life according to a rhythm based on prayers, which were often sung. Two main types of daily liturgical practices were Mass and Divine Office (*Officium Divinum*). The former originates from rituals centred around celebrations of the Last Supper. The name *Officium Divinum* was given to those religious practices that emerged in the first three centuries of Christianity. A basic programme of the Office consisted of a psalm, a reading from the Scriptures, and a hymn, i.e. a metrical laudatory song of Greek origin. According to Psalm 119, lines 164 ("Seven times a day I praise you") and 62 ("At midnight I rise to give you thanks"), seven Divine Offices have been ordered for the day (matins, prime, terce, sext, none, vespers and compline) and one for the night (nocturne).[105] Moreover, a liturgical order of each of the Office's eight hours was established. Basically, *Regularis concordia* remains faithful to these rules. The programme of the Office, which has been called Divine Work (*Opus Dei*) by St. Benedict, was supplemented by Anglo-Saxon reformers with numerous devotional practices, especially prayers for the royal court, but without changing the order of the eight-hour Office.

The life of a monk was determined by sunrise and sunset. Since both day and night were twelve hours long, winter daytime was shorter than in summer. Accordingly, singing of shorter hymns was advised in winter. One could get a good night's sleep though, because nighttime was longer. It was only the mechanical clock, introduced in the 14th century that allowed dividing the twenty-four hours into segments of equal length, thus establishing a single order of the day regardless of the season.[106] Earlier on, no one bothered to determine the Office hours precisely. As a result of this, "an hour of time" (*hora quoad tempus*) rarely equalled "an hour of office" (*hora quoad officium*).[107] Naturally, it was the sacred time produced by the monks' performance that was privileged. *Regularis concordia* advised extended use of variously sized bells, in accordance with the English tradition. They would indicate the time for key liturgical performances both to monks and people living in the monastery's neighbourhood. The beginning of work was signalled by striking wooden tablets.

2. In his introduction to the classic edition of the Latin text of *Regularis concordia*, Dom Thomas Symons included a hypothetical reconstruction of monks' duties

---

105   *RB* 16.
106   Kobialka (1999, 258).
107   Dorn-van Rossum (1996, 32).

in winter working days, i.e. from 1 November until Lent (with only one meal a day), and in summer, from Easter to 14 September (with two meals a day).[108] Investigation of both schedules leads to interesting conclusions. Daytime offices were definitely shorter than nighttime ones. Regardless of the season, a greater part of the night would be spent on singing psalms. In winter, monks would eat only once a day, late, but would also work once. Apart from psalms and prayers for the royal court[109], *Regularis concordia* supplements the daily liturgy with a series of Offices for the dead[110] as well as gradual[111] and penitentiary psalms.[112]

WINTER HORARIUM		SUMMER HORARIUM	
		ca. 1.30	Rise *Trina oratio*[113] Gradual Psalms
		2	NOCTURNS Psalms for the Royal House Short interval
ca. 2.30	Rise *Trina oratio*[113] Gradual Psalms		
3	NOCTURNS[114] Psalms for the Royal House Vigil of the Dead Matins of the Dead Matins of All Saints	3.30 / 4	MATINS of the day (ending *luce diei*) *Miserere* (Psalm 51) Psalms for the Royal House Anthems Matins of All Saints Matins of the Dead Interval (if day: change shoes, wash etc.; if dark: sleep for those who wish)
		ca. 5	*Trina oratio*
5	*Lectio* (reading)		*Lectio*

---

108 *RC*, pp. xliii–xliv.
109 With separate ones for the king, the queen, and the benefactors.
110 Offices for the dead were celebrated daily in the years 800–1971. Initially, in the 9th century, the ceremony took place after the funeral, with the deceased "speaking" through the celebrant, or the community, expressing bitterness and terror on the one hand, and remorse and faith on the other. This office was made part of daily singing of hours after recommendation by Benedict of Aniane at the Council of Aix-la-Chapelle in 817. Cf. Ottosen (1996, 171–172).
111 Fifteen psalms (nos. 120–134) performed in three groups of five, kneeling after each of the three parts. They were usually sung on the steps to the altar (*gradus* in Latin) or the bishop's rostrum; hence the name.
112 Psalms 6, 32, 38, 51, 102, 130 and 142.
113 So-called "triple prayer" in praise of Holy Trinity, said three times a day.
114 The night-time Office, the longest one, was traditionally devoted to singing psalms.

WINTER HORARIUM		SUMMER HORARIUM	
6	MATINS of the day (at dawn)[115] *Miserere* (Psalm 51) Psalms for the Royal House Anthems	6	PRIME[116] Four psalms, Penitential psalms, Litany MORROW MASS Chapter
6.45	PRIME[116] Four psalms, Penitential psalms, Litany		Five psalms (for the Dead)
7.30	*lectio* (*usque horam secundam*)	7.30	Work
8	Interval (change shoes, wash etc.) *Trina oratio* TIERCE[117] Psalms for the Royal House Morrow mass Chapter[118] Five psalms (for the Dead)[119]	8	TIERCE[117] Psalms for the Royal House PRINCIPAL MASS
		9.30	Lectio
ca. 9.45	Work		
		11.30	SEXT[120] Psalms for the Royal House
12	SEXT[120] Psalms for the Royal House PRINCIPAL MASS	12	*Prandium* (first meal)
		ca. 13	Siesta
ca. 13.30	NONE[121] Psalms for the Royal House		
ca. 14	*Cena* (the one meal *ad nonam*)		
		14.30	NONE Psalms for the Royal House Drink
ca. 14.45	*Lectio* or *Work* VESPERS of the day[122] Psalms for the Royal House Anthems (as after Matins) Vespers of All Saints Vespers of the Dead Change to night shoes Drink	ca. 15	Work VESPERS of the day[122] *Miserere* (Psalm 51) Psalms for the Royal House Anthems Vespers of All Saints

---

115 First hour of the Office.
116 Second hour.
117 Third hour.
118 A monastic parliament, during which the Rule or that day's passages from Gospels would be read, among other activities, including confession of sins in front of the entire community.
119 Psalms 5, 6, 116, 116b and 130.
120 Fourth hour.
121 Fifth hour.
122 Sixth hour.

WINTER HORARIUM		SUMMER HORARIUM	
18	*Collatio* (readings)[123]		Vespers of the Dead
18.15	COMPLINE[124] *Miserere* (Psalm 51) Psalms for the Royal House *Trina oratio*		*Cena* (second meal) Vigils of the Dead
18.30	Retire		
		19.30	Change to night shoes *Collatio* (readings)[123]
		20	COMPLINE[124] *Miserere* (Psalm 51) Psalms for the Royal House
		ca. 20.15	*Trina oratio* Retire

3. The performative character of monastic culture found its fullest expression in music. In the 4th and 5th century, Christian ascetics would recite mantra-like, never-ending strings of psalms during the night to keep awake. St. Benedict ordered performing the entire psalter, i.e. all one hundred and fifty psalms, in a weekly cycle during the offices, primarily the longest one at night, in line with the ancient tradition of the hermits. In contrast to prayers and readings, psalms were always sung. As Isidore of Seville wrote, "[a] lesson is so called because it is not sung, like a psalm or hymn, but only read."[125]

Psalms, however, were performed in a remarkable manner. The main part of the text was sung using a single note, known as the "reciting tone" or *tenor* (from Latin *tenere*, meaning "to hold").[126] The proper tenor was established through a several-syllable-long intonation (from *initium*, meaning "beginning"), from which the psalm would begin. It was performed by the soloist called *precentor*. The intonation was always rising, with the first syllable of a psalm sung on the lowest sound, the next on a higher one, and the last – in the case of three-syllable intonation – on the highest, which in turn became the tenor for further recitation performed by the choir. In case of longer lines, the tenor was repeated, which reinforced the performance's monotonous character. The end of every half-line was also signalled by short, several-syllable-long musical ornaments. At the end of

---

123 *RB* 42.3: "Someone should read from the Conference or the Lives of the Fathers or at any rate something else that will benefit the hearers."
124 The seventh and last hour of the Divine Office, celebrated usually after sunset.
125 Isidore, *Etymologiae* 6.19.9: "Lectio dicitur quia non cantatur, ut psalmus vel hymnus, sed legitur tantum."
126 Ilnitchi (2001, 647–648).

the first half-line, monks would sing the so-called mediant (*mediatio*), a musical formula that split the verse, like a comma or semi-colon, into two half-lines. The second part began once again from the tenor, and the last syllables of the ending (*terminatio*), sometimes called a cadence (*cadere* – "to fall"), would be sung using falling sounds.

The custom of monotonous singing has its origin in the earliest ritual practices. Richard Taruskin argues that it features traces of the very beginnings of music. In Western church, first mentions of psalm tones date back to early 8th century. With time, the Roman liturgy adopted the habit of using eight basic tones and an additional one called *tonus peregrinus* ("wandering" or "migrant")[127] when the tenor of the first half-line differed from that of the second. *Tonus peregrinus*, used to perform only two psalms (nos. 113 and 114), testifies to pre-Christian vocal practices. Yemeni Jews used this technique to perform the same texts.[128] Monotonous musical performances based on an archaic tone of recitation created a sacred "acoustic space," stimulating internal transformation of the performer similarly to the "vibrating songs" practiced towards the end of the 20th century by Jerzy Grotowski. The vibration of his performers would efficiently convert "heavy energy" into "subtle" one, also in members of the audience, which I have experienced myself watching *Akcja* (*Action*) in Wrocław's Ossoliński Library in 1996.

4. Initially, psalms were probably performed by two dialoguing choirs. Multi-choir antiphons are described in the Bible; in 445 BC the priest Nehemiah blessed the walls of Jerusalem he rebuilt himself, and placed two thanksgiving choirs at the battlements on two sides of the gate, both joyfully praising God.[129] Another testimony to early performances is contained in the unique structure of psalms themselves. Each verse is comprised by two half-lines that express the same thought in different words. However, Christian psalmody does not originate from Jewish temple rituals, but rather from the monotonous, night-time performances at vigils practiced by early Christians.[130] In a letter to the clergy at Neocaesarea written in 375, St. Basil[131] mentions that when ascetics of Caesarea met at night in the prayer house, they formed two choirs in order to take turns in singing psalms.

In his account of monasticism at the turn of the 4th and 5th century, John Cassian (ca. 360–435) observes that already at this stage the singing of psalms was

---

127 Lundberg (2011).
128 Appel (1958, 509). Cf. Lundberg (2011, 276–277).
129 Nehemiah 12:27–43. Cf. Taruskin (2005, 1.9–11).
130 Taruskin (2005, 1.7–9).
131 St. Basil, *Ep.* 207.3, ed. Courtonne, vol. 2, p. 186.

prolonged by using "antiphonal melodies" (*antiphonarum melodiis*) and "some modulation" (*quarundam modulationum*).[132] However, Cassian does not clarify these terms. According to Amalarius of Metz (d. 850), towards the end of the 8th century the term antiphon referred to refrains that the choir repeated after each line of the psalm.[133] St. Benedict, however, allowed skipping of antiphons in order to lessen the Office's burden on smaller communities.[134] Antiphons were most often sung only at the beginning and at the end of psalms. These were short songs with simple melodies, whose lyrics were usually derived from the psalm they accompanied. Antiphons were also added to biblical songs lifted from the Gospel of Luke, such as *Magnificat* or *Benedictus*. They were also composed for special occasions like the Palm Sunday procession. In mediaeval Europe, antiphon was the most widespread musical genre.

5. The relationship between text and music has three dimensions: syllabic, neumatic and melismatic. In the simplest compositions each syllable was assigned one tone. In the more complex songs, one syllable could be sung using entire cascades of tones, which were called melismas. Christian mystics considered melismatic singing as the highest form of religious expression. St. Augustine wrote: "Qui iubilat, non verba dicit, sed sonus quidam est laetitiae sine verbis vox est enim animi diffusi laetitia."[135] The term *jubilus* ("cry of joy") – the only Latin word originating from the root of the interjection *ju* – was commonly used to refer to the main melisma at the end of the phrase.

In neumatic songs, on the other hand, a single syllable was sung using two or three tones. The word "neuma," etymologically derived from the Greek *pneūma* ("breath"), was used in reference to the kind of musical phrase it was possible to sing in one breath. Carolinian scholars developed a system of graphic signs to denote the neume. Soon after the Synod of Winchester, neumes were used to preserve the earliest known examples of liturgical polyphony in a manuscript

---

132 Cassian, *De institutis coenobiorum* 2.2 (PL 49.78bc). Cf. Raasted (1996, 78–79).
133 Amalarius, *Liber de ordine antiphonarii* 3.4, ed. Hanssens, p. 24: "ex senis antiphonis quas uicissim chori per singulos uersus repetunt." For more information on psalm singing see: Dyer (1989).
134 *RB* 17.6: "If the community is rather large, refrains are used with psalms, if it is smaller, the psalms are said without refrain."
135 Augustine, *In psalmum* 94.4 (PL 37.1272): "One who jubilates does not speak words, but it is rather a sort of sound of joy without words, since it is the voice of a soul poured out in joy" (trans. McKinnon 1987, 158). Cf. Wiora (1962); Taruskin (2005, 1.11).

now kept in Cambridge.[136] Among other works it contains one of the earliest examples of musical score to the performance *Visitatio Sepulchri*. The document was made 150 years prior to the next known collection of liturgical polyphonies. This proves that Anglo-Saxon monks displayed exceptional competence in the art of performance.

Today it seems impossible to reconstruct melodies basing only on neumes, which were added to the text without additional lines, using "cheironomic" notation (*cheirnomía* means "gesticulation" in Greek). The name derives from a performative practice: teachers would instruct how to sing, while cantors conducted the performance by air-drawing the course of the melody so that the singers would imitate gestures in song. Cheironomic neumes did not define the precise pitch and intervals, nor would they provide any rhythm. Cheironomic signs only assisted singers who already knew the melody. The song could survive only by being performed. It was only at the beginning of the 11th century that the line notation was developed. Clearly determined intervals allowed separating music from its performance. Monks at St. Gallen, where the first collections of antiphons were created, made manuscripts with cheironomic neumes until the 15th century.[137] Singing was taught there through performance, not by developing a notation.

6. Singing antiphons with the psalms was a relatively easy task in comparison to the performance of the responsorium. Although the shorter *responsoria brevia* were similar to most antiphons insofar as they featured simple musical structures, the longer *responsoria prolixa* were distinguished by elaborate ornamentation and highly developed melodic phrases. The most competent musicians were needed to perform them properly. Based largely on never-ending streams of melismas, *responsoria* created a unique opportunity to meditate on a text one has just heard.[138] During matins, *responsoria* always followed readings from the Bible or the lives of saints. They also distinguished themselves clearly from the monotonous psalmodies with musical richness and an originality of composition. Their text could be either in verse or in prose.

Performances of *responsoria* could be fascinating. Traditional dialogues between the soloist and the choir were elevated to absolute artistic heights. The cantor would only sing a simple verse, usually in a monotonous, psalmodic style, whereas the response – the most developed part in terms of music – would be sung

---

136 MS 473, Corpus Christi College, Cambridge. For attempted transcription see: Holschneider (1968).
137 Taruskin (2005, 1.16–17).
138 Edwards (1996, 50).

by the entire choir. Such a response would often comprise many different musical phrases, sometimes quite long due to the extension of syllables in key words with melismas. Poets had to be highly ingenious in order to position the crucial word four or five syllables before the end, because it was there – according to the tradition – that the longest melismas would be found.[139] The choral responses reinforced a sense of the community coming together, perfectly rendering the idea of a single universal church believing in the one and only God.

7. *Regularis concordia* advised monks to receive the Eucharist every day.[140] No other document mentions the existence of such a practice in the 10th century, although it was commonplace then to celebrate Mass every day, either the morning one or the main one. Monks were supposed to be assisted in their preparations for receiving Communion by taking the "healing remedy" (*salubre remedium*), i.e. going to a sacramental confession.[141] It was usually the abbot who acted as the confessor, and custom demanded one do so once a week or more often if a brother's individual conscience required this.[142] Monks were obliged to remain truthful, even if this entailed testifying against oneself.[143] This obligation was a true cornerstone and involved the compulsion to propagate truth. Every performance in a monastic complex was supposed to testify to the truth. One of the key spiritual experiences of every monk was the chapter meeting when excerpts from the Rule and Acts of the Martyrs were read, and sins were confessed publicly. Sometimes a monk would confess himself, and sometimes he would be accused by the abbot or an older brother; however, in neither case was he allowed to defend himself. He would have to lie prostrate on the ground and remain silent until the abbot allowed him to speak.[144] Once this duty, the "spiritual purgation," was over, it was necessary to sing five psalms for dead brothers.[145]

One special form of giving testimony was engaging in charitable activities.[146] *Regularis concordia* recommended mercy for the poor as a fundamental duty applying to all members of the community, from the smallest boy to the abbot himself, the "assistant to Christ." A special place was even set up where the poor would be received. Not only would they be given alms, but also three selected people

---

139   Edwards (1996, 51); Ilnitchi (2001, 661–663).
140   *RC* 23, p. 19.
141   *RC* 22, p. 18. The phrase recurs in many prayers said during Ash Wednesday.
142   *RC* 27, p. 23.
143   See Kobialka (1999, 63), who cites lectures by Michel Foucault.
144   *RC* 21, p. 17.
145   Psalms 5, 6, 116, 116b and 130.
146   *RC* 62 and 63, p. 61 and 62.

would be invited to eat with the monks. Moreover, every day the monks would follow the continental custom and wash the feet of at least three poor, despite the fact that they were required to wash their own only once a week, on Saturday.[147] Even when he was old and weak, Oswald – one of the initiators of monastic reform – would fast and wash the feet of twelve poor people every day. He died on the next day after fulfilling this duty on the third Sunday of Lent in 992.[148] According to Symons, "the picture drawn by the *Concordia* of the love and reverent care lavished on the poor has not its like in any contemporary consuetudinary."[149] Anglo-Saxon monks supported the poorest and the excluded, humbling themselves before the sick, and generously giving to people who had nothing to give back. Monks did not disdain human corporeality. Through everyday performances they restored dignity and a spiritual dimension of the often sick and mutilated body. Every body was reminiscent of the Incarnation. As St. Augustine taught, "[o]ne does not enter into truth except through charity."[150]

---

147   *RC* 25, p. 22.
148   *RC*, p. xxvii.
149   *RC*, p. xxxvii.
150   Augustine, *Contra Faustum* 32.18: "non intratur in ueritatem, nisi per caritatem."

Bodily Performances

1. The manuscript *Cotton Tiberius A.iii* from Canterbury – which also contains the Latin text of *Regularis concordia* with Old English glosses, as well as a selection of Benedictine texts – features a catalogue of 127 monastic gestures (Latin *indicia*, Old English *tacn*). Admittedly, *Regularis concordia* somewhat softened the strict injunction to remain silent, formulated by Benedict in the Rule[151]; silent conversations were allowed "at the proper time and touching necessary affairs,"[152] although the document generally prescribed that monks should refrain from speaking. Strict silence was obligatory all through the night, from vespers until chapter on the following day. The said catalogue of gestures, composed in Old English, was meant to provide the monks with means of communication in an emergency, without having to break the rule of silence.[153]

The first lexicon of monastic signs was created in Cluny, in Burgundy.[154] This abbey, founded in 910, originally did not differ from others, but it initiated a thorough reform of monasticism, which was corrupted by two centuries of Scandinavian raids. Life in Cluny rested on three fundamental principles: vowing absolute sexual abstinence, singing developed and prolonged psalmodies, and remaining entirely and piously silent. Monks of Cluny were the first to recognize silence as a powerful facilitator of transformation and a virtue in itself.[155] Absolute silence during night and day on the territory of the entire abbey was in force for a week during the octaves of Christmas and Easter. The silent performance was supposed to anticipate "the eternal silence to come."[156] In Cluny, refraining from speech not only protected from the "sin of language," but also helped imitate angels in accordance with the order of Duke William I of Aquitaine.[157] The Duke inclined monks to desire and seek the "heavenly" way of life "with full commitment and

---

151 *RB* 42.1: Monks should diligently cultivate silence at all time.
152 *RC* 56, p. 55: "opportuno tamen tempore de rebus necessariis."
153 Banham (1991).
154 Initially, the signs were not recorded, and knowledge of them was passed orally. Copies of the lexicon emerged only ca. 1080 as chapters in consuetudines, i.e. detailed accounts of monastic practices, made by Bernard of Cluny and Ulrich of Zell. Cf. Bruce (2007, 9–10 and 69–70).
155 Bruce (2007, 3).
156 Bruce (2007, 27). Cf. John of Salerno, *Vita Odonis* 1.32 (*PL* 133.57a): "aeternum silentium."
157 Mediaeval sources often compared monks to angels. See: Frank (1964); Leclercq (1961, 15–42).

inner ardour."[158] Odon, the second abbot of Cluny (925–942), perceived monastic life as the imitation of angels – *coelestis disciplina*.[159]

2. The silence kept by monks in Cluny symbolized the silent omnipresence of God. It was already Gregory the Great who stated that after the resurrection of chosen ones at the end of time, the Word of God will fill everyone silently, penetrating every mind with its power of internal light.[160] The silent performances of the monks expressed the final nature of reality and attempted to convey it in terms fit for this earthly world. In order to avoid breaking the pious silence, an appropriately silent language, mainly utilizing hands, was introduced in Cluny.[161]

The dictionary of gestures from Cluny describes one hundred and eighteen signs. They mainly represent nouns – only fifteen denote verbs or abstract notions. However, this artificial system of communication was not invented to replace spoken language. The signs were only supposed to aid in emergency, e.g. while preparing food in the kitchen, where absolute silence was in order.[162] The first part of the catalogue contains thirty-five signs related to nourishment. The list opens with "bread" (*panis*): "make a complete circle using each thumb and the next two fingers, the reason being that bread is usually round."[163] Further signs refer to matters related to clothing, the Divine Office, people and events. This catalogue throws unique light on everyday life at the abbey.

3. Anglo-Saxon monks adopted the signs used in Cluny through the mediation of Fleury, but arranged them differently. The Canterbury catalogue begins by enumerating the seven main "officials" at the monastery, with the abbot heading the list. Subsequent signs are related to liturgy, food, hygiene, clothing, and the last group contains gestures denoting king, queen, bishop, monk and lay persons. The catalogue was made in Old English in order to make it more accessible for those without knowledge of Latin. A similar goal motivated Old English glossas added to the Latin text of *Regularis concordia* contained in the same manuscript.

---

158 *Charta qua Vuillelmus, comes et dux, fundat monasterium cluniacense* (no. 120): "conuersatioque celestis omni desideratio et ardore intimo perquiratur et expetatur" (Bruce 2007, 17).

159 Odon of Cluny, *Sermo 3. De Sancto Benedicto abbate* (PL 133.722a). Cf. Asad (1993, 137) and Bruce (2007, 20).

160 George I the Great, *Moralium libri* 30.4.17 (PL 76.533ab): "mentes nostras vi intimae illustrationis penetrat." Cf. Bruce (2007, 28).

161 Jarecki (1981).

162 Bruce (2007, 79–83).

163 Bruce (2007, 177).

Knowledge of Latin was not universal among monks, and the success of reforms demanded that everyone understand the new rules of monastic life.

The Canterbury lexicon also contains new signs. Particularly striking is the attention to hygiene, greater than in Cluny. No other catalogue features signs from this category. Other novel gestures include ones denoting king and queen, which may be seen as the acknowledgment of royal patronage over English monasticism. Both signs were made by putting one's hand, with fingers apart, in front of one's bowing head. In Cluny it meant the psalter, since the gesture referred to King David, author of Psalms. In Canterbury, verbs were entirely dropped so as to prevent excessive "garrulousness" and reinforce discipline.[164] Towards the end of the 12th century, Gerald from Wales (d. ca. 1223) would be outraged at the monks in Canterbury for undue gesturing during meals. Moreover, they would hiss and whistle (*sibilis*) instead of talking, in which they seemed to Gerald like actors or clowns (he refers to *ludos scenicos, histriones* and *joculatores*). His opinions, however, have to be taken with a pinch of salt. The Welshman was not particularly fond of the Canterbury monks, because their archbishop supported English bishops for filling dioceses in Wales; later, they would efficiently employ excommunication to block regional uprisings.[165]

4. Items were identified using two methods: either by imitating their use or by showing how they were made. If a monk asked for a candlestick (*candel sticca*, no. 26[166]), he slightly clenched his fist as if he held one, and blew at his index finger. A knife (*syx*, no. 55) was shown by cutting one finger with another; a small drinking cup (*lytel drencefœt*, no. 82) – by putting the index finger on one's lips and lifting it as if to drink; water (*wœter*, no. 97) – by suggesting easing of hands; comb (*camb*, no. 100) – by combing; scissors (*sceara*, no. 109) – by cutting with two hands; chisel (*grœf*, no. 112) – by writing with the index finger extended; beer (*beor*, no. 85) – by rubbing hands, which was imitative of the beverage's production process; finally, a herbal potion (*wyrtdrenc*, no. 86) was indicated by pressing the index finger on the lips as if one were crushing herbs.

---

164 Bruce (2007, 116–117).
165 Giraldus Cambrensis, *De rebus a se gestis* 11.5, ed. Brewer, vol. 1, p. 51. Cf. *MES* 33 (A19). For more information on the ambiguity of terms referring to mediaeval performers see: Ogilvy (1963) and Baldwin (1997). Gerald's views are discussed by Bartlett (1982, 48–57).
166 All names in Old English and sign numbers after: Banham (1991). Cf. Dodwell (2000, 146–147).

A completely different technique was used to identify people. Usually, the symbol of their office was demonstrated: a crown made from hands denoted king (*cyning*, no. 118) and queen (*cyninges wif*, no. 119). A characteristic element of clothing could be recalled, as in the case of the nun's veil (*mynecenu*, no. 122), or a woman's band (*ungehadod wif*, no. 127). Activities would be demonstrated – the cellar keeper was signified by opening the door (*hordere*, no. 4). All of these signs aided communication, but could not convey feelings or moods. In late Anglo-Saxon miniatures illustrating biblical themes it is possible to identify such arrangements of hands and body that express the thoughts and emotions of figures from the Scripture. After long and painstaking studies of manuscripts, Charles Reginald Dodwell discovered that the most common gestures painted by Anglo-Saxon illuminators stem from Roman theatre.

5. Twelve illuminated manuscripts of plays by Terence have been preserved. Works by this poet were particularly popular and frequently imitated in the Middle Ages. Three earliest and best preserved codices[167] were made at the turn of the 9th and 10th century. Each contains six comedies, and the scenes are accompanied by drawings depicting the dramatis personae – 144 miniatures in total. Dodwell meticulously analysed the gestures made by figures from Terence's comedies and found six of them in somewhat later Anglo-Saxon miniatures. None of these gestures appear earlier in Christian sources[168]:

- puzzlement or perplexity – two fingers, or one, pointing to the forehead or face;
- grief or sadness – bent or straight hand on a cheek;
- approval or acquiescence – bent thumb and index finger, or the ring one, or the middle one, formed in a circle;
- supplication – arms extended in a typical gesture of begging;
- fear or anxiety – hands facing outwards, with elbows touching the corpus;
- pondering or reflecting – a clenched fist propping the chin.

Dodwell confirmed that the miniatures accompanying Terence's plays date back to the 3rd century AD by comparing them to Roman artworks made in the same period. Although it seems that the classical author was inspired by literature rather than theatrical representations, the drawings clearly depict a consistent code of

---

167 *Vaticanus latinus* 3868, *Parisinus latinus* 7899, and Milano, *Ambrosianus* S.P.4bis (formerly H.75). Codex Oxoniensis (Auct. F.2.13) was created in the 12th century and is now deposited in Oxford, in the Bodleian Library. Reproduced in: Jones & Morey (1930–1931). Cf. Kocur (2005, 176–177).
168 Dodwell (2000, 101–154).

gestures, which suggests that they accurately render the means of expression used by Roman comedy actors. Anglo-Saxon monks reproduced those gestures on their miniatures, displaying a deep understanding of the meaning behind each of the signs. Thus, biblical stories were illustrated in a language borrowed from pagan comedies steeped in a morality that radically differed from the Christian one. Terence's plays feature a protagonist who disguised himself as a eunuch to rape a woman from a harem, a slave surpassing his master with intellect, and a hetaera coveted by a young man. St. Augustine condemned the Roman poet for encouraging young people to become promiscuous.[169] On the other hand, however, he never stopped quoting Terence as a source of true *eloquentia*.[170]

Was the influence of Roman theatrical gestures limited to visual arts? Perhaps the monks who made the miniatures absorbed this code, learning Latin from works by Terence and their illustrations. The popularity of these gestures in 11th-century works of art, including sculptures, proves that there had to be people who understood this language, perhaps because they used it on a daily basis themselves.

6. Bodies of all members of the monastic community were subject to strict control so that they would metamorphose into angelic ones already while living in this world. During the liturgy monks would have to stand, kneel or fall face down at designated moments. During procession they were supposed to walk slowly and with dignity. If one fell asleep during a night vigil, *circator* – the brother who "wandered" around the monastery ensuring that silence and discipline are preserved – would stand a lit lamp in front of the sleepy monk.[171] If a boy wanted to ask the abbot at night to allow him to leave and relieve himself, he could only express his need by using a gesture recommended by the monastic lexicon. If a monk was afraid of something, or begged, he could use the gestures of Roman ac-

---

169 Augustine, *De civitate Dei* 2.12 (*PL* 41.57): "adolescentium nequitiam concitaret." Augustine quoted scene five from the third act of *Eunuch*, where Chaerea boasted that he seduced a girl by imitating the tricks used by Jupiter (lines 584–590).
170 Cf. e.g. *De Trinitate* 13.7 (*PL* 42.21). Augustine quotes from the comedy *Andria* (lines 305–6): "quoniam non potest id fieri quo vis, / id velis quo possi[t]" ("since you can't have what you want, want what you can have," trans. J. Barsby). In one of his letters (*Ep.* 155, ed. Goldbacher, p. 444), Augustine even called Terence "ille comicus, sicut luculentis ingeniis non defit resplendentia veritatis" ("the comic poet, whose shining wit contains rays of truth," trans. E.M. Atkins). This remark refers to the famous line 77 from the comedy *Heautontimorumenos*: "homo sum, humani nil a me alieno puto" ("I'm human, and I regard no human business as other people's," trans. J. Barsby).
171 *RC* 57, p. 56.

tors preserved on miniatures accompanying plays by Terence (Dodwell suspected that they were available in England since the end of the 10th century).

Monks would have to almost completely renounce the reactions and gestures that were considered "natural" outside the monastery. Their bodies were forced to learn new ones in order to radically transform their innermost nature. Monks were performers who "imitated" the Other so that they would become the Other. However, preserving silence meant that monks were forced to make gestures, just like actors, to point to objects, people and perhaps even their own emotions and mental states. Life in a monastery consisted of strings of performances. However, although some of them might have been borrowed from Roman comedians, it does not mean that monks were actors. New light was thrown on the monks' body language by groundbreaking studies on sign language, initiated in 1960 by William Stokoe. In *Sign Language Structure*, he gave a "phonological" description of the American Sign Language, demonstrating that its structure and grammar are as complex as those of spoken English. Since then, scholars described the creation of advanced sign languages in communities of people without hearing disabilities, e.g. in contexts that precluded speaking for some reason, as in the case of the language developed by Aboriginal women in Australia.[172] Contrary to the intentions of authors who wrote codices listing monastic gestures, silent monks may also have developed a fully-fledged body language that could entirely replace speech. Perhaps Gerald from Wales did in fact meet "garrulous" brothers in Canterbury.

---

172   Kendon (1988).

Part two: Liturgical Performances

While the liturgical day comprised a cycle of offices, and the monastic week a cycle of psalms, the church calendar itself was framed as an annual cycle of commemorative holidays, which developed with time into quite spectacular performative events. The liturgical year (*temporale*) was determined by celebrations of events in the life of Christ, which were ordered into two cycles connected with two crucial ceremonies: Christmas and Easter. They were supplemented with festive celebrations of saints (*sanctorale*). The Christmas cycle, defined in accordance with the Roman calendar – secular and solar – began with Advent, i.e. four weeks of solemn preparations, and ended with Epiphany. The Easter cycle, defined in accordance with the Jewish lunar calendar, was modified at the Synod of Whitby to ensure that Easter falls on a Sunday defined using the Roman method, and not the Celtic one. It began with forty days of Lent and ended with Pentecost.

The liturgical calendar defined all people's rhythm of everyday life, because there was no alternative way of measuring time in the Middle Ages. Anniversaries or birthdays were referred to using names of religious holidays occurring on the same day. Holidays determined the rhythm of work at courts of law and other public institutions. Marriage was impossible during the four weeks of Advent and the six weeks of Lent. During Lent one was supposed to withhold not only from eating meat, but also from consuming any eggs and dairy produce. Strict fasting was also in order during many other holidays such as the Eve of Christmas and Pentecost, or the Assumption Day.[173]

---

173 Duffy (1992, 41).

Christmas

1. "On the Vigil of Christmas," *Regularis concordia* rules, "the brethren shall all rise together and then genuflect, giving thanks to the unspeakable lovingkindness of our Lord Who came down to redeem the world from the snares of the devil." During certain particularly festive vespers it was ordered that "the psalms shall be sung with proper antiphons suitable to the fullness of time."[174] Monastic collections of antiphons from the 10th and 11th century provide different works of this type. Here is an example from a collection deemed to be the most mature, i.e. the one made by Leofric, Bishop of Exeter (1050–1072)[175]:

SUPER PSALMOS [Ant.] *Iudea et Heirusalem, nolite timere, cras egrediemini et dominus erit vobiscum.*

[Ant.] *Judea and Jerusalem, do not be afraid, tomorrow you will go forth and the Lord will be with you* (Corinthians 2:17).

ANT. *Orietur sicut sol salvator mundi et descendet in uterum virginis sicut ymber super gramen, alleluia.*

ANT. *The Saviour of the world will rise like the sun and descend in the womb of the virgin like rain over the grass, alleluia.*

ANT. *Dum ortus fuerit sol de celo, videbitis regem regum procedentem tanquam sponsum de thalamo suo.*

ANT. *When the sun is rising in the sky, you will see the king of kings proceeding like a bridegroom from his marriage-bed.*

ANT. *Gaude et letare, Hierusalem, quia rex tuus venit tibi, de quo prophete praedixerunt, quem angeli semper adorant, cui cherubin et seraphin sanctus, sanctus, sanctus proclamant.*

ANT. *Rejoice and be glad, Jerusalem, because your king comes to you, about whom the prophets prophesied, whom angels perpetually adore, to whom cherubim and seraphim proclaim, "Holy, Holy, Holy."*

Christ is the sun, while the celebrating community – the people of Jerusalem. The key event would happen "tomorrow." Singing this or similar antiphons at dusk, monks would wait "in darkness" for the Saviour to come, just like the people of Jerusalem once did. Metaphors of light prevailed during Christmas as awaiting Christ also meant longing for "the real sun." Images of light reflect the biblical language used to speak of God. In Malachi 3:20 the coming of Messiah entails that "the sun of justice will arise." Performing songs in darkness allowed the singers to experience the reality of awaiting the Saviour.

---

174 RC 31, p. 28: "Vigilia Natalis Domini [...] omnes pariter surgentes genua flectent, gratias agentes propter eius ineffabilem pietatem qua mundum a laqueis diaboli redempturus descendit. [...] Vespere canantur antiphonae congruae de ipsa completione temporis ad psalmos."

175 *The Leofric Collectar*, eds. Dewick and Frere, p. 19. MS *Harley 2961*, British Library, London. Trans. Bedingfield (2002, 27).

2. *Regularis concordia* recommends attending a morning Mass precisely early at the break of day.[176] During Christmas, the triumph of light over darkness was celebrated using the natural circumstances of the sun rising. This "natural performance" occurred in reality – it was no illusion or representation. The Gospel of John is particularly emphatic in identifying the figure of Christ with bright light. Since early 4th century, Christians have celebrated the birth of Christ on 25 December, the day of winter solstice, when pagans celebrated in Rome *dies natalis Solis Invicti* (the birth of the godly *Sol Invictus*, or the "Unconquered Sun"[177]). Archaeological works under St. Peter's basilica in Rome revealed that the ceiling of one of the tombs features a mosaic depicting Christ as the Sun God riding a chariot with four white horses.[178] A real sunrise initiated an actual transformation of the world, which had slumbered in the dark just a minute before. An equally fundamental metamorphosis ought to occur among members of the community celebrating the birth of Christ.

Regularis concordia ordered that on Christmas Day special confessions be made during the collect[179]:

Finita prima, uenientes ad capitulum, post cetera spiritualis aedificationis colloquia petant humili deuotione omnes fratres ueniam ab abbate, qui uices Christi agit, postulantes multiplicium indulgentiam excessuum, dicentes: *Confiteor*[180]; et abbas respondeat *Misereatur*[181]. Demum ipse abbas, solotenus se prosternens, eadem a fratribus petat.	After Prime they shall assemble for Chapter at which, when words of spiritual edification have been spoken, the brethren shall all, with lowly devotion, beg pardon of the abbot, who takes the place of Christ, and asks forgiveness of their many failings, saying the *Confiteor*. To this the abbot shall answer *Misereatur* and then, prostrate on the ground, he himself shall ask pardon of the brethren.

Confession confirmed the birth of a new man, proclaiming new life. Just like the sun brings rebirth and illuminates the world, so Christ cleanses the monk's body, strengthening it. Prayers said during the main Mass of the day confirmed the renewed unity of the faithful and God.[182]

---

176 *RC* 31, p. 29: "in lucis crepusculo."
177 *Solus Invictus* most probably originates from the Graeco-Roman Helios. On 25 December 274, a special temple was devoted to him in Rome (in *regio* VII). *DNP* 11.693–695.
178 The Christ/Apollo Mosaic, Vatican Necropolis. Fig. 9 in: Jensen (2006, 570–571).
179 Die "Regularis Concordia," ed. Kornexl, p. 60; *RC* 31, p. 29.
180 The first word and the name of the prayer initiating general confession.
181 Prayer ending general confession.
182 Bedingfield (2002, 31–32).

3. According to *Regularis concordia*, the Christmas octave was celebrated with particular solemnity[183]:

ad nocturnam et ad uesperam uti ad missam, sicut in usum huius patriae indigenae tenent, omnia signa pulsentur. Nam honestos huius patriae mores ad Deum pertinentes, quos ueterum usu didicimus, nullo modo abicere, sed undique, uti diximus, corroborare decreuimus. Ad matutinas uero ob rem praedictam, licet *Te Deum laudamus* non canatur et euangelium minime festiuo more legatur, cerei tamen accendantur et signa pulsentur omnia et turribulum turificando deportetur.	all the bells shall ring at Nocturns and Vespers as at Mass, as is the custom among the people of this country. For we have ordained that the goodly religious customs of this land, which we have learned from our fathers before us, be in no wise cast off but confirmed on all hands. For the same reason candles shall be lit at Matins and all the bells shall peal and thurible shall be carried round although the *Te Deum laudamus* is not sung nor the gospel read in the manner of a feast day.

The performances of monks transformed ordinary days into festive ones, which was proclaimed, loudly and joyously, to all people in the vicinity. One particularly striking characteristic is the striving to preserve the local tradition. Anglo-Saxon monastic communities did not isolate themselves from local people, as was common in continental monasteries. Monks lived among common folk and never ceased to carry on their missionary activities. The language of tradition facilitated better communication. Pealing bells and lit candles sacralised time and space around the monastic complex, at the same time providing rhythm to the lives of people outside. In this way, the activities of monks functioned as transformative performances.

---

183   Die *"Regularis Concordia,"* ed. Kornexl, pp. 61–62; *RC* 32, p. 30.

Feast of the Purification of the Virgin

1. According to the Mosaic law, forty days after giving birth to a first-born son his mother should purify herself during a special ceremony. Accordingly, the Feast of the Purification of the Virgin commemorates the purification of Virgin Mary. Bede states that as early as in the 8th century this holiday was celebrated by both the people and the clergy, all participating in a festive procession on 2 February, whose route included "churches and selected places in the town." Everyone would sing holy hymns and carry lit candles donated by the Pope. This ceremony replaced the pagan procession during *Lustratio*, which took place every five years to expiate the "earthly kingdom."[184]

The English name for the Feast of the Purification of the Virgin is Candlemas, which has roots in the Old English word *candel-mæsse*, meaning "mass with candles." It referred to what was considered the main event during the holiday: the blessing of wax candles and the procession of people carrying them. Candles were of crucial importance. In the Salisbury Mass Book[185] the first of five prayers containing blessings for the Candlemas ascribes apotropaic features to blessed wax, i.e. the ability to drive away evil powers. After the celebrations, parishioners would take candles home and light them during storm or in sickness. Moreover, they would be put in the hands of deceased.

2. *Regularis concordia* (33, pp. 30–31) also recommends that priests take part in the processions. First, however, the blessed candles would have to be placed in a selected church, probably outside the monastic complex because some sources suggest that processions included laymen. Ælfric of Eynsham (ca. 950–1010) – one of the most learned people of his time and disciple of Bishop Æthelwold – describes people marching with the procession in a letter to Wulfstan using the phrase *ge hadode ge læwede*, meaning "both monks and laity." Additionally, in one of his sermons he preached that if someone from the procession cannot sing, they should at least carry a candle.[186] This suggests the participation of lay people, who were unprofessional performers in comparison with the monks.

---

184 Beda, *De temporum ratione* 12, ed. Jones, p. 323: "cum in mense eodem die sanctae Mariae plebs uniuersa cum sacerdotibus ac ministris hymnis modula deuotis per ecclesias perque congrua urbis loca procedit, datasque a pontifice cuncti cereas in manibus gestant ardentes. [...] non utique in lustrationem terrestris imperii quinquennum." Cf. Clayton (1990, 36–37).
185 *Missale Sarum*, ed. Dickinson, col. 697.
186 *Die Hirtenbriefe Ælfric's*, ed. Fehr, p. 215; *Ælfric's Catholic Homilies* 1, Homilia 9, ed. Clemoes, pp. 256–257. Cf. Bedingfield (2002, 54–55).

Monks, wearing albs if the weather permitted, would head towards the church where candles had been placed earlier, marching solemnly and focusing on psalms. After entering, they would intone antiphons and collects in honour of the saint in whose name the church was consecrated. Then, the abbot, dressed in a stole and a cope, would bless the candles, sprinkling them with holy water and incensing with a thurible. Next, the church's caretaker would hand the abbot a blessed candle, upon which singing would begin, with other monks receiving and lighting their own candles. The titles of the three antiphons performed during the passing of blessed candles have been preserved in the *Canterbury Benedictional*[187] – one of the most important testimonies to Anglo-Saxon liturgy[188]:

Puer Ihesus proficiebat aetate et sapientia coram deo et hominibus.	*The boy Jesus grew in age and in wisdom in the sight of God and of men* (Luke 2:52).
Nunc dimittis, domine, seruum tuum in pace, quia uiderunt oculi mei salutare tuum.	*Now you are dismissing, Lord, your servant in peace, because my eyes have seen your salvation* (Luke 2:29–30).
Lumen ad reuelationem gentium et gloriam plebis tuae Israhel.	*A light for the revelation of men and the glory of your people Israel* (Luke 2:32).

The above lines were taken from the Gospel of Luke, and the two last sentences were uttered by Simeon when he recognized the Child Jesus and took him in his arms. A citizen of Jerusalem, Simeon was a "righteous and devout" man to whom the Holy Spirit revealed "that he would not see death before he had seen the Lord's Messiah."

3. Although the ceremony did not theatralize Luke's account, an unusual performance would take place during the distributing and lighting of candles. Participants would sing Simeon's words and repeat the gesture he made by lifting a lit candle, just like Simeon raised the Child Jesus. Thus, everyone would play the role of Simeon, which surely augmented the experience of being in the presence of a newborn God, and facilitated internal transformation among the performers. Therefore, the holiday's essence consisted not in repeating the events described by Luke, but rather in recognizing Jesus in the light of the candle, accepting and raising Him, as well as praising God for allowing a glimpse of the divine.[189]

---

187   MS *Harley 2892*, British Library, London.
188   *The Canterbury Benedictional*, ed. Woolley, p. 83. Trans. Bedingfield (2002, 61).
189   Bedingfield (2002, 61).

3. *The Presentation of Christ to Simeon. Benedictional of Æthelwold. MS Additional 49598, fol. 34v* © British Library board. All Rights Reserved 2016

Consequently, the Feast of the Purification of the Virgin was not focused on the purification of Mary, but on the contemplation of Jesus as light. The ceremony culminated in a procession that led back to the main church at the monastic complex. Everyone carried a blessed candle, imitating Simeon who lifted the Child Jesus. This spectacular performance made God's earthly presence real, especially when the procession moved along the streets, as was probably the case in Canterbury and Winchester.[190] Jesus, "a light for the revelation of men and the glory of your people," was present in the glow of the candle's flame.

4. At the gate of the monastery's church everyone would sing the antiphon *Responsum accepit Symeon*, which quotes the Gospel of Luke (2:26): "It had been revealed to him by the Holy Spirit that he would not die before he had seen the Lord's Messiah." After entering the temple, they would perform the responsory *Cum inducerent Puerum*, once again referencing the said evangelist (2:27–28): "When the parents brought in the child Jesus to do for him what the custom of the Law required, Simeon took him in his arms." Crossing the temple's threshold was supposed to change the life of everyone participating in the procession, just like Simeon's fate was once changed.

Celebrations ended with a purification Mass – *In purificatione sancte Marie* – during which the blessed candles were still held in hands. After the offertory, when God is offered the gifts of bread and wine, everyone would pass their candles to the priest, alluding in this way to the offering of the Eucharist, which probably reinforced the connection between the blessed candles and Christ. This ended the holiday, during which the faithful reiterated the old man Simeon's performance, recognizing Jesus as the light that illuminates the road to salvation.

5. One intriguing dimension of this holiday was the gender status of the Incarnation. Jesus would reveal himself both as a man and as a woman's son identical with the body of the mother. Re-enacting holy events allowed to experience the power of the Incarnation, revealing that it obliterates the oppositions between the human and the divine, as well as between the male and the female.[191] This context also provides a possibility to interpret a fascinating document made somewhere between November 1388 and February 1389 in Beverley: a license issued to the guild of Blessed Virgin Mary, formed in the 1350s. It contains a description of Candlemas held in the local parish.[192] The elaborate "theatricality" of the cer-

---

190 For a discussion of testimonies see: Bedingfield (2002, 58–59).
191 Hill-Vásquez (2007, 156).
192 Latin text in: Young (1933, 2.252–253). Cf. Duffy (1992, 15–22); Hill-Vásquez (2007, 162).

emony was perhaps supposed to stimulate the faithful to eagerly participate in it, and aid them in internalizing the liturgical actions.

Every year, on the morning of the holiday "all the brothers and sisters of the guild" (*omnes fratres et sorores eiusdem gilde*) would meet at a certain distance from the church. One of the brothers (*quidam de gilda*), dignified and meticulously dressed as the Virgin Queen Mary, would carry in his arms a figurine representing Christ (*habend quasi Filium in vlnis suis*). Two other brothers were dressed as Joseph and Simeon (*assimulantes Ioseph et Simeonem*), and another two, wearing costumes of angels, would carry a candlestick with twenty-four thick wax candles. Surrounded with bright light, music and joy (*cum omni melodia et exultacione*), they proceeded to the church. At the front, just behind the Blessed Virgin, two guild sisters would follow, with brothers behind them, everyone marching in twos and carrying half-pound candles. In the church, at the main altar, the Virgin would offer her Son to Simeon, upon which all the other guild members would offer, one after the other, a candle and a penny each.

6. Women played a prominent role in Beverley, marching at the head of the procession. Queen Mary, however, was represented by a man, "someone from the guild" (*quidam de gilda*). Dressed festively, he carried in his arms the figurine of Jesus. Liturgical realism would thus merge with theatrical fiction. Representing a woman by a man allowed to retain liturgical distance to the represented figure, just like in the case of revealing Christ in candlelight. The figure in the man's arms, however, belonged to an entirely different ontological order because it created an illusion. Control over the performance was held by a lay guild. In the 14th century, craftsmen helped theatre penetrate into the liturgy. It needs to be emphasized, however, that even the most spectacular liturgical performances in England were modest in comparison to the shows delivered on the continent. In the 15th century, the Florentine Compagnia delle Purificazione would celebrate the Feast of the Purification of the Virgin not only by employing the key figures and using a wide range of props, but also engaging a huge number of angels and twenty prophets, on one occasion even using a whale.[193]

On 26 July 1512, on the feast of St. Anne, the play *Candlemes Day and the Kyllyng of þe Children of Israelle*[194] was performed, perhaps in Chelmsford[195] in Essex.

193　Newbigin (1990, 363–368); Davidson (2007, 20–21).
194　The play has been preserved in one manuscript only: MS Digby 133, Bodleian Library, Oxford (fol. 146r-157v). Text in: *The Digby Plays*, eds. Baker, Murphy & Hall, pp. 96–115. Cf. Kocur (2012, 266–292).
195　Coldewey (1975).

It was partially inspired by the Feast of the Purification. This unusual text begins with a scene featuring Herodotus, soldiers, and the Massacre of the Innocents, as related by Matthew and Luke. It ends with a reference to the rite of purification. The play contains many quotations from the liturgy, and has preserved an unusually elaborate account of the procession. The prophetess Anne, sometimes identified as the grandmother of Jesus, would lead a choir of virgins to the Temple, which was accompanied by singing the antiphon *Nunc dimittis*, just as in the liturgy. Simeon would conduct the procession as if he were a priest, concluding it with a short sermon. He would recommend everyone to praise Our Lady and her mother Saint Anne in a spirit of joy (line 533: *glad in myn inward mende*). Virgins would dance during the finale. The guild holiday in Beverley also ended joyously, *cum gaudio*. 16th-century theatre would substantially adopt and develop both the means of expression invented by monks for the purpose of liturgical performances, and elements of folk culture in the form of dance.

Lent

During the first three weeks of the forty days of fasting, monks were not supposed to shave themselves.[196] Beginning from Ash Wednesday, a procession was in order on every Wednesday and Friday. On Ash Wednesday, after none, the abbot dressed in stole would bless the ashes and sprinkle them over each monk's head, ordering them to do penance. Afterwards, with psalms and antiphons on their lips, everyone would go to another church, where litanies would be intoned among other activities. Finally, they would return to the main church to attend a regular Mass. The priest, deacon and subdeacon would appear in chasuble, although the subdeacon would take it off when reading letters. When beginning to read from the Gospels, the deacon would also take the chasuble off, fold it and throw over his left arm, strapping one end to the alb's belt. Instructions detailing this specific "play" with the chasuble have been preserved only in *Regularis concordia* (34, p. 33). While handling the sacred texts, the celebrants would "bare" themselves, taking off the liturgical "costume." The central theme of Lent was the performance of penance.

On Ash Wednesday, "blatant sinners" would be expelled. Wulfstan, Archbishop of York (1002–1023), explained the meaning of this performance in a special sermon composed for this particular occasion[197]:

And sume men syndon eac þe nyde sculan of cyricgemanan þas halgan tid ascadene mid rihte weorðan for healican synnan, ealswa Adam wearð of engla gemanan þa ða he forworðe þa myclan myrhðe þe he on wunode ær ðam þe he syngode […]. Leofan men, on Wodnesdæg, þe byð *caput ieiunii*, bisceopas ascadað on manegum stowan ut of cyrican for heora agenan þearfe þa ðe healice on openlican synnan hy sylfe forgyltan. And eft on Dunresdæg ær Eastran hy geinniað into cyrican þa ðe geornlice þæt Lencten heora synna betað, swa swa hym man wissað; þonne *absolutionem* bisceopas ofer hy rædað 7 for hi þingiað 7 mid þam heora synna þurh Godes mildheortnesse myclum gelyhtaþ.	And there are some men also who rightly must in this holy time be expelled from the church community for high sins, just as was Adam from the community of angels when he forsook the great joy in which he dwelt before he sinned […]. Dear men, on Wednesday, which is *caput ieiunii*[198], bishops expel in many places out from the church for their own need those who have made themselves highly guilty in open sins. And afterwards on Thursday before Easter they reenter the church, those who zealously during Lent atone for their sins, just as one instructs them. Then bishops read the absolution over them, and pray for them, and with that alleviate their sins through God's great mercy.

---

196 *RC* 35, p. 34.
197 For the Old English text see: *The Homilies of Wulfstan*, ed. Bethurum, pp. 234–235. Trans. Bedingfield (2002, 82).
198 The phrase *caput ieiunii* means literally "head [hence: beginning] of Lent."

Later sources provide more details.[199] Public sinners would usually gather outside the cathedral; all of them, both the rich and the poor, would stand there barefoot, clad in coarse hair shirts, with heads bent meekly. The bishop, accompanied by canons, would assign each sinner individual penance, depending on the gravity of their offences. Then, he would grab one of them by the hand and lead to the church; others would follow, one after another, holding hands. In front of the altar all would recite seven penitentiary psalms. The bishop would touch everyone with his hands, sprinkle holy water over them, and pour blessed water over their heads. Everyone would then receive a hair shirt tunic. Then, the penitents would be led out of the church and ordered not to return before Holy Thursday. They would be forced to spend Lent away from their monastic communities, in places of voluntary seclusion, where they would fill their time with prayer as well as physical and charity work. Throughout Lent they would walk barefoot and sleep on straw, on bare earth. Moreover, it was forbidden to speak to anyone and cut one's hair. This custom survived until the 14th century.

---

[199] Weiser (1958, 175); Hardison (1965, 98). Cf. the description of excommunication provided by Gratian, quoted below, in the chapter *Ordo representacionis Ade*.

Palm Sunday

4. The Entry into Jerusalem. Benedictional of Æthelwold. MS Additional 49598, fol. 45v
© British Library board. All Rights Reserved 2016

The Palm Sunday celebrations, testified to have been held already in the 4th century, constitute the oldest and grandest procession-based rite in Western Church. During this immensely popular holiday an important role was played, from the very beginning, by lay participants. In the Anglo-Saxon church, the great procession would begin with a morning Mass. Just like on the Feast of the Purification of the Virgin, monks wearing albs and focusing on psalmodies would first head towards the church where palm twigs had been previously placed.[200] There they would recite prayers praising the patron saint, asking for intercession and help. Then the deacon would read from the Gospel of John (12:12–19), beginning from the passage: "The next day the great crowd that had come for the festival heard that Jesus was on his way to Jerusalem. They took palm branches and went out to meet him." During the reading, palms would be blessed, sprinkled with holy water and incensed. Twigs were distributed as children sang antiphons[201]:

Pueri ebreorum tollentes ramos olivarum obviaverunt domino, clamantes et dicentes, „Osanna in excelsis".	*The sons of the Hebrews, carrying olive branches, came to meet Lord, crying out and saying, "Hosannah in the highest."*
Pueri ebreorum vestimenta prosternebant in via et clamabant, dicentes: „Osanna filio David, benedictus qui venit in nomine domini"	*The sons of the Hebrews spread out their cloaks on the way and cried out, saying, "Hosannah to the sons of God, blessed is he who comes in the name of the Lord."*

Mention of olive branches in the first of the two quoted antiphons reflects the confusion related to practicing this rite in a country where no palm trees grow. There was no agreement among the four evangelists as to the origin of palm branches. It is only John who speaks directly of palms; Matthew and Mark mention "leafy branches," while Luke does not provide any details whatsoever. Apart from flowers, willow twigs were used as well as branches of "other trees."[202] In the Salisbury Missal, willow is mentioned alongside yew and boxwood.[203] Flower or branch, the substitute for palm played an active role in the procession: this symbol of victory could turn into a cross. According to *The Old English Life of St. Machutus*, Christ

---

200 Unfortunately, *Regularis concordia* does not make it clear, just as in the case of the Feast of the Purification of the Virgin, where this church would be located. Many monastic complexes contained more than one church, so the procession could have been held inside the walls of one such complex. See: Spurell (1992, 167).
201 *The Canterbury Benedictional*, ed. Woolley, p. 25. Trans. Bedingfield (2002, 101).
202 For a discussion of testimonies see: Bedingfield (2002, 94).
203 *Missale Sarum*, ed. Dickinson, col. 253–257. Cf. Duffy (1992, 23).

was crucified on a cross made from palm tree.[204] After the procession, the blessed palms would be often taken home as people believed they would protect them from evil and sickness.

These processions also culminated in the "return." Children would be sent forth in order to await inside the church, behind closed doors, in accordance with Matthew's account (21:8–9) of how the gathered parted into "crowds that went ahead of him and that followed."[205] When the palm-carrying procession stopped in front of the closed church doors, from its inside – which represented Jerusalem – children's singing would resound, to which everyone would respond as the custom dictated. Children would sing the refrain at the beginning and end of each verse of the song *Gloria laus*, which was written by Theodulph, Bishop of Orléans (d. 821). The elaborate dialogue between members of the procession and children elevated the event to a mystical plane as the two sides would not see each other, but only hear.

The song *Gloria laus*, preserved in *The Canterbury Benedictional*, praises Christ as the Saviour and the king who crushed death. Jesus was also depicted as a triumphant figure who will redeem the world with his own blood. In this sense, the Palm Sunday heralded the Holy Week – the most important cycle of ceremonies in Christianity.

Then the cantor would intone the response[206]:

Ingrediente domino in sanctam civitatem, With the Lord entering into the holy city,
Hebreorum pueri, resurrectionem vitae the sons of the Hebrews, announcing the
pronuntiantes, cum ramis palmarum resurrection of life, cried out with palm
osanna clamabat in excelsis branches, "Hosannah in the highest."

After the opening of the gates the procession would enter the church, or "Jerusalem." Mention of the "resurrection of life" heralded the culmination of the Easter celebrations: the discovery of the empty tomb, with real Christ absent because he had risen from the dead. On Palm Sunday, however, the drama's main hero – Jesus – was in fact present.

In Germany, already towards the end of the 10th century, a wooden figure of Christ on a mule (*Palmesel*) would be used during the Palm Sunday procession.[207]

---

204 *The Old English Life of St. Machutus*, ed. Yerkes, p. 31. Cf. Bedingfield (2002, 106–108).
205 Matthew (21:15) also recalls "children crying out in the temple, 'Hosanna to the Son of David.'" However, the presence of children in the procession – not confirmed by the Gospels – seems to be a liturgical invention. Cf. King (2006, 132).
206 *The Leofric Collector*, ed. Dewick and Frere, p. 123.
207 Young (1933, 1.94); MES 66–67.

Ca. 1078, Lafranc ordered the use of the Blessed Host during the procession. In other countries, the "role" of Jesus would be played by the Gospels or a cross. However, no source testifies to similar practices on the British Isles during the Anglo-Saxon period.[208] Later it became popular in England to use the Host during processions on the occasion of the Blessed Sacrament, which is confirmed by the Salisbury Missal; moreover, Eamon Duffy considered this to be one of the hallmarks of the English church.[209] English liturgy moved beyond the theatralization of the Gospels by using a wooden prop, just like in Germany. The Host did not resemble Jesus physically, but was His body in a much more essential way. It was in the Sacrament that the faithful could experience the real presence of God, "here and now," which probably efficiently mobilized people to participate in the celebrations: the real Sacrament (Christ) entered the church (Jerusalem). The Host was rarely brought outside the church. The other holiday during which this was practiced was Corpus Christi, which was celebrated in England since 1318, to a large extent following the model of Palm Sunday.

---

208 Bedingfield (2002, 95–96).
209 *Missale Sarum*, ed. Dickinson, col. 258–262; MES 63–66. Cf. Duffy (1992, 26).

Holy Thursday

During the night-time offices, just before dawn on Holy Thursday, Good Friday and Easter Eve, all candles would be extinguished in the church, one by one, which was supposed to symbolize Jesus leaving his disciples. This custom, known as *Tenebrae* ("Darkness"), made a spectacular impression and was known already to Amalarius.[210] In his second letter to Wulfstan, Ælfric wrote that during the rite of *Tenebrae* twenty-four candles would be extinguished, one after each psalm with an antiphon.[211] Authors of *Regularis concordia* (37, pp. 36–37) describe yet another performance characterized by immense expressive force, designed "in order to augment the trembling of the soul." On that occasion, they make reference to customs popular *in quorundam religiosorum ecclesiis*, i.e. "in churches of certain pious people," although the term *religiosorum* most probably refers to monastic communities, perhaps also continental ones.[212]

After completing all songs from the night-time offices, when the antiphon to the *Benedictus* song from the Gospels was finished and not a single candle was left burning to denote that the light of Christ had been extinguished, on the right side of the choir a pair of boys' clear voices would resound signing *Kyrie eleison*, "God, have mercy!" On the left, two others would respond with *Christe eleison*, "Christ, have mercy!" In the western part of the choir, another pair would intone *Domine misere nobis*, "Lord, have mercy on us!" Finally, all monks would sing together *Christus Dominus factus est oboediens usque ad mortem*[213] – "Christ, our Lord, has become obedient until His death." The entire cycle would be repeated thrice.

Kneeling in complete darkness, the monks would hear clear voices of children from three sides, calling out to the absent God. After each of the three cycles, everyone would respond in powerful unison that Christ is dead. Then they would pray on their knees in silence. World without God was dark and empty. The performance must have aroused strong emotions because the authors of *Regularis concordia* made it clear that nobody should be forced to partake in such practices, explaining that it was the Catholics who developed such means of inciting religious terror in order to make the horror of darkness during the Passion evident to the ignoramuses, as well as to introduce the meaning of apostolic consolation,

---

210   Amalarius, *De ordine antiphonarii* 44. *De exstinctione luminum circa sepulturam Domini* (*PL* 105.1293 bc).
211   *Die Hirtenbriefe Ælfric's*, ed. Fehr, p. 154.
212   *RC*, p. 36; Bedingfield (2002, 119).
213   *Flp* 2.8.

which shows the world Christ who remained obedient to his own Father until the very end in order to redeem humankind.

After prime, which was celebrated at dawn, monks would sing in unison the entire psalter, which was followed by reciting a litany while lying prostrate on the ground. Then, after taking their shoes off the brothers would wash the floors, while priests washed the altar with holy water. Later, while singing antiphons, the monks would wash, dry and kiss the feet of poor people, finally giving them food and money, as ordered by the abbot. In the evening, the abbot would wash the feet of selected monks, and then, in the refectory, drink to the health of every brother and kiss their hands. In Latin texts, Holy Thursday is usually referred to as *Cena Domini*, or Lord's Supper. Performances of humility instructed monks what gestures to make and how to behave so that they would renounce themselves in order to embrace Christ.

Nevertheless, before brothers proceeded to the refectory, after the none they would approach the church doors dressed in liturgical attire and carrying a staff *cum imagine serpentis*, i.e. "with the apparition of the snake," as a "secret sign of a certain mystery."[214] Then they would use the flint to strike fire and light the candle put in the mouth of the snake on the staff. The abbot would bless this "new fire," which was used to light a single candle, in turn becoming the source of light for all the candles extinguished later during *Tenebrae* on three days of the Holy Week. Whereas the rite of *Tenebrae* prefigured the Passion, the blessing of the new fire heralded the Resurrection.[215] These spectacular performances re-enacted historical events; after all, three evangelists recall that after Christ died, "from noon on, darkness came over the whole land until three in the afternoon."[216] However, their primary aim was to recreate the emotional experience. The reality of Passion and Resurrection was brought about through anxiety and mounting fear. In the face of terror, man would testify to the Truth, or – to employ Martin Heidegger's philosophical idiom – his being would reveal itself as "care" (*Sorge*).[217]

The shocking performance of *Tenebrae*, repeated also on Good Friday and Easter Eve, made everyone experience the death of God. Christ, who was celebrated

---

214 *RC* 41, p. 39: "ob arcanum cuiusdam mysterii." This is a reference to the secret of redemption, and perhaps an allusion to John 3:14.
215 Bedingfield (2002, 121).
216 However, it was no ordinary eclipse of the sun, because – as Biblia Tyniecka, a classic Polish edition of the Bible, tells us – there was full moon on that day (Matthew 27:45; Mark 15:33; Luke 23:44).
217 See Chapter 6, § 39 of Martin Heidegger's *Sein und Zeit*.

during Christmas as light, would now pass away, extinguishing all the brightness that illuminated people's world and endowed their lives with meaning. Kneeling in utter darkness allowed one to experience the reality of God's death in His absence. Christ's death was a crucial event because it made Resurrection possible. In both of these events, however, Christ was absent. In order to become incarnated in an ordinary man and then die, God had to "empty" himself of all divinity. Presence by way of absence may be difficult to grasp with reason alone, but the paradox can be experienced emotionally during a specially designed performance. Thus, emotion would become the vehicle of cognition and understanding of that which cannot be put properly into words.

Good Friday

1. After the night-time rite of *Tenebrae*, monks would take off their shoes and participate barefoot in all the celebrations related to the Adoration of the Cross. The *Adoratio Crucis* ceremony developed from the cult of the relics of the real Cross in Jerusalem. From 8 am till late afternoon, the wooden Cross would be worshipped in Jerusalem's Golgota Church. Then, descriptions of Passion would be read until 2.30 pm (or until none, the ninth hour of the Divine Office). This practice spread from Jerusalem to Ireland and then to Great Britain, finally reaching continental Europe.[218] The Anglo-Saxon church adored the Cross no later than in the 8th century.

In accordance with the provisions of *Regularis concordia* (43–47, pp. 41–46), the main celebrations began at *hora nona*, "the hour of the none." After readings from Hosea (6:1–6) and Exodus (12:1–11), separated with responses and solemn prayers, with everyone kneeling, Psalm 140 would be sung: *Eripe me Domine* ("Deliver me, O Lord"). Then, the deacon would commence reading the description of the Passion from the Gospel of John. Upon reaching the words *Partiti sunt vestimenta mea* ("They divided my clothes among themselves"), two deacons would snatch – "like thieves"[219] – the tablecloth from the altar where gospels lay. The deacons would thus repeat the gestures of the soldiers who stole Jesus's clothes after crucifixion. They did not pretend, however, to be soldiers. The liturgical performance produced real experiences among the participants: being a thief on the one hand, and witnessing the theft of a holy object on the other.

After the reading from John, the abbot would intone *orationes sollemnes*, i.e. solemn prayers, also known as "universal" ones. They comprise some of the earliest evidence of the Western Church. Prayers would be said for everyone: the Pope, Emperor, King, new catechumens, heretics and schismatics, pagans, and even Jews, who killed Christ.[220] Everyone would kneel during each but the first prayer. Then, the proper part of the *Adoratio Crucis* ceremony would begin.

2. The cross, "wrapped in cloth,"[221] would be placed at some distance in front of the altar, with two deacons supporting it from the sides, singing *Popule meus* ("O my people"), the first antiphon from the cycle *Improperia* (*Reproaches*). It refers

---

218 Holloway (1990, 31–42); Bedingfield (2002, 125–126).
219 *RC* 43, p. 42: "in modum furantis."
220 De Clerk (1977, 125–143) (testimonies). Cf. Bedingfield (2002, 126–127).
221 *Die Hirtenbriefe Ælfric's*, ed. Fehr, p. 163: "mid hrægle be-wæfred." Cf. Bedingfield (2002, 128).

to Christ speaking reproachfully about those evildoers who contributed to His Passion. The song, which uses the first person, transformed those who participated in the celebrations into the ones causing Christ to suffer. One could not be a mere "onlooker" or indifferent witness in the face of the Passion, even if it was only represented as part of a liturgical ceremony.

After each of the following *Reproaches* sung by the deacons, two subdeacons would respond in Greek: *Agios o Theos*, while *schola* (boy choir) would do so in Latin: *Sanctus Deus*. They reminded everyone that the Holy Spirit had spoken to them. When the first responses were heard, deacons would bring the Cross, still covered in cloth, erect it at the altar and place on a pillow carried by an acolyte. After the second *Reproach* – *Quia eduxi vos per desertum* ("For I have led you through the desert") – and the second round of responses, the deacons would raise the Cross and sing the third *Reproach*: *Qui ultra* ("What else were I to do for you"). Next, the Cross would be revealed and oriented towards the clergy. Antiphons would be intoned, beginning with *Ecce lignum crucis* ("Here is the tree of the cross") and *Crucem tuam adoramus Domine* ("We adore your cross, Lord"). The abbot and all brothers would fall thrice on their knees before the Cross, face to the ground, and sing penitentiary psalms together, *cum magno cordis suspirio* ("with a deep, heartfelt sigh"), praying to the Cross.

3. Prayers to the Cross are also quoted in *Regularis concordia*, which unusually provides their entire text. The first one begins with the words: *Domine Ihesu Christe, adoro te* ("Lord, Jesus Christ, I adore you"), and praises the God who mounts the Cross; the wounded; the one placed in the tomb; the one entering hell; the one raising from the dead; the one ascending to heaven; and finally, the one returning for the Last Judgement. After two other prayers separated with psalms, the abbot would kiss the Cross, and was followed in this by all brothers, the entire clergy, and other people.

The main actor in these performances was the Cross itself: not only the key prop, an instrument of torture, but also the subject of most actions. "The wood of the Cross" played the role of Christ: it was the Cross that reproached people, was bared, adored and prayed to. In Old English texts the Cross was often endowed with powers attributed to Christ: healing, saving and conquering darkness with light. Some prayers were not addressed directly towards Christ, but indirectly to the Cross. One fascinating demonstration of the power of the Cross is found in one of the earliest Old English poems, *The Dream of the Rood*.[222] The vision

---

222 The poem has been preserved in manuscript in the cathedral library in Vercelli, in northern Italy; hence the name *Vercelli Codex*. For the complete text see: *The Vercelli*

descended upon the poet *to midre nihte*, "in the middle of the night." He saw the Cross *lēohte bewunden*, "bathed in light." The poet, *forwunded mid wommum* ("wounded with sins"), humbly admires the tree of glory, shining joyously, covered in gold, jewels and red blood. According to the account of the Cross, Christ *mē wolde on gestīgan* ("wanted to scale me"), and climbs it, thus opening the most dramatic part of the poem:

[40] *Gestāh hē on gealgan hēanne,*	[40] He ascended onto the high gallows,
mōdig on manigra gesyhðe,	brave in the sight of many, there,
þā hē wolde mancyn lȳsan.	[since] he wished to release mankind.
Bifode ic þā mē se beorn ymbclypte.	I trembled when the man embraced me.
Ne dorste ic hwæðre būgan tō eorðan,	However, I dared not bow down to the earth,
feallan tō foldan scēatum,	fall to the surface of the earth,
ac ic sceolde fæste standan.	but I had to stand fast.
Rōd wæs ic ārǣred.	I was raised [as a] cross.
Āhōf ic rīcne cyning,	I lifted up the mighty king,
[45] *heofona hlāford,*	[45] the lord of the heavens;
hyldan mē ne dorste.	I dared not bend down.
Þurhdrifan hī mē mid deorcan nǣglum.	They pierced me with dark nails.
On mē syndon þā dolg gesīene,	On me, the scars are visible,
opene inwidhlemmas.	open malicious wounds.
Ne dorste ic hira ǣnigum sceððan.	I did not dare injure any of them.
Bysmeredon hīe unc būtū ætgædere.	They mocked both of us, together.
Eall ic wæs mid blōde bestēmed,	I was all drenched with blood,
begoten of þæs guman sīdan,	covered from the man's side,
siððan hē hæfde his gāst onsended.	after he had sent forth his spirit.

The account of the Cross shows Crucifixion from a surprising perspective. The Cross suffered just like Christ, and was also wounded. Many scholars have linked the astounding dramatic tension of *The Dream of the Rood* to the performances centred around the Adoration of the Cross. The poem was widely known. In the years 730–750, when Anglo-Saxons controlled the northern shores of Solway

---

Book, ed. Krapp, pp. 61–65. There is a website devoted to the work, containing its text, transcriptions, facsimiles, translations and commentaries: http://www.dreamofrood.co.uk. The translation quoted here is the one provided on this website.

Firth, four sentences from the poem were carved in runes on a stone cross from Ruthwell (Dumfriesshire in Scotland).[223] This six-metre-high monument, lavishly decorated in low reliefs, is considered today as the prime example of the "Northumbrian Renaissance". Julia Bolton Holloway compared the poem with the liturgy, and arrived at the conclusion that the *Adoratio Crucis* ceremony, in which the Cross played an equally dramatic role as in *The Dream of the Rood*, constitutes the source of liturgical drama in the West.[224]

4. Authors of *Regularis concordia* provided an additional performance for Good Friday, just like in the case of Holy Thursday. It was practiced by certain "pious people," i.e. *religiosorum*, and was worth imitating in order to "strengthen the faith of the ignorant people [*indocti vulgi*] and neophytes."[225] At the altar, *quaedam assimilatio sepulchri* was erected – "something reminiscent of a tomb," covered with a veil. It was the place where the Cross was supposed to be placed. The deacons who held the Cross before were now supposed to wrap it in a shawl and ceremoniously transfer to the place where the tomb stood, singing the antiphons *In pace in idipsum*, *Habitabit* and *Caro mea requiescet in spe*.[226] Next, they would place the Cross in the tomb, *ac si Domini nostri Ihesu Christi corpore sepulto*, "as if burying the body of Our Lord, Jesus Christ," singing the antiphon *Sepulto Domino, signatum est monumentum, ponentes milites qui custodirent eum*.[227] The Cross was meant to be watched over until Resurrection by two, three or more monks – depending on the size of the community – standing on "holy guard" and singing psalms.

The faith of simple people was supposed to be reinforced by this liturgical show, especially by the sight of Christ, wrapped in a shawl and carried to the tomb by two deacons reminiscent of Joseph and Nicodemus, who wrapped and buried Christ according to John. However, the liturgical performances did not focus on reconstructing events in terms of their appearance. The deacons would not pretend to be Joseph and Nicodemus, but rather commemorated the deeds of historical figures through gestures and liturgical means, such as procession or

---

223   Éamonn Ó Carragáin, *Ruthwell Cross*, in: Lapidge (1999, 403–404). Cf. Cassidy (1992).
224   Holloway (1990, 29).
225   RC 46, p. 44: "ad fidem indocti uulgi ac neophytorum corroborandam."
226   Respectively: Psalm 4:9: "O Lord, make me lie down in safety"; adaptation of Psalm 15:1: "O Lord, who may abide in your tent? Who may dwell on your holy hill?"; Psalm 16:9: "my body also rests secure."
227   Cf. Matthew 27:66: "So they went with the guard and made the tomb secure by sealing the stone."

singing of antiphons. The performance was delivered using means of expression appropriate for the liturgy. The faithful would understand this language, because liturgical performances shaped the identity of all Christians.

5. After the *Depositio* ceremony referring to the entombment, the deacon and the subdeacon would carry the Lord's corpus, "left from the day before" (the Host was not consecrated on Good Friday and Easter Eve), and a cup of non-consecrated wine. The abbot would intone a series of prayers; then, he would silently put the offering in the cup. Everyone would receive communion in silence. Finally, all would say vespers privately and retreat to the refectory. In the evening, they were allowed to shave and bathe; this was important if the community was large and not everyone could wash on Easter Eve.

Instructions regarding the Adoration of the Cross contained in *Regularis concordia* are addressed not only to monks, but also to lay people. The presence of guests from outside the monastery probably depended on its location. M. Brandford Bedingfield imagined that in a monastic cathedral like the one in Winchester, the Adoration of the Cross was attended by an entire spectrum of the Anglo-Saxon society: from king to slave. The key performers, however, were the brothers and the abbot. They presented *Depositio* as a performance for the *indocti vulgi*. They intoned Christ's *Reproaches* and kissed the Cross. Even if they were treated as witnesses to Crucifixion, lay people remained mere audience. If we are to say that modern theatre was born then, its first actor was the wooden cross, and its first "stage" – a makeshift tomb.[228]

---

228   Sheingorn (1987, 3).

Easter Eve

1. During the night, the *Tenebrae* rite was performed for the third time. Proper celebrations began at none. When the abbot entered the church in the company of brothers, a new source of light was brought inside and used to light the paschal candle, which was then placed in front of the altar. After blessing the paschal candle, the second one, "*alter cereus*," was lit. Acolytes would hold them at the sides of the altar. The subdeacon began with a reading from Genesis 1:1: *In principio creavit* ("In the beginning God created"; Revised Standard Version). This was followed, in turns, by prayers and readings from Exodus and Isaiah. After prayers, litanies would be intoned, which was concluded by the *magister scholae*, the choir master, singing in high voice *Accendite* (*Light up*). The church would suddenly become illuminated with the glow of all candles, and was filled with the joyful song *Gloria in excelsis*. This multimedia performance, which referred once more to the symbolism of light and darkness, naturally heralded Resurrection. Prior to this, Christ remained under the ground.

Traditionally, Easter Eve was considered to be the day when Christ descended to hell, although Anglo-Saxon sources are not clear on this matter, while *Regularis concordia* (31, p. 28) mentions this event only by heralding it in instructions related to celebrating Christmas. The term "Harrowing of Hell" is ambiguous, since according to OED "to harrow" can mean "to break up," "to crush," and "to pulverize with a harrow." The Old English verb *herȝian* meant "to harry," "to rob," and "to spoil." Thus, Christ came down to hell by bursting through its gates and robbing Satan of his spoils, i.e. the souls of the just.[229] In the Old English translation of the apocryphal Gospel of Nicodemus – the key witness who related the Harrowing of Hell – the event is presented in equally dramatic terms.[230]

2. *The Book of Cerne*[231] – a compilation of religious texts copied in the first half of the 9th century – contains an intriguing document: a Latin version of the Harrowing of Hell in the form of a dialogue. David Dumville, one of the contemporary publishers of the manuscript, suggested that it may be the earliest example of a "liturgical drama" in England.[232] The text consists of alternating parts of the nar-

---

229 Tamburr (2007, 1).
230 For a complete text see: Izydorczyk (1997). Cf. Tamburr (2007, 102–147).
231 MS Ll.1.10, University Library, Cambridge. For a complete text see: Dumville (1972).
232 Dumville (1972, 381). In Poland, Juliusz Lewański differentiated "liturgical drama" from "dialogue-based officium" and "dramatic officium." However, I neglect these literary categories here because they are not useful in reconstructing the performances of Anglo-Saxon monks.

rator and the choir of the just, as well as voices of Adam and Eve. In narrative sections, written in red ink, verbs are usually (though not always) in the present tense, which seems to indicate that the text could have been used during the liturgy. Such directions contained in liturgical books came to be known as "rubrics" because the red ink was derived from "red clay" (*rubrica* in Latin). Some verbs, however, are in the past tense. One reason for this inconsistency might be lack of care in adapting the original account, probably inspired by Nicodemus's Gospel, for the purposes of the performance. Enunciations of the dramatis personae constitute a series of solemn but conventional prayers. Any ties to an actual performance are suggested only by the narration itself. Therefore, they are quoted below in their entirety, along with a summary of other passages.[233]

[NARRATION]

Hæc est oratio innumerabilis sanctorum populi qui tenebantur in inferni captiuitate. Lacrimabili uoce et obsecratione Saluatorem deposcunt, dicentes, quando ad infernos discendit:	This is a prayer of innumerable saints, held hostage in hell. With tearful voices, they turn to the Saviour imploringly, speaking as he descends to hell:

[CHOIR OF THE JUST]

You have come, O Saviour of the world; the one we have been awaiting each day with great hope. You have come, O light of the future, which was promised by the prophets. You have come, sacrificing your living flesh to redeem the sins of the world. Save the lost prisoners of hell! [Then the choir would intensify its cries for help, while Christ established the sign of the cross in hell.]

[NARRATION]

Postquam autem audita est postulatio et obsecratio innumerabilium captiuorum, statim iubente Domini omnes antiqui iusti, sine aliqua mora ad imperium Domini Saluatoris resolutis uinculis, Domini Saluatoris genibus obuoluti, humili supplicatione cum ineffabili gaudio, clamantes:[234]	Later, when the complaints of countless imploring prisoners have been heard, on Lord's command all the ancient just are immediately released from captivity by the order of the Lord and Saviour, standing on their knees before the Lord and Saviour, meekly begging and crying with indescribable joy:

---

233   MS Ll.1.10, fol. 98v–99v. Cf. Dumville (1972, 376–377); Bedingfield (2002, 147); *MET* 38–39.
234   The text appears to be incorrectly constructed, as there is no main verb. Cf. Dumville (1972, 382).

[CHOIR OF THE JUST]

Lord, you have freed us from our ties! [Short prayer follows.]

[NARRATION]

Adam autem et Eua adhuc non sunt desoluti de uinculis. Tunc Adam, lugubri ac miserabili uoce, clamabat ad Dominum, dicens:	However, Adam and Eve are not free from their ties. Now Adam, tears dripping, cries mournfully to the Lord, saying:

[ADAM]

Have mercy on my soul, O Lord! [Further prayers inspired by psalms use the first person singular, the voice begging to be set free from "the house of bondage and the shadow of death."]

[NARRATION]

Tunc, Domino miserante, Adam, e uinculis resolutus, Iesu Christi genibus prouolutus:	Now, when the Lord showed pity, Adam, free from ties, falls on his knees before Jesus Christ:

[ADAM]

Bless, O Lord, my soul! [A thanksgiving prayer follows, asking for forgiveness of offences, without any references to hell.]

[NARRATION]

Adhuc Eua persistit in fletu, dicens:	And Eve still cries, saying:

[EVE]

You are just, Lord! [Prayer for mercy follows, without any references to staying in hell.]

The text breaks off abruptly. Homilies, from which it is derived, elaborate further the themes of freeing Eve and her being thankful, finally giving voice to the praising choir of freed souls. The parts of the three soloists and of the choir were all sung.

3. Dumville made efforts to prove that the version of the text preserved in *The Book of Cerne* is actually a copy of an earlier text created in Northumbria in the 8th century. On this basis he claims that the "liturgical drama" did not develop on the continent, but rather in Anglo-Saxon England as a result of Irish influences.[235]

---

235 Dumville (1972, 381–382). However, caution in judgment was advised by P. Dronke (*Nine Medieval Latin Plays*, pp. xxvi–xxviii) and M.P. Brown (1996, 146).

However, there is no proof that the dialogue quoted above was actually incorporated into the liturgy. The entire passage might have just as well been meant to be read during a private church service. However, the specific form of the narrative sections – i.e. the use of red ink and verbs in the present tense – seems to indicate the performative purpose of this text. Considering it in the categories of a "drama" is an anachronistic imposition of inadequate contemporary categories on historical material. The confrontation of three singing soloists and the choir comprises an intriguing yet probably unintentional reworking of the fundamental structure of the ancient, non-illusionistic religious performance. Introduction of the singing narrator hindered the development of mimetic illusion and lent the performance an air of liturgical truth. The narrator would proclaim who is going to speak, and explain all the gestures and actions of the performers. Just like the deacons holding the Cross during *Adoratio* on Good Friday, the soloists would sing the parts of Adam and Eve, but would not have to pretend that they become these figures. Regardless of the context in which the performance could be delivered, it retained its liturgical character.

Sadness is the dominant mood in this ceremony, which is full of humble imploring. Although the gates of hell are crushed, nobody relishes the new freedom: after his ties are cut, Adam falls on his knees, while Eve weeps. Similar reactions are conveyed in iconographical sources. One illumination from a mid-11th-century psalter shows the scene of freeing the just from hell.[236] It is dominated by a giant Christ, who leans over little figures extending their arms up high in a beseeching gesture.

The disturbing and emotional interpretation of the Harrowing of Hell developed by Anglo-Saxon monks proved to be a lasting one. In the 14th century, nuns from Barking near London elaborated on this liturgical performance, turning it into a spectacular show, preserving at the same time the supplicatory and thanksgiving dimension of the liturgy.[237] Satan also did not make an appearance in Barking. The absence of Christ's chief adversary in Latin liturgical texts was meant to deprive him of his evil powers. By exaggerating the figure of Christ[238] – as in the psalter drawing reproduced here – the liturgy focused on the saving dimension of Christ's actions. Satan appeared only in the English versions of texts describing

---

236 MS *Cotton Tiberius C.IV*, fol. 14r, British Library, London.
237 For more information about the performances of nuns in Barking see the chapter on liturgical performances after the 10th century.
238 William Langland refers later to this tradition by showing a giant Christ descending to hell in *Piers Plowman* (Passus XVIII).

the Harrowing of Hell. However, these accounts were not meant to be performed as part of the Easter liturgy. One case in point is the Old English *Harrowing of Hell* preserved in several versions in manuscripts from the end of the 13th century and the first half of the 14th century.[239] Even if these texts were performed in religious communities, there is no indication in them that it was done inside a church. Almost half of the text is devoted to a debate between Christ and Satan on the question whether it is right to free the just from hell. In later biblical cycles performed in York and Chester appearances of Satan served as an occasion for ludicrous antics and vulgar jokes.

---

239 The earliest manuscript – MS *Digby 86* (Bodleian Library, Oxford) – was created in the years 1272–1282. Cf. Hulme (1961).

Easter

1. At night, before the bells pealed signalling the first nocturne, the sacristan would lift the Cross from the tomb, where it was placed on Good Friday, and put it "at the proper place." Celebrations began at the night-time office. After prayer, antiphons and psalms were sung, which was followed by readings. *Regularis concordia* describes a special performance for this occasion. These are the instructions[240]:

Dum tertia recitatur lectio, iiii fratres induant se, quorum unus, alba indutus ac si ad aliud agendum, ingrediatur atque latenter sepulchri locum adeat ibique, manu tenens palmam, quietus sedeat. Dumque tertium percelebratur responsorium, residui tres succedant, omnes quidem cappis induti, turribula cum incensu manibus gestantes, ac, pedetemptim ad similitudinem quaerentium quid, ueniant ante locum sepulchri. Aguntur enim haec ad imitationem angeli sedentis in monumento, atque mulierum cum aromatibus uenientium, ut ungerent corpus Ihesu. Cum ergo ille residens tres uelut erraneos ac aliquid quaerentes, uiderit sibi adproximare, incipiat mediocri uoce dulcisone cantare:	During the reading of the third lesson, four brothers change their clothes. One of them, dressed in an alb, pretending as if he were to do something else, sneaks to the tomb, where he sits silently, holding a palm in his hand. While singing the third responsory, three others approach, all dressed in copes and carrying thuribles. Step by step, as if looking for something, they approach the tomb. This is done to imitate the angel sitting on the tomb and the women[241] who came with oils to anoint the body of Jesus. And when the sitting one sees the three [figures] approaching, as if they were lost and looking for something, he begins to sing delicately in a sweet voice:
Quem quaeritis?	*Who are you looking for [...]?*
Quo decantato finetenus, respondeat hi tres, uno ore:	When he finishes singing[242] the other three respond in unison:
Ihesum Nazarenum.	*Jesus of Nazarene.*
Quibus ille:	Then he [the sitting one] responds:
Non est hic. Surrexit sicut praedixerat. Ite, nuntiate quia surrexit a mortuis.	*He is not here. He rose, as he said. Go and spread the word that he rose from the dead.*
Cuius iussionis uoce uertant se illi tres ad chorum, dicentes:	On this command the three turn towards the choir, saying:

---

240 *Die "Regularis Concordia,"* ed. Kornexl, pp. 104–107; *RC* 51–52, pp. 49–51.
241 According to Mark 16:1, there were Mary Magdalene, and Mary, mother to James and Salome. Matthew lists only two Marys, Luke mentions women in general, while John says the tomb was approached by Mary Magdalene alone.
242 *Regularis concordia* quotes only the first words of the dialogue. The entire line is "Who are you looking for, Christian women?" The entire trope is reconstructed below.

Alleluia. Resurrexit Dominus.
Dicto hoc, rursus ille residens, uelut reuocans illos dicat antiphonam:
Venite et uidete locum.
Haec uero dicens, surgat et erigat uelum ostendatque eis locum cruce nudatum sed tantum linteamina posita, quibus crux inuoluta erat. Quo uiso, deponant turribula, quae gestauerant in eodem sepulchro sumantque linteum et extendant contra clerum ac, ueluti ostendentes quod surrexerit Dominus etiam non sit illo inuolutus, hanc canant antiphonam:
Surrexit Dominus de speulchro,
superponantque linteum altari. [52] Finita antiphona prior, congaudens pro triumpho regis nostri quod deuicta morte surrexit, incipiat hymnum

Te Deum laudamus;
quo incepto una pulsantur omnia signa. Post cuius finem dicat sacerdos uersum
[*Surrexit Dominus de sepulchro*]
uerbotenus et initiet matutinas.

Halleluia. The Lord rose from the dead.
After saying this, the sitting one, as if calling them to return, says the antiphon:
Come and see the place.
Then he rises, lifts the veil and shows the others the place where there is no Cross, but only the cloth it was wrapped in before. Upon seeing this, they place their thuribles in the tomb, lift the cloth and stand before the clergy, as if demonstrating that the Lord has risen from the dead and is no longer wrapped in this [cloth], singing the antiphon:

The Lord has risen from the tomb [...],
and putting the cloth on the altar. [52] After the antiphon is finished, the abbot, rejoicing in the triumph of our King, who conquered death by rising from the dead, intones the hymn:

We praise Thee, O God [...].
Then all the bells peal. After this, the priest quotes the entire line[243]:
[*The Lord has risen from the grave*]
and begins the morning Mass.

2. The real presence of resurrected Jesus, the key figure in the Easter liturgical performance, was conveyed through the lack of His body. The first great role in the Christian theatre was thus played by absence, emptiness. In contrast to the ancient temple of Dionysus, the mediaeval church was supposed to foster the revelation of Truth, not to create a convincing illusion. If Jesus really was who he said he was, then he rose from the dead and his body had to disappear from the grave. The reality of the empty grave testified to the truth of the Incarnation. Presence in absence: this is the mode in which Christ appeared in the Eucharist.[244] The liturgical performance theatralized the Sacrament.[245] One characteristic feature

---

243 The entire line is: "The Lord has risen from the grave, the one who hung on the tree for us."
244 Kocur (2007, 200–204).
245 Sarah Beckwith analyses the pheonomenon of "sacramental theatre" in the third part of her book *Signifying God* (2001, 59–117); for more information on *Quem quaeritis* see pages 72–74.

is that it was the strict monastic rule, which introduced absolute control over the corporeality of monks, that assumed the absence of the body as the model of a fully real presence.

Holy Week was celebrated as a series of extraordinary performances focusing on the fundamental theme of the death of God. These performances, realized in the context of the liturgy, would not theatralize biblical events by confirming their fictional character, but restored their real nature, locating them in the time and space of those who participated in the celebrations. Nobody could remain indifferent in the face of Passion, because its subsequent stages occurred "here and now." The four monks who participated in the performance were not actors but performers of rites.[246] Dressed in liturgical vestments, appropriate for the solemn occasion, they wielded liturgical objects: thuribles, tools of the monastic profession, as well as palm branches symbolizing Christ's conquest of death. The three brothers were three women looking for the Holy Sepulchre and yet remained themselves, i.e. monks testifying to the truth of the Resurrection. In the same way, during the *Adoratio Crucis* celebration, the Cross was both the tortured Christ and the wooden instrument of torture. In the Anglo-Saxon monasteries a new kind of theatre was born, one that was fundamentally different from the ancient one. Performers in this theatre would not wear masks, but rather bare themselves radically, making honest and authentic confession the essence of their art. The face had to be clearly visible in order to reveal the surreptitious trembling of the soul.

3. The structure of the *Visitatio Sepulchri* performance intriguingly combined details and themes derived from various evangelical accounts. The culmination of the Visit to the Sepulchre was the demonstration of the shroud. Showing it to the clergy, the monks made everyone in the church become witnesses to Resurrection; thus, everyone was also one of the three "women." In the Gospels, the shroud was discovered by men, the Apostles. *Regularis concordia* instructs women to lift the shroud from the grave, which was probably inspired by the liturgical tradition. The dialogue *Quem quaeritis*, confirmed to be an earlier source than the *Visitatio Sepulchri* performances, must have been used by monks during Easter Mass for a long time. The liturgy also had an impact on iconography. Carol Heitz published a series of ivory tiles made in the 9th and 10th century featuring scenes from the Visit to the Sepulchre, with three Marys looking more like monks than women: one even carries a thurible, a liturgical accessory that is never mentioned in any biblical account. According to Heitz, these tiles present monastic performances.[247]

---

246   Boor (1967, 9).
247   Heitz (1963, 172–273).

5. Visitatio Sepulchri. *Benedictional of Æthelwold. MS Additional 49598, fol. 51v*
© British Library board. All Rights Reserved 2016

The *Æthelwold Benedictional*, composed in the years 963–984, contains an illustration depicting the Visit to the Sepulchre, with an angel sitting on the tomb and three women, one of whom also holds a thurible.[248] The shroud, which is mentioned only by two evangelists: John and Luke, is also clearly exposed. The artist presented the event by referring to the liturgical performance, which he probably witnessed himself on many occasions. Monastic culture was fundamentally performative; in the liturgy, performance could be as important as words.

---

248   MS Additional 49598, fol. 51v, British Library, London. Cf. Bedingfield (2002, 157 [pl. 5], 169).

Quem Quaeritis

1. It is traditionally considered that the main part and source of the *Visitatio Sepulchri* performance is a sung dialogue which begins with the question *quem quaeritis*: "Whom are you looking for?" However, these words do not appear in biblical accounts of the Resurrection, but in John's description of the arrest at Gethsemane (John 18:5–7). Jesus asks the guards twice who they are looking for and they answer twice that it is Jesus of Nazareth they want to find. Posing the same question in a radically different context, i.e. after Resurrection, lent the phrase *quem quaeritis* incredible symbolic power, perhaps making it the chief vehicle of Christian performance. Every man and women would respond with their lives and deeds to the key question posed by God: Whom are you looking for?

Regularis concordia instructs that the dialogue *Quem quaeritis* ought to be sung at the end of the night-time Divine Office. The existence of a similar practice was later confirmed by documents from northern Europe, southern and eastern France, as well as Rhineland. In southern France, Catalonia and Italy, as well as in several places in the eastern parts of the Franks' country – i.e. St. Gallen, Rheinau, Heidenheim or Minden – the dialogue was sung as a trope before the first Mass on Easter.

2. Tropes are special vocal compositions invented in the 9th century, probably for educational purposes. Church reformers from the circle of Charlemagne initiated the practice of adding introductions to existing liturgical songs in order to emphasize their basic message. This tradition was developed by Benedictine reformers of monasteries, who were active in the country of Franks. It was considered that the inventor and greatest author of tropes was the monk Tuotilo (d. 915), who spent all his life in St. Gallen. This abbey, along with the St. Martial monastery in Limoges as well as sites in south-western France (Aquitaine), was among the chief centres where collections of tropes (tropers) would be created and stored in manuscripts. This form would be greatly developed with time, since it allowed creative composers to enrich the liturgy with new works, without interfering with the integrity and structure of the rite.

Initially, tropes were often added to the introit – the choral singing that opened the Mass.[249] "Parmi les nouvelles création liturgiques," claims Ritva Jonsson (1975, 11–12) in the introduction to the first volume of the monumental work *Corpus Troporum*, "les tropes représenta le genre musical et poétique le mieux intègre à

---

249   Young (1933, 1.182).

la messe, si étroitement même que trope et texte liturgique de base forment une symbiose".[250] The trope would offer a specific commentary on the entire Mass. The earliest testimonies confirming such use of the trope *Quem quaeritis* have been preserved in a manuscript written at the beginning of the 10th century in St. Martial, which is now stored in Paris.[251] The main part of the dialogue is preceded by a special rubric. The letter "*R*" (short for *responsio*) suggests that these are vocal parts meant to be sung by two or more singers. Texts of tropes were always supplemented with music: St. Martial Troper also contains neumes, written above the words.

Quem queritis in sepulchro, o[252] *christicole?*	*Whom are you seeking in the sepulchre, O followers of Christ?*
R[ESPONSIO]	RESPONSE
Ihesum Nazarenum crucifixum, o celicole.	*Jesus of Nazareth who was crucified, O heaven-dwellers.*
R[ESPONSIO]	RESPONSE
Non est hic, surrexit sicut ipse dixit; ite, nunciate quia surrexit.	*He is not here; he has risen as he foretold; go, announce that he has risen.*
Alleluia, resurrexit Dominus hodie: resurrexit leo fortis Cristus filius Dei. Deo gratias dicite eia.	*Alleluia! The Lord has risen today. The strong lion, Christ, has risen, the Son of God. Thanks be to God. Sing eya!*
[INTROIT]	INTROIT
Resurrexi…	*I have risen…* (singing commences, inaugurating the proper Easter Mass).

Although the music to the trope is difficult to reconstruct (neumes were written using cheironomic notation), the melody seems to feature a distinct culmination:

---

250 "Among the new liturgical creations, the tropes represent the musical and poetical genre best integrated into the Mass, even to the extent that trope and liturgical base text form a symbiosis." Trans. Petersen (2007, 345).

251 MS lat. 1240 (fol. 30 verso), Bibliothèque Nationale, Paris (Young 1933, 1.210; facsimilie of the page from the manuscript is on the page opposite to p. 210).

252 The origins of the letter "o" lie in musical performance. The word *sepulchro* ("grave") was sung by prolonging the last syllable: sepulchro-o-o-o. The copyist, who had musical expertise, added the letter "o." Later writers, who had lesser knowledge of music, treated the "o" as an exclamation. Cf. Hughes (1991, 46–47); Smoldon (1980, 80–81).

the words *Non est hic* are accompanied by decidedly higher notes.[253] The crucial part of the musical performance was the revelation of the empty grave: "He is not here!" Music preserved in the St. Martial manuscript thus confirms that the main subject of the Easter performance was "absence" – lack of the body, which constitutes proof of Resurrection. This specific realism also dominates in visual arts: paintings and sculptures created in the 10th and 11th century often show an angel pointing to the grave which was empty save for the shroud.[254]

3. The shortest version of the *Quem quaeritis* trope has been preserved in the manuscript created and still stored in the Abbey of St. Gall (il. 6).[255] The document was copied ca. 950, slightly later than the manuscript from St. Martial. It is another case in which the trope precedes the introit of the Easter Mass. Musical notation was added over the text, just as in the St. Martial text, in the form of cheironomic neumes, while individual utterances are preceded by rubrics informing which line is the "question" (INT[ERROGATIO]), and which the "response" (R[ESPONSIO]).

INT[ERROGATIO]	QUESTION
Quem queritis in sepulchro, christicole?	Whom are you seeking in the sepulchre, followers of Christ?
R[ESPONSIO]	RESPONSE
Iesum Nazarenum crucifixum, o caelicolae.	Jesus of Nazareth who was crucified, O heaven-dwellers.
Non est hic, surrexit sicut predixerat: ite nuntiate quia surrexit de sepulchro.	He is not here; he has risen as he had foretold. Go, announce that he has risen from the sepulchre.
[INTROIT]	INTROIT
Ressurexi...	I have risen... (singing commences, inaugurating the proper Easter Mass).

---

253 Rankin (1990, 318–319).
254 For examples in iconography see: Schiller (1971, 310–329). Cf. Campbell (2001, 622–625).
255 MS 484, Stiftsbibliothek, St. Gallen (Young 1933, 1.201; facsimile of page 111 of the manuscript, featuring the trope, on the page opposite to p. 202).

6. *The simplest version of the trope* Quem quaeritis, *MS Cod. Sang. 484, p. 111. St. Gallen, Stiftsbibliothek*

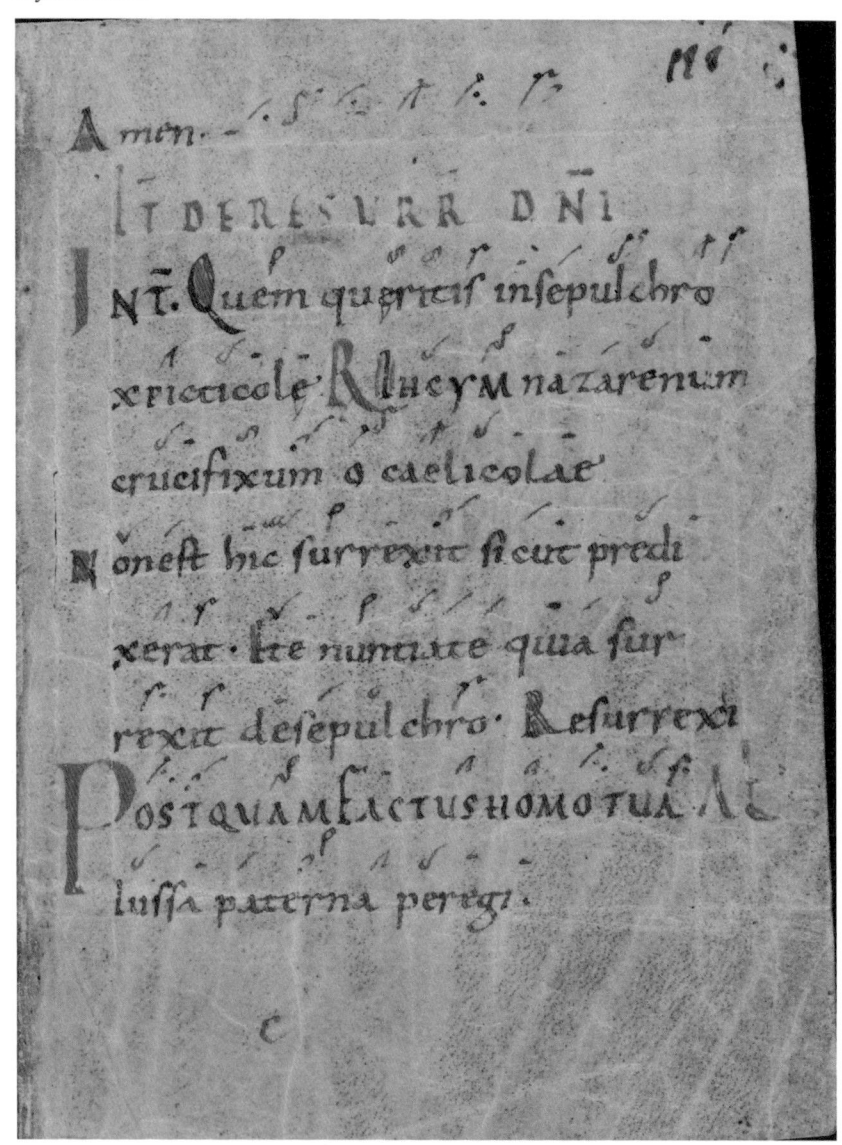

ITEM DE RESURR DNI

INT. Quem queritis in sepulchro
xpicticole R Ihesum nazarenum
crucifixum o caelicolae
N oneft hic surrexit sicut predi
xerat. Ite nuntiate quia sur
rexit de sepulchro. Resurrexi
Postquam factus homo tua
Iussa paterna peregi.

7. The transcription into modern notation of the trope Quem quaeritis *from St Gallen*

[Musical notation with the following text underlay:]

Interrogatio: Quem quae - ri - tis in se - pul - chro, o Chri - sti - co - lae?

Responsorium: Je - sum Na - za - re - num cru - ci - fi - xum, o cae - li - co - lae.

Non est hic, sur - re - xit si - cut prae - di - xe - rat; i - te, nun - ti - a - te

Introit: qui - a sur - re - xit de se - pul - chro. Re - sur - re - xi ... etc.

Just like in the St. Martin manuscript, the sentence *Non est hic* is highlighted with higher notes as the melody suddenly rises.

4. In the classic influential work *The Drama of the Medieval Church* (1933), Karl Young claims that the trope *Quem quaeritis* was created as an extra-liturgical addition to the antiphon to the introit of the Easter Mass, then was separated from the introit and attached to the procession, and finally incorporated into the finale of the matins (as *Regularis concordia* recommends, among other sources); only at that stage could it emerge as a separate theatrical performance.[256] However, later studies question this theory. In mid-1960s, O.B. Hardison called the Mass itself a "sacred drama."[257] Timothy McGee questioned the possibility of "tropes migrating" between liturgies, and proved in 1976 that the dialogue *Quem quaeritis* was sometimes part of the ceremony preceding the Easter Mass (*Collecta*). In her groundbreaking analyses of the music accompanying mediaeval performances, Susan Rankin compared tropes created in the 10th and 11th century in Aquitaine, and concluded that from a musicological perspective the dialogue *Quem quaeritis* fundamentally differs from the introit *Ressurexi*.[258] Andrew Hughes, on the other hand, brought attention to intrigu-

---

256 Young (1933, 1.178–238).
257 Hardison (1965, 35–79).
258 Rankin (1989, 1.22).

ing similarities between the staff version of music to *Quem quaeritis* and the matins *responsoria*.[259]

English testimonies also provoke many debates. Two earliest documents containing music to *Quem quaeritis* – the Winchester Tropers[260] – seem to make a connection between this trope and various liturgies. The Oxford Troper[261] has preserved *Quem quaeritis* between tropes for Palm Sunday and the rubric inaugurating the ceremony of blessing the paschal candle on Easter Eve: *Sabbato S[an]c[t]o primu[m] Benedictio cerei*. The Cambridge Troper[262] contains *Quem quaeritis*, which is placed after songs for Palm Sunday and before the rubric *Tropi in die Christi resurrectione*, which may suggest – according to many scholars[263] – that the trope *Quem quaeritis* preserved in this manuscript constitutes a part of Easter matins, in contrast to the Oxford document, but in line with *Regularis concordia*.

However, careful consideration of the manuscripts containing collections of tropes from Winchester leads to the conclusion that there is no reason to identify, as most scholars do, a particular trope with the rubric that appears directly after it (e.g. *Quem quaeritis* with Easter Eve, as is suggested in the case of the Oxford manuscript). The monastery scribe who worked on the manuscript preserved in Cambridge might have just as well skipped Easter

---

259 Hughes (1991, 56–60). The responsorial structure of the trope was identified earlier by Theo Semmler (1970) and Hans-Jürgen Diller (1973).
260 MS 775, Bodleian Library, Oxford; MS 473, Corpus Christi College Library, Cambridge. For transcriptions see: Rankin (1989, 2.17–29, and 1.26–28 for commentary). The latest critical edition is contained in: CT 3.2, pp. 256–260 (as well as pp. 217–222 and p. 281). See also: Planchart (1977, 1.17–43: 50–55, and 2.37–41: 234–240).
261 Holschneider (1968, 24–25) and later Planchart (1977, 1.40) date the entire manuscript to the middle of the 11th century. At the same time, however, they prove that the Oxford manuscript (MS 775) contains tropes in versions that are earlier than the document preserved in Cambridge (MS 473). The date of creation of the section containing *quem quaeritis* has been estimated by them to be 978–980.
262 The first part of the manuscript, which contains *quem quaeritis*, is dated by Holschneider (1968, 20) and Planchart (1977, 1.18 and 26–32) to the years 996–1006.
263 Some – e.g. Chambers (1903, 2.15), Young (1933, 1.587), Woolf (1972, 343) and Planchart (1977, 1.239–240) – claim that the Oxford manuscript 775 (Bodleian Library) contains a mistake made by the copyist. On the other hand, Hardison (1965, 190–192) argues that the position of the trope in MS 775 is correct and proves the existence of a tradition according to which *quem quaeritis* was performed on Easter Eve. Petersom (2000, 115–117) argues that the trope was sung during procession on Easter night before the main daytime Mass.

Eve for some reason. Accepting such a hypothesis leads to intriguing conclusions. Both collections of tropes would have to be considered as testimonies to one and the same ceremony of *Quem quaeritis*.[264] Moreover, the texts of the tropes – similar yet not identical – might prove the existence of a performative practice among monks from the Old Minster Abbey in Winchester in the times of the famed synod, which reformed monastic life in England. An earlier variant would have to be assumed as the original text of the trope: one created before 980 and preserved in a troper now kept in Oxford. However, the version of *Quem quaeritis* preserved in *Regularis concordia* differs slightly from the texts contained in both tropers. After all, the aim of the Synod of Winchester was not to decree or describe the local tradition of performance, but rather to create a model performance which would be adopted in all monasteries. Sadly, no text fully compliant with the model recommended in *Regularis concordia* has been preserved.

5. *Regularis concordia* belongs with the *ordinarium*, the part of liturgy that is not subject to change. This explains why only the first words of dialogues and antiphons are quoted in the text. Musical notation is also missing. In the 10th and 11th century, complete music scores with the text of the liturgy were usually recorded in tropers. Two such documents from Winchester – MS 775 (Bodleian Library in Oxford) and MS 473 (Corpus Christi College Library in Cambridge) – are the only tropers preserved in England which contain music to *Quem quaeritis*.[265] In both of them, music is recorded only using Anglo-Saxon cheironomic neumes, which does not allow for an unambiguous reconstruction of the melody. The Oxford one, however, resembles – in terms of text and music – the earliest example of

Quem quaeritis from the collection of tropes from St. Martial de Limoges. Although the St. Martial manuscript also contains only cheironomic signs, comparison with later collections made in St. Martial, which employ neumatic or staff notation, allowed scholars to reconstruct the hypothetical height of tones in the Winchester troper.[266]

---

264 Petersen (2000, 110–111).
265 Dolan (1975, 21–44); Smoldon (1980, 89–100).
266 Dolan (1975, 28–29); Smoldon (1980, 94–95); *REED Kent: Diocese of Canterbury 978–981* (commentary, transcription, facsimile).

8. Quem quaeritis, *Winchester troper, MS 775, fol. 17r.* The Bodleian Libraries, University of Oxford

9. Quem quaeritis, *Winchester troper, MS 775, fol.17v.* The Bodleian Libraries, University of Oxford

ANGELICE UOCES CONSOLATUS·
Non est hic surrexit sicut predixerat
ite nunciate quia surrexit dicentes.
SCARU MULIERU ADONNE CLERU MODULATIO·
Alleluia resurrexit dominus hodie leo
fortis xpō filius dei deo gratias dicite eia·
Uenite & uidete locum ubi DICAT ANGELUS.
positus erat dominus alleluia. alia ITERU
Cito euntes dicite discipulis DICAT ANGELUS.
quia surrexit dominus alleluia. alia·
MULIERU UNA UOCE CANAN IUBILANTES·
Surrexit dominus de sepulchro qui
pro nobis pependit in ligno alleluia·
SABBATO SCO PRIMU BENEDICTIO CEREI. DE
In principio creauit ds INDE LECTIO· SINE
Ds qui mirabiliter CANTICO· SEQUIT ORATIO

10. *The transcription into modern notation of the trope* Quem quaeritis *from Winchester troper*

ANGELICA DE CHRISTI RESURRECTIONE:
Quem quae - ri - tis in se - pul - chro, Chri - sti - co - lae?

SANCTARUM MULIERUM RESPONSIO:
Ie - sum Na - za - re - num cru - ci - fix - um, O cae - li - co - la.

ANGELICAE VOCIS CONSOLATUS:
Non est hic; sur - re - xit si - cut prae - di - xe - rat.
I - te nun - ti - a - te qui - a sur - re - xit di - cen - tes:

SANCTARUM MULIERUM AD OMNEM CLERUM MODULATIO:
Al - le - lu - ia. Re - sur - re - xit Do - mi - nus ho - di - e, le - o for - tis,
Chri - stus fi - li - us De - i; De - o gra - ti - as di - ci - te, ei - a.

DICAT ANGELUS:
Ue - ni - te et ui - de - te lo - cum u - bi po - si - tus e - rat Do - mi - nus, al - le - lu - ia, al - le - lu - ia.

ITERUM DICAT ANGELUS:
Ci - to e - un - tes di - ci - te di - sci - pu - lis qui - a sur - re - xit Do - mi - nus, al - le - lu - ia, al - le - lu - ia.

MULIERES UNA UOCE CANANT IUBILANTES:
Sur - re - xit Do - mi - nus de se - pul - chro qui pro no - bis pe - pen - dit in li - gno, al - le - lu - ia.

The Oxford manuscript preserves developed rubrics, written in red capital letters, offering instructions for performers[267]:

ANGELICA DE CHRISTI RESURRECTIONE:	ANGELIC PROCLAMATION OF THE RESURRECTION OF CHRIST:
Quem quaeritis in sepulchro, Christocolae?	*Whom do you seek in the sepulchre, O followers of Christ?*
SNACTARUM MULIERUM RESPONSIO:	THE RESPONSE OF THE HOLY WOMEN:
Iesum Nazarenum crucifixum, o caelicola.	*Jesus of Nazareth who was crucified, O heaven-dwellers.*
ANGELICAE UOCES CONSOLATUS:	THE CONSOLATION OF THE ANGELIC VOICE:
Non est hic; surrexit sicut predixerat. Ite nuntiate quia surrexit dicentes:	*He is not here, he has risen as he had predicted; go, announce that he has risen, saying:*
SANCTUARUM MULIERUM AD OMNEM CLERUM MODULATIO:	THE SONG OF THE HOLY WOMEN TO ALL THE CLERGY:
Alleluia. Resurrexit Dominus hodie, leo fortis, Christus filius Dei; Deo gratias dicite eia.	*Alleluia! The Lord has risen today, the mighty lion, Christ, the Son of God. Praise be to God, say it indeed!*
DICAT ANGELUS:	LET THE ANGEL SAY:
Uenite et uidete locum ubi positus erat Dominus, alleluia, alleluia.	*Come and see the place where the Lord had been laid, alleluia, alleluia.*
ITERUM DICAT ANGELUS:	AGAIN LET THE ANGEL SAY:
Cito euntes dicite discipulis quia surrexit Dominus, alleluia, alleluia.	*Going quickly, tell the disciples that the Lord has risen, alleluia, alleluia.*
MULIERES UNA UOCE CANANT IUBILANTES:	LET THE WOMEN WITH ONE VOICE SING REJOICING:
Surrexit Dominus de sepulchro qui pro nobis pependit in ligno, alleluia.	*The Lord has risen from the sepulchre, who for us hung on the wood, alleluia.*

As far as the melodic line is concerned, what draws attention is the sudden heightening of sounds accompanying the words *Non est hic* and *Alleluia* – key moments in the performance of the Resurrection. Therefore, the trope does not only constitute an organic part of the liturgy, but also introduces new elements to the

---

267 Oxford, Bodleian Library, MS 775, fol. 17r-17v. Trans. *Medieval Drama* 29 (Bevington), modified.

ceremony. Since the 9th century, the *Alleluia* song has been identified with the singing of angels. Rubrics from the Winchester troper emphasize the angelic and metaphysical dimension of the trope. Just as in the case of earlier manuscripts from St. Martial or St. Gallen, the high notes accompanying the line *Non est hic* accentuate the lack of body, at the same time reinforcing and authenticating the fundamental message conveyed by the Easter liturgy: the truth of the Resurrection. Surely, the *Quem quaeritis* trope was not an extra-liturgical addition to monastic ceremonies as Karl Young argued.

6. Young also offered a Darwinian interpretation of the trope's evolution, i.e. one leading from the simplest version, contained in the St. Gallen manuscript, through the more developed one, as in the St. Martial manuscript, to the most elaborate and multi-layered performances of later ages.[268] This evolutionary theory has been definitively and soundly disproved by Hardison. Rankin, on the other hand, has proven that in musical terms the five-line version (St. Martial) – in opposition to the three-line version (St. Gallen) – "forms a coherent and balanced structure."[269]

The *Quem quaeritis* dialogue was sung during various liturgical ceremonies – introit, *Collecta*, procession, matins – but it always comprised their organic part. Elaborate performances like *Visitatio Sepulchri* were probably created, just like tropes, not only out of didactic needs, but also out of the impulse to enrich and beautify the liturgy. The oldest documents do not necessarily have to contain the earliest versions of the trope. Analyses of hundreds of surviving examples of *Quem quaeritis*, mainly found in continental Europe, reveal complex and sometimes unclear relations or dependencies existing between the dialogue and the liturgy. In her unpublished doctoral dissertation, Sister Marie Delores Moore analyses over three hundred early manuscripts of *Quem quaeritis*. She created chronological tables, from which it is clear that in the 10th and 11th century it was most often the case, though not always, that the dialogue preceded Mass; since the early 12th century it appeared more often at the end of matins, and since the 13th century – only as part of matins.[270] Thus, scholars abandoned any search for the first, original trope.[271]

---

268 Young (1933, 1.178–410).
269 Hardison (1965, 1–34 & 178–252); Rankin (1985, 1.191).
270 After McGee (1976, 17).
271 Petersen (2007, 342).

7. The *Visitatio Sepulchri* performance described in *Regularis concordia* contains a more elaborate form of the *Quem quaeritis* dialogue than the trope preserved in the St. Gallen manuscript. This is the reconstruction of the entire text[272]:

Quem quaeritis in sepulchro, Christicolae?	*Whom are you seeking in the sepulchre, followers of Christ?*
Jesum Nazarenum crucifixum, o caelicolae.	*Jesus of Nazareth who was crucified, O heaven-dwellers.*
Non est hic, surrexit sicut praedixerat. Ite nuntiate quia surrexit a mortuis.	*He is not here; he has risen as he had foretold. Go, announce that he has risen from the dead.*
Alleluia, resurrexit Dominus hodie, leo fortis, Christus, filius dei, deo gratia dicite eia.	*Alleluia, the Lord has risen today, the strong lion, Christ, has risen, the Son of God, thanks be to God, sing eya.*
Uenite et uidete locum ubi positus erat dominus, alleluia, alleluia.	*Come and see the place where the Lord was laid, alleluia, alleluia.*
Surrexit dominus de sepulchro qui pro nobis pependit in ligno, alleluia.	*The Lord has risen from the sepulchre, who for us hung on the wood, alleluia.*

The last antiphon proclaimed the good news about the Resurrection. "Women" would reveal the empty shroud to all those participating in the ceremony, which turned everyone into witnesses to this event. The Resurrection would occur "here and now." The abbot would joyously intone the hymn *Te Deum laudamus*; then, all the bells would peal, and the priest would carry on with the words *Surrexit Dominus de sepulchro*. The *Quem quaeritis* performance legitimized the actions of the abbot, the priest, and the bell-ringer, giving them meaning and explaining the ritual that followed. It was also a rite in itself, which forced all those present to partake in the experience. Therefore, the text of *Regularis concordia* does not allow separating the trope *Quem quaeritis* from the liturgical context as an example of "drama."[273]

8. The question *quem quaeritis* served special performative functions in the monastic context. It is quite telling that according to instructions contained in *Regularis concordia* it was compulsory to partake in *Visitatio Sepulchri*, as opposed to *Tenebrae* or *Depositio Crucis*. The verb *quaerere* ("to seek") aptly rendered the specificity of monastic life, which was concentrated on ceaseless looking for traces

---

272 Basing on the catalogue of tropes in: Planchart (1977, 2.37 & 40). Cf. *REED Kent: Diocese of Canterbury* 3–27.
273 Petersen (2003).

of divinity, and sought union with transcendence, as ordered by the Scriptures. In the Latin Vulgate, the term *quaerere* appears in Psalms and Gospels[274]: *Quaerite Dominum, et confirmamini; Quaerite faciem eius semper*[275] (Psalm 105:4); *Et sperent in te, qui noverunt nomen tuum; quoniam non dereliquisti quaerentes te, Domine*[276] (Psalm 9:10); *Petite, et dabitur vobis; quaerite, et invenietis*[277] (Matthew 7:7). It is the Song of Solomon that expresses most fully the meaning of monastic yearning for mystical union with God (3:1–2): *In lectulo meo, per noctes, quaesivi quem diligit anima mea, quaesivi illum, et non inveni. Surgam, et circuibo civitatem, per vicos et plateas. Quaeram quem diligit anima mea, quaesivi illum, et non inveni.*[278] In the performance of the Visitation, the question "Whom are you looking for?" is posed by God, using an angel as intermediary, not only to the women or three brothers wielding thuribles, but also to all monks gathered in the church. This question expressed the deepest sense of monastic life. Seeking Christ and finding an empty grave also provoked deep emotions among all the faithful. After all, witnessing Christ's Resurrection heralded the joyful end of all people's striving for God.[279]

---

274   After Flanigan (1996, 15).
275   "Seek the Lord and his strength, seek his presence continually!"
276   "And those who know thy name put their trust in thee, for thou, O Lord, hast not forsaken those who seek thee."
277   "Ask, and it will be given you; seek, and you will find."
278   "Upon my bed by night / I sought him whom my soul loves; / I sought him, but found him not; / I called him, but he gave no answer. / I will rise now and go about the city, / in the streets and in the squares; / I will seek him whom my soul loves. / I sought him, but found him not."
279   Coldewey (2004, 34).

The Second Birth of Theatre

1. It is generally assumed that Christian theatre was born during Easter, the first example of drama being the trope *Quem quaeritis* preserved in *Regularis concordia*.[280] Scholars supporting this view differ only in how they define theatre. E.K. Chambers considers dialogue to be the key criterion[281]; the trope *Quem quaeritis* meets this requirement since it features an exchange of songs between the angel and the women. Karl Young and Joy Enders discern the category of theatrical "impersonation"[282] which consists in playing a certain figure, as in the case of monks imitating the angel and the women. O.B. Hardison criticizes the evolutionary approach of Chambers and Young, and reduces liturgical performances to literature, borrowing his definition of theatre from Aristotle's *Poetics*: Resurrection would feature the Aristotelian "turn" of action (*peripéteia*) and "recognition" (*anagnōrisis*).[283] In the latest monograph on Anglo-Saxon "dramatic liturgy," M. Bradford Bedingfield considers performances related to the liturgical year –processions on the Feast of the Purification of the Virgin, and on Palm Sunday, as well as ceremonies like *Tenebrae, Adoratio Crucis, Depositio Crucis* and *Visitatio Sepulchri* – to be liturgies displaying a specifically English aesthetic, distinguished by its "dramatic character."[284] Each of those diagnoses offers interesting insight into early modern theatre, but all of them are marked by anachronism insofar as they describe mediaeval culture using concepts derived from the ancient times or the 20th century.

Regularis concordia does not use the words "theatre," "drama" or "dramatic quality." In the 10th century these terms had an entirely different meaning than in the 5th century BC or in the 20th century. The word "drama" does not occur at all in the *Middle English Dictionary*. The revered *Oxford English Dictionary* dates its first use back to ca. 1515, quoting the *Eclogues* collection by a Scottish poet Alexander Barclay. Although the Greek word *drāma* meant "deed," "action," "story" and "drama," it was already Isidore, Bishop of Seville, who defined the term

---

280 This opinion is unreflectively repeated for example by Lucia Kornexl in the fabulous compendium *The Blackwell Encyclopaedia of Anglo-Saxon England* (Lapidge 1999, p. 389, entry: *Regularis concordia*). Cf. Kocur (2007a).
281 Chambers (1903, 1.81).
282 Young (1933, 1.80); Enders (1992, 65).
283 Hardison (1965, 178). L. Goldstein (2004, 24–33) accuses Hardison of excessively simplifying the positions of Young and Chambers, quoting Engels, and praises the use of *Poetics* in descriptions of mediaeval theatre.
284 Bedingfield (2007, 228).

dramaticum at the beginning of the 7th century as a mode of speech in which "the poet never speaks, as in comedies and tragedies."[285] Thus, in a "dramatic" work the voice of author or narrator is replaced by the voices of characters. This is how mediaeval scholars understood ancient drama. Since Origen's commentaries, the most famous example of a Christian "dramatic" text has been the Song of Solomon. Isidore even claimed that "wedding songs" (*epithalamium*) used to be sung "by rhetoricians in honour of the bride and groom. Solomon first composed these in praise of the Church and of Christ"; pagans would first perform them on stage, and only later at weddings.[286] Bishop of Seville definitely differentiated Christian practices from ancient ones. Scholastic choirs would not impersonate the bride and the groom while singing the Song of Solomon, unlike pagans who performed on the theatre stage. Thus, liturgy was a drama in the mediaeval sense, since choirs of monks, and cantors would sing texts in turns, but it was not a drama in the sense given to the term in ancient or contemporary times, because monks would not render the dialogues mimetically, pretending to be lovers. The real presence of Christ in the ceremony would not be possible if the celebrants behaved like actors because they would produce only a professional illusion without bearing true testimony.

2. Another reason why early mediaeval authors did not interpret the term "drama" in theatrical categories is that there were no buildings that could act as a theatrical stage. Theatre could only be associated with ancient ruins and the condemned, pagan past. Isidore harboured no illusions about this subject (*Etymologiae* 18.42.2): "*theatrum* is the same as a brothel [*prostibulum*], because when the plays are finished prostitutes 'stretch themselves out' [*prostrari*] there." In the Middle Ages, the term *theatrum* would be often accompanied by such words as *impudicitia* (prostitution), *spurcitia* (filth), *impuritas* (impurity), *turpitudo* (dishonour), *licentia* (dissolution), *luxuria* (superfluity) or *obscenitas* (obscenity). "When clerics begin to represent Rachel and the *Quem quaeritis* within the church and at the altar, there would have been no reason to identify these liturgical responses with the *theatrum* because the church was a sacred place and the action cultic and

---

285 *Etymologiae* 8.7.10: "dramaticum, in quo nusquam poeta loquitur, ut est in comoediis et tragoediis."
286 *Etymologiae* 1.39.18: "Epithalamia sunt carmina nubentium, quae decantantur ab scholasticis in honorem sponsi et sponsae. Haec primum Salomon edidit in laudem Ecclesiae et Christi. Ex quo gentiles sibi epithalamium uindicarunt, et istius generis carmen adsumptum est. Quod genus primum a gentilibus in scenis celebrabatur, postea tantum in nuptiis haesit."

symbolic."[287] Hugh (1096–1141), a scholar from the St. Victor Abbey in Paris, considered *theatrica* to be a mechanical art, listing it alongside hunting, agriculture, and weaving, i.e. fundamental human practices. Although he could distinguish reciting epic poems from acting in a mask, all his references to theatre are in the past tense and all the examples he discusses come from ancient times.[288]

Another problem is related to the term "liturgy," because nobody actually used it in the Middle Ages. New research has revealed that a surprising capacity characterized Christian rites. Many ritual functions were performed by lay people, especially during ceremonies in parish churches. Festive processions constituted a perfect occasion for demonstrations of power. There was no clear boundary between "official" liturgical practices and what was later designated by the Counter-Reformation as para-liturgical or even extra-liturgical activities.[289] The earliest performative work that displays clear independence from church rites is contained in a 12th-century manuscript and titled *Ordo representacionis Ade*, which has been translated by David Bevington as *The Service for Representing Adam*. The word *ordo* carried strong liturgical connotations, since it was used to denote, among other things, the "order" of the Mass (*Ordo Missae* – the Rite of Holy Mass). By extending beyond text, the mediaeval understanding of "liturgy" allowed to incorporate into the rite a surprising variety of diverse performative practices. Every performance made during liturgy became its part. However, if the same performance were to be made in a different context, it could lose its liturgical dimension.

3. In a widely debated article from 1974, titled "The Roman Rite and the Origins of the Liturgical Drama," Clifford Flanigan develops a brilliant hypothesis about the genesis of elaborate liturgical performances. At the turn of the 8th and 9th century, Pepin, Charlemagne and their successors introduced the duty to celebrate liturgy in accordance with the Roman Rite in all places where the Gallican Rite had developed and become dominant, i.e. chiefly on the territories of the Franks. According to Flanigan, the Gallican Rite was exuberant, full of elation, and lengthy. It abounded in long and flowery prayers, as well as spectacular actions, with rhetoric, ornamentation and showiness prevailing. The Roman Rite, on the other

---

287 Clopper (2001, 2). Cf. Bigongiari (1946).
288 Hugh of Saint Victor, *Didascalion* 2.27; *MES* 43 (A30). For more information on Hugh's original perspective, as well as his predecessors (Isidore) and followers (Bonaventura, Vincent de Beauvais, Reisch, Alsted) see: Tatarkiewicz (1965). Cf. Dox (2004, 85–87); Lerud (2008, 33).
289 Flanigan, Ashley & Sheingorn (2001, 699); Flanigan (1996, 15–16).

hand, was defined by Flanigan as simple, stiff, cold, as well as deprived of liveliness and any theatricality. The scholar estimates that imposing the austere rite did not eradicate the "dramatic instinct" among the Franks, allowing the exuberant performative elements of the older rite to seep into the new one.

In the 12th century – along with the arrival of new religious practices, and with more and more people from outside the monasteries attempting to meet the requirements posed as the Christian model[290] – monks began to develop liturgical performances to such an extent that they would transform them into autonomous literary works, although they were still delivered as part of the liturgical calendar. When ten such texts were copied in one hand in a separate manuscript in Fleury or close by (including an extended version of *Visitatio Sepulchri*), they were given a new meaning. Perhaps they were distinguished in this way precisely because – as Flanigan suggested in 1985 – all of them shared one special characteristic: they could be staged as independent plays.[291] Moreover, the entire collection came to be known as "the Fleury plays."

4. The spectacular quality was a natural component of Christian liturgy. After all, the fundamental events in this religion involve incidents of cosmic proportions, e.g. the Incarnation – the epiphany of God in the body of an ordinary human being. Living among the people, Jesus taught using parables, demonstration, and his own example. The source of Christianity's main ritual is the Last Supper, during which Jesus pointed to bread and said "This is my body."[292] Soon thereafter – according to John 19:5 – Pilate brought forth the tormented Jesus, wearing a crown of thorns and purple cloak, and showed him to the people saying "This is the man." This scene has become the icon of Christianity. The final moments of God on earth comprise a series of spectacular events: Crucifixion, Entombment and Resurrection. Rites and liturgical performances re-enacted these "shows" by employing liturgical means of expression, thus allowing the faithful to experience them over and over as something occurring "here and now." Making Christ

---

290 For more information on the crisis of monasticism in the years 1050–1150 see: Van Engel (1986).
291 Flanigan (1985, 17; MS 201 [previously 178], Bibliothèque de la Ville in Orléans, pp. 176–243). The manuscript has 251 pages, the first 175 containing homilies and religious texts, the last ones (pp. 244–251) – hymns and prose. "Plays" are found in the middle part.
292 This sentence has been preserved, in three versions, in three Gospels: Matthew 26:26 ("Take, eat; this is my body"), Mark 14:22 ("Take; this is my body"), and Luke 22:19 ("This is my body which is given for you"). The earliest account comes from St. Paul (1 Corinthians 11:24). Cf. below, the chapter on Mass.

present was rendered mainly by appealing to the sense of sight. The key actions of the monks during the Visitation, which involves the lack of body and an empty shroud, are described in *Regularis concordia* with the term *ostendere*, meaning "to show," "to demonstrate," and "to point out."[293] Such indications conveyed the main message of the Easter liturgy, as recommended by *Regularis concordia*.

After saying "Come and see the place," the angel "shall rise and lift the veil and show [*ostendat*] to them the place bare of the cross but only the linen cloths, in which the cross had been wrapped [...]. Seeing this they should lay down the thuribles which they had carried in the same sepulchre, and they shall take the linen and hold it out facing the clergy, and, as if showing [*ostendentes*] that the Lord has risen." Singing the words of the dialogue and performing the actions specified in rubrics, the monks most probably used gestures to indicate the key symbols of Resurrection. Image served the fundamental purpose in all liturgical performances commemorating and re-enacting events from the life of Christ. The art of memory was based, after all, on visualization of space.

5. Mnemotechnics was invented by ancient Greeks and developed by Romans, while mediaeval scholars elaborated it further, transforming rhetoric into ethics – Albert the Great and St. Thomas Aquinas considered memory to be a vital component of the virtue of prudence.[294] The art of memory, however, has preserved its architectonic nature, according to its legendary genesis. After the collapse of a banquet hall, Simonides of Keos could remember where everyone sat, and helped the families identify the massacred bodies, which inspired him to discover that spatial order supported memory. As Cicero remarked while commenting on this, in order to remember certain facts, it is necessary to link their mental representations with particular locations (*loci*), or "record" images in space: "We shall employ the localities and images respectively as a wax writing tablet and the letters written on it."[295] Liturgical performances were also closely tied to specific locations (*loci*) that carried precise connotations. The Easter cycle would be centred around the sepulchre, initially positioned in the free space around the altar – the place where Christ's sacrifice was commemorated and made present every day during Mass. Processions on Candlemas or Palm Sunday followed a predefined route, incorporating various contemporary buildings into the liturgical reconstruction, thus furnishing them with new mean-

---

293 Campbell (2001, 627).
294 Carruthers (2008, 81–89); Yates (1966).
295 Cicero, *De oratore* 2.87.354: "res autem ipsas rerum effigies notaret, atque ut locis pro cera, simulacris pro litteris uteremur." Trans. E.W. Sutton.

ings. Such "places" (*loci*) were anchoring points for memory. The description of spatial practices among monks is suited perfectly by two terms employed in analyses of mediaeval and Renaissance theatre[296]: *platea* (the "square" where the play was performed, or a place in the real world) and *locus* ("place" in the world of performance, e.g. God's mansion). Generally speaking, *platea* refers to "non-localizable space": it is not mimetic, and does not represent anything but itself. In this space, actors would address the audience directly. *Locus*, on the other hand, stands for mimetic and signifying space where actors would create a particular setting for the plot, distancing themselves from the audience. During *Visitatio Sepulchri* the interior of the church is *platea*, while the sepulchre is *locus*. Medieval performance art was in fact rooted in mnemotechnics, the art of memory.

In his commentary to the Simonides anecdote, Cicero emphasized that it is sight that plays the crucial role in remembering, being "the keenest of all our senses."[297] This opinion was also spread by the treatise *Rhetorica ad Herennium*, which was popular in the Middle Ages, and attributed to Cicero; it also emphasized that memory ought to be closely tied only to such images (*imagines*) that can "do something."[298] Ca. 680, Benedict Biscop, founder of the Wearmouth Abbey, brought from Rome many images, which he used to adorn the walls of St. Peter's church, where they inspired and taught all who entered the building, even if they could not read.[299] In subsequent centuries, the art of illuminating manuscripts flourished in English monasteries. The great illuminators included Dunstan, reformer of monasticism, and primarily Æthelwold, who made Winchester a great artistic centre.[300] It was there that ca. 980 a certain monk, probably Godeman, fabulously illuminated a liturgical book, thus creating a masterpiece of Anglo-Saxon manuscript illumination, known today as *The Benedictional of St. Æthelwold*.[301] Images also came to dominate the texts of blessings. St. Thomas Aquinas called sight "the most spiritual, the highest of the senses, with the widest range of objects," adding that "fantasy and imagination is, as it were, a treasure-

---

296   Weimann (1978, 73–85); (2000, 180–215); Counsell (1996, 17–19); Dillon (2006, 4–16).
297   Cicero, *De oratore* 2.87.357: "acerrimum autem ex omnibus nostris sensibus esse sensum uidendi."
298   *Rhetorica ad Herennium* 3.12.37: "aliquid agentes imagines."
299   Bede, *Historia abbatum*, ch. 6, ed. Plummer, pp. 369–370.
300   Knowles (1963, 528–534).
301   Additional MS 49598, British Library, London (Temple 1976, no. 23, figs. 85, 86, 88, 90 & 91). For facsimiles see: Prescott (2002). For commentary see: Deshman (1995).

store of forms received through the senses."[302] He also claimed that the soul better remembers subtle and spiritual things if they are clad in "corporeal similitudes."[303]

6. Modern science confirms these intuitions. According to anthropologists, the sense of sight is dominant among all primates, which may probably result from the way in which our old ancestors adapted to living on trees. An *Ardipithecus* who missed a branch would fall and die, therefore not replicating her genotype. In a forest only sight can provide all the necessary information about the shape, size and position of distant objects.[304] Neuroscience proves, on the other hand, that images impact humans so strongly because the exact same areas of the cerebral cortex are active while perceiving and visualizing; moreover, they probably condition linguistic competences.[305] At the beginning of the 1990s, a team led by Giacomo Rizzolatti from the University of Parma discovered "mirror neurons" in the frontal lobes of primates, specifically in two macaques.[306] They activated both when the animal performed a certain manual action, for example while grabbing an object, and when they observed such actions. Soon after, "mirror neurons" have also been found in human brain. Rizzolatti explains that they "allow us to grasp the minds of others not through conceptual reasoning but through direct simulation. By feeling, not by thinking."[307]

Not long ago, the same team discovered a mirror neuron that activates when a monkey performs or only hears a communicative vocal signal.[308] Perhaps the origins of human language lie in making gestures.[309] In monasteries, gestures often replaced speech. During liturgy, the movement of the celebrants' bodies stimulated specific performances of memory. Living images – Aquinas's "treasure-stores of forms received through the senses" – stimulated the imagination of the faithful and communicated the truth about biblical events. In liturgical performances, it was not the word that functioned as the most important element, but image.

---

302 Aquinas, *Summa Theologiae* 1a.78.3–4, ed. Gilby, p. 132: "maxime spiritualis, et perfectior inter omnes sensus, et communior […] phantasia sive imaginatio quasi thesaurus quidam formarum per sensum acceptarum." Trans. T. Suttor.
303 Yates (1966, 85).
304 Armstrong & Wilcox (2007, 13–14). For more information on *Ardipithecus* see: *Science* 326, 74 (2009); Kocur (2016, 60–65).
305 Miyashita (1995); Bressloff *et al.* (2000) (mathematical models of hallucination).
306 Rizzolatti & Sinigalia (2006); Arbib (2012); Kocur (2016, 83–88).
307 After Blakeslee (2006). For more information on mirror neurons and empathy see, among other places: Gallese (2003 & 2008). For critical discussion see Hickok (2014).
308 Ferrari *et al.* (2003).
309 Armstrong & Wilcox (2007); Kocur (2016, 73–82).

Words would, at most, provide commentary and explain the performance. Sung dialogues or monologues, addressed directly to the faithful, conveyed a religious message and were not meant to describe the characters of a drama. Liturgical performances were composed of multiple series of "resounding images," which were "staged" in places ripe with meaning in order to enliven the memory of all those participating in the ceremony.

7. To sum up, in the 10th century, "theatre" was born for the second time, but not in the form of ancient or contemporary performing arts. Christian theatre was developed by monks whose calling demanded they imitate Christ, and who were performers out of duty. By developing a coherent programme of liturgical performances, monks developed and sanctioned new artistic practices. Many of them were talented in literature, music or – primarily – visual arts. Naturally, they did not consider their performances as "theatre," but rather as exercises in the art of memory. In fact, they had little understanding of how ancient theatre worked. Many thought that on Greek or Roman stages the silent actors, who made gestures only, were accompanied by someone reciting the parts of all characters. Monks were able to lay the foundations for a new kind of theatre precisely because they were accomplished artists who did not associate their own performances with theatre, which they piously condemned and shunned. Any attempts at describing their achievements using terms derived from ancient Greece have no historical grounding. Monastic performativity is fundamentally different from the ancient one.[310]

Reconstruction of the early history of mediaeval theatre is made difficult not only by shortage of sources (in England large amounts of documentation were destroyed during Reformation), but also by the fact that any public activity occurred in the religious context. To employ a metaphor, mediaeval theatre never left the church. It is impossible to ascertain any date when theatre was born in the Middle Ages, just like it is unthinkable to point to any such date in ancient Greece. Both kinds of theatre developed, however, within the framework of a cult, and never cut off their ties to religion. Nor does the birth of commercial theatre in Elizabethan England provide any clear dividing line. Sacral elements persisted in plays until the 17th century, both in those staged in London and in the provinces.[311] Catholicism is still discernible in works by Shakespeare.[312]

---

310 More on this subject below, in the chapter titled "Towards Christian Performativity."
311 White (2008, 4–5).
312 Groves (2007).

Monks created a surprisingly lasting artistic project, because their main goal was not to make art, but to transform themselves and the world through confessing and testifying to the truth. The form of their performances stemmed from human biology. In 2008, Vittorio Gallese, one of the scientists who discovered mirror neurons, published an intriguing vision of a "performative body." In *Il corpo teatrale*, he cites results of many years of in-depth studies and experiments conducted recently by the most prestigious scientific institutes. This research confirms the existence of a neuronal, i.e. corporeal foundation of all interpersonal communication, including the art of performance. By developing and enriching liturgy, monks developed a religious "theatre of memory." They testified to the truth of their faith with their own bodies, with their own voices and gestures – means that we now consider to be artistic because we have lost the religious zeal of Anglo-Saxon monks.

Liturgical Performances after the 10th Century

1. In ancient Greece, theatre buildings usually belonged to temples, and dramas were performed in public only as part of religious ceremonies. When church replaced theatre as the place of worship, the term *theatrum* was endowed with new meanings. Associated with former pagan rituals, which were wrongly interpreted, it became a handy metaphor for denoting everything that was considered to be debauched and devilish, or simply not part of the church. The metaphor of theatre was used – according to an accurate description provided by Lawrence M. Clopper (2001, 50) – as part of "a rhetoric of abuse." This rhetoric particularly intensified in the 12th and 13th century, when the first texts written entirely in Anglo-Norman French emerged: *Ordo representacionis Ade* and *La Seinte Resureccion*. It was still the official language at the English court. Both texts contain elements that reveal their liturgical origin; nevertheless, their purpose was to be performed outside the liturgy. They might be called "plays" because they are not simple translations from Latin, but rather have roots in the ludic tradition, which was independent from the liturgy and being increasingly influential penetrated into church culture. Theatre metaphors stigmatized all activities that were considered to be non-Christian (*ludi inhonesti*), or regarded as posing a threat to the sacredness and dignity of the cult.

Perhaps some kind of abuse was involved. Already in the middle of the 12th century, Æthelred, who was the abbot of the wealthy Cistercian Rievaulx monastery in Northern Yorkshire in the years 1150–1166, criticized the performances of some choir singers[313]:

Interim histrionicis quibusdam gestibus totum corpus agitatur, torquentur labia, rotant, ludunt humeri; et ad singulas quasque notas digitorum flexus respondet. […] Stans interea vulgus […] non sine cachinno, risuque intuetur, ut eos non ad oratorium, sed ad theatrum, nec ad orandum, sed ad spectandum aestimes convenisse.	Meanwhile the whole body is agitated by actorly movements; the lips are twisted, the shoulders turn and play, and the fingers move in response to certain individual notes. […] The crowd stands looking on […] not without laughter and derision, so that you would think they had gathered not at a place of prayer but at a theatre, not to pray but to watch a show.

---

313 Æthelred, *Speculum charitatis* 2.33. For Latin text see: *PL* 195.571; Chambers (1903, 1.81); Young (1933, 1.548). Trans. *MES* 32, A17 (N. Davis).

It remains unclear, however, what Æthelred understood by *theatrum*. Definitely he could not mean modern theatre, because nothing approximating it existed at that time. Nor did the abbot condemn all liturgical performances, because he considered that the Church Fathers rightly established them in order to reassure the weak in faith (*ut infirmi excitarentur ad affectum pietatis*). He levelled his criticism mainly against all those who distorted the liturgy and transformed it into a non-Christian ritual.

Similar examples of abuse are also found in continental Europe, including Poland. In 1207 Pope Innocent III issued a decree to the archbishop and bishops of the Gniezno province, drawing their attention to *ludi theatrales* and masks (*larvae*), which were especially popular during Christmas[314]:

Interdum ludi fiunt in eisdem ecclesiis theatrales, et non solum ad ludibriorum spectacula introducuntur in eis monstra larvarum, verum etiam in aliquibus anni festivitatibus, quae continue natalem Christi sequuntur, diaconi, presbyteri ac subdiaconi vicissim insaniae suae ludibria exercere praesumunt, per gesticulationum suarum debacchationes obscoenas in conspectu populi decus faciunt clericale vilescere.	From time to time public spectacles are made in certain churches, and not only are masks of monsters introduced in derisive spectacle, but in truth during other feast days of the year which follow immediately after the birth of Christ, deacons, presbyters and subdeacons in turn presume to exercise their insane mockeries [and] by the gestures of their obscene rages demean their clerical office in the sight of the people.

Such *ludi theatrales* were naturally to be immediately suppressed.

2. In England, after the Norman Conquest, monks and the clergy continued and developed the tradition of liturgical performances, as can be inferred from scarce evidence from Durham, York, Beverley, Lincoln, Lichfield, Norwich, Salisbury and Wells.[315] Ca. 1150, Laurentius, the prior of Durham, composed in Latin the dialogue *Peregrinus* (*Pilgrim*), now lost, which describes a meeting of Christ and two disciples on the road to Emmaus after Resurrection.[316] Slightly later, in the years 1188–1198, texts in English and Latin were created in the Lichfield diocese, which are now referred to as "the Shrewsbury fragments" (they have been discovered towards the end of the 19th century in a local school library). These "fragments"

---

314 *CIC* 2.452 (*Decretales Gregorii* IX, 3.1.12). Trans. Clopper (2001, 55). Cf. Chambers (1903, 1.279); *MES* 114 (B27a).
315 In the largest yet still incomplete collection of testimonies, Walther Lipphardt cites 833 texts, out of which only 28 are from the British Isles (*Leteinische Osterfeiern und Osterspiele*).
316 *DTRB*, no. 620: *Rithmus Laurentii de Christo et eius Discipulis*. Cf. Lipphardt 5.1615–1633, no. 809–810.

are in fact copies of roles written for the following characters: Third Shepherd in the "shepherd's play" (*representacio pastorum* performed at Christmas); Third Mary in the "Resurrection play"; and finally, Disciple Cleopas in the "pilgrim's play" (*representacio peregrinorum*). The manuscripts also contain the last words of preceding parts and partial musical scores.[317] They constitute a unique testimony to the lasting character of performative practices. Their form also resembles that of actors' texts or parts used in ancient and Elizabethan times.[318] Those parts would be handed to performers and contained only one character's text, at best supplemented with cues.

In the years 1277–1370 another document was created which describes Easter performances delivered by Benedictine monks in Norwich. The local cathedral would provide space for the performance of *Depositio*, *Elevatio*, and primarily *Visitatio Sepulchri* with three Marys whose parts were supposed to be played with special piety.[319]

3. One unique testimony to women's performative tradition survived the turmoil of Reformation, detailing performances from the Benedictine abbey in Barking near London. It was the biggest and wealthiest convent. Although the manuscript[320] dates back to the 15th century, it refers to reforms introduced by the venerable lady Katherine of Sutton, abbess in the years 1363–1376, who was hailed by Nancy Cotton in 1978 as "the first English dramatist." Venerabilis Domina Katerina reformed the celebrations, "desiring to get rid of the said torpor completely and more to excite the devotion of the faithful to a such renowned [Easter] celebration."[321] According to William Tydeman, the abbess was not motivated by missionary goals, but rather desired to stimulate and strengthen faith among women who were already initiated into the mysteries.[322] Although this seems

---

317 *DTRB*, no. 843. For reconstruction attempts see: Davies (1970, xiv–xxii, 1–7); Young (1933, 2.514–523); Smoldon (1980, 394–399).
318 Kocur (2008); Palfrey and Stern (2007).
319 Norwich, *Consuetudines* 1277–1370, Cambridge, Corpus Christi College, MS 465, fol. 62v, 65v, 66r (Lipphardt no. 4111): "Dum legitur iii. lectio eant se preparare tres marie cum magna reuerencia in deuotione." Cf. Sheingorn (1987, 249–250).
320 University College, Oxford, MS 169, Ordinale Berkingense. *DTRB*, no. 362. Cf. Young (1933, 1.164–166 & 381–384 [text and commentary]); Tolhurst (1927-8, 1.106–110, [text]); *MES* 83–87 (English translation). For photographs of the manuscript see: Sheingorn (1987, figs. 10–17).
321 Young (1933, 1.165, 2.411): "torporem penitus extirpare et fidelium deuocionem ad tam celebrem celebracionem magis excitare."
322 Tydeman (1994, 8).

plausible, the exuberant theatricality also seems to suggest other, more important sources of this reform. The Barking convent was located on the outskirts of London, where the aristocratic abbess held a large landed estate and controlled numerous parishes. During her lifetime protests against monastic landowners intensified. Riots became more and more common. In 1378 the convent in Hatfield was burned, and three years later the same fate was shared by archives at the Waltham Abbey. Perhaps the spectacular attempt at inciting piety also constituted the abbey's attempt to address revolts.[323]

Descriptions of ceremonies performed at Barking also contain unique "stage directions" for liturgical performances. The entire convent would actively participate in all celebrations, assuming ever new performative roles. Performances were delivered as part of the liturgy; therefore, the ceremony could be led only by an ordained priest.

During the Burial (*Depositio*) it was men who carried the Cross to the Tomb, while women accompanied them only by singing antiphons. The crucial symbolic gesture, however, was made by the abbess. After laying the Cross at the Tomb, she would light the candle that burned before the Tomb until Resurrection on Easter night. The specifically understood realism of *The Deposition of the Cross* demanded that the priests play the roles of Joseph and Nicodemus, as well as cleanse Christ's wounds, which were probably painted directly on the Cross. *Depositio* would always follow, as provided in *Regularis concordia*, after the reading on Passion from the Gospel of John. Such readings were sometimes augmented with suspenseful singing in several voices. There are preserved rubrics detailing instructions for performers. Singers would probably accentuate key passages with gestures, while the choir represented the gathered faithful.[324]

[DEPOSITIO CRUCIS][325]	THE BURIAL OF THE CROSS
Cum autem santa crux fuerit adorata, sacerdotes de loco predicto crucem eleuantes incipiant antiphonam:	When, however, the holy cross has been adored, the priests, raising the cross from the aforesaid place, shall begin the antiphon:

---

323 Lindenbaum (2007, 393).
324 Davidson (2007, 29).
325 University College, Oxford, MS 169, pp. 108–109. For Latin text see: Young (1933, 1.164–165); Sheingorn (1987, 132). Original orthography is preserved. Trans. *MES* 83–87, B10.

Super omnia ligna [cedrorum, tu sola excelsior, in qua vita mundi pependit, in qua Christus triumphavit, et mors mortem superavit in eternum], et choro illo subsequente totam concinant, cantrice incipiente deferant crucem ad magnum altare. ibique in specie ioseph et nichodemi de ligno deponentes ymaginem, uulnera crucifixi uino abluant et aqua. Dum autem hec fiunt, concinat conuentus Responsorium:

Ecce quomodo moritur iustus, [et nemo percipit corde, et viri iusti tolluntur et nemo considerat; a facie iniquitatis sublatus est iustus. Et erit in pace memoria ejus],

sacerdote incipiente et cantrice respondente et conuentu succinente. post uulnerum ablucionem cum candelabris et turribulo deferant illam ad sepulcrum hac canentes antiphonas: *In pace in idipsum [dormiam et requiescam].*

Antiphona: *Habitabit [in tabernaculo tuo requiescet in monte sancto tuo].*

Antiphona: *Caro mea [requiescet in spe].*

Cumque in predictum locum tapetum palleo auriculari quoque et lintheis nitidissimis decenter ornatum illam cum reuerencia locauerint, claudat sacerdos sepulcrum et incipiat Responsorium:

Sepulto Domino, [signatum est monumentum].

Above all the cedar threes [you alone excel on whom hung the life of the world, on whom Christ was victorious and death overcame death.], and with the choir following they shall all sing it together, the *cantrix*[326] beginning. They shall carry the cross to the high altar and there, as though they were Joseph and Nicodemus, taking down the image from the wood, they shall wash the wounds of the Crucified with wine and water. While they are doing this, the convent shall join in the responsory:

Behold how the just [man] dies [and no one feels it in his heart: the just men are killed and no one heeds it: the just man is killed by the working of evil and his memory shall be in peace.],

the priest beginning, the *cantrix* replying and the convent joining them. After washing the wounds they shall bear it [the image[327]] with candles and censer to the sepulchre, singing these antiphons: *In peace itself [I shall sleep and rest.]*

Ant. *He shall dwell [in your tabernacle: he shall rest in your holy mountain];*

Ant. *My flesh [shall rest in hope].*

And when they have placed it reverently in the aforesaid place, fittingly decorated with a covering of hangings, with a pillow also, and with most beautiful linen cloths, the priest shall close the sepulchre and begin the responsory:

The Lord being buried [the sepulchre was sealed].

---

326 *Cantrix*, the main singer, would conduct the choir of nuns during many liturgies. The nun selected for this position would have to have deep knowledge of liturgical texts. Latin handbooks allowed a lot of leeway for her own decisions (*ad uolantatem cantricis*), e.g. what melody to choose for Kyrie during the feast of St. Andrew (University College, Oxford, MS 169, p. 166). Cf. Lindenbaum (2007, 394).

327 It was probably not the cross, but only *Imago Crucifixi*, the Host hidden in a crystal monstrance, that was placed in the Tomb, as it arises from rubrics related to the next performance, *Elevatio Hostiae*.

Et tunc abbatissa offerat cereum, qui iugiter ardeat ante sepulcrum, nec extinguatur donec ymago in nocte pasche post matutinas de sepulcro cum cereis et thure et processione resumpta, suo reponatur in loco. Hiis itaque gestis, redeat conuentus in chorum, et sacerdos in uestiarium.	And then the abbes shall offer a candle which shall burn continually in front of the sepulchre, and shall not be extinguished until the image, taken from the sepulchre after Matins of the night of Easter with candles, incense, and procession, shall be put back in its place. And so, these things being done, the convent shall return to the quire and the priest to the vestry.

Another performance, *The Harrowing of Hell*, was separated in the manuscript from the *Deposition* with a short digression calling for piety, and would begin with a spectacular procession of the entire convent accompanied by men who – just like during Easter Eve – carried palms and unlit candles. Spatial features also reinforced the impression of descending into the "abyss." The chapel of St. Mary Magdalene, where the procession would be headed, was located in the lower left part of the Barking Abbey. Both directions suggested moving away from God.[328] The chapel symbolized hell itself. All nuns would be locked in there, become for a period of time the souls of Old Testament patriarchs waiting for Christ to come. In the procession that completed the performance, nuns would leave the abysmal chapel, emerging as resurrected souls: "The earth shook, and the rocks were split; the tombs also were opened, and many bodies of the saints who had fallen asleep were raised" (Matthew 27:51–52).

The Harrowing of Hell was performed at dawn, at the end of the Easter morning Mass. The rising sun was meant to augment the spectacular effect of releasing humankind from the abyss of hell. Unlike in Anglo-Saxon liturgy, in Barking no individual names were given to the souls of the just. The entire convent was "released" from the chapel to signify the freeing of entire humankind.

---

328 Faulkner (1992, 146).

[DESCENSUS CHRISTI AD INFEROS][329]

In primis eat domina abbatissa cum toto conuentu et quibusdam sacerdotibus et clericis capis indutis quolibet sacerdote et clerico palmam et candelam extinctam manu deferente intrent capellam sancte marie magdalene. ffigurantes animas sanctorum patrum ante aduentum christi ad inferos descendentes, et claudant sibi ostium dicte capelle. deinde superueniens sacerdos ebdomadarius[330] ad dictam capellam approprians alba indutus et capa cum duobus diaconis, vno Crucem deferente cum uexillo dominico desuper pendente, altero cum turibulo manu sua baiulante et aliis sacerdotibus et clericis cum duobus pueris cereos deferentibus, ad ostium dicte capelle incipiens ter hanc antiphonam:

Tollite portas, [principes, vestras, et elevamini, portae aeternales].[331]

qui quidem sacerdos representabit personam christi ad inferos descensuram et portas inferni dirupturam. et predicta antiphona vnaquaque uice in altiori uoce incipiatur, quam clerici tociens eandem repetant et ad quamquam incepcionem pulset cum cruce ad predictum ostium. figurans dirupcionem portarum inferni. et tercia pulsacione ostium aperiat. deinde ingrediatur ille cum ministris suis. interim incipiat quidam sacerdos in capella existens antiphonam:

A porta inferi [erue, Domine, meam animam],

quam subinferat cantrix cum toto conuentu: *Erue Domine,* etc.

THE DESCENT OF CHRIST INTO HELL

First the lady abbess shall go with all the convent and with certain priests and clerks dressed in copes, and with each priest and clerk carrying in his hand a palm and an unlit candle. They shall enter the chapel of St Mary Magdalene, signifying the souls of the holy Fathers descending into Hell before the coming of the Christ; and they shall shut the door of the aforesaid chapel on themselves. Then the priest *hebdomadarius*[4], dressed in alb and cope, coming to the said chapel with two deacons, one carrying a cross with the Lord's banner hanging from the top, the other carrying the censer in his hand, and with other priest and clerks and with two boys carrying candles, approaching the door of the said chapel, shall begin three times this antiphon:

Raise your gates, [princes, and be lifted up, you eternal gates].

This priest indeed shall represent the person of Christ about to descend to Hell and break down the gates of Hell. And the aforesaid antiphon shall be begun at each repetition in a louder voice which the clerks repeat the same number of times, and at the beginning, each time, he shall beat with the cross at the aforesaid doors, signifying the breaking down of the gates of Hell. And at the third knock, the door shall open. Then he shall go in with his ministers. Meanwhile a certain priest being inside the chapel shall begin the antiphon: *From the gates of hell [O Lord, rescue my soul],*

which the *cantrix* shall take up, with the whole community: *O Lord, rescue* etc.

---

329 University College, Oxford, MS 169, pp. 119–120. For Latin text see: Young (1933, 1.165–166); Sheingorn (1987, 133).

330 *Hebdomadarius*, literally meaning "seven-day," was the priest designated to perform duties at the convent for one week.

331 Antiphon to Psalm 24:7.

Deinde extrahet sacerdos ebdomadarius omnes essentes in capella predicta. et interim incipit sacerdos antiphonam: *Domine abstraxisti, [ab inferis animam meam],* et cantrix subsequatur: *Ab inferis.* Tunc omnes exeant de capella id est de limbo patrum. et cantent sacerdotes et clerici antiphonam: *Cum Rex glorie,* processionaliter per medium chori ad sepulcrum portantes singuli palmam et candelam designantes victoriam de hoste recuperatam subsequentibus domina abbatissa priorissa et toto conuentu sicut sunt priores.	Then the priest *hebdomadarius* shall lead out all those who were inside the aforesaid chapel, and in the meantime the priest shall begin the antiphon: *O Lord you have taken out [my soul from hell],* and the *cantrix* shall follow: *From hell.* Then all shall go out from the chapel, that is, from the Limbo of the Fathers, and the priests and clerks shall sing the antiphon: *When the king of Glory* in the procession through the middle of the quire to the sepulchre, each one carrying a palm and a candle, signifying victory recovered from the enemy, with the lady abbess, the prioress, and all the convent following, as if they are the early Fathers.

The finale to the *Harrowing of Hell* took the form of a triumphal procession. The popular hymn *Cum Rex glorie*, often sung during Easter processions, was known as *Canticum triumphalis (Song of triumph)*.

The Elevation of the Host directly followed the *Harrowing*. In his reconstruction, Karl Young emphasizes that the above are two parts of a single ceremony. Once again, the specific realism of the performance seems striking. The Host, closed in a crystal monstrance, was radically separated from the Cross, which may have been impacted by the cult of Corpus Christi, popular in England since the 14th century.

[ELEVATIO HOSTIAE][332] Et cum sepulcrum peruenerint, sacerdos ebdomadarius sepulcrum thurificet et intret sepulcrum incipiendo versum: *Consurgit.* Deinde subsequatur cantrix: *Christus tumulo [victor redit de baratro, tyrannum trudens uvinculo, et reserans paradisum].*	THE ELEVATION OF THE HOST And when they have reached the sepulchre, the priest *hebdomadarius* shall cense and enter the sepulchre, beginning the verse: *He rises.* Then the *cantrix* shall follow with: *Christ from the tomb, [The victor returns from the pit Thrusting down the tyrant in chains And unlocking Paradise].*

---

332 University College, Oxford, MS 169, p. 121. For Latin text see: Young (1933, 1.166); Sheingorn (1987, 134).

Versus: *Quesumus, auctor [omnium, in hoc paschali gaudio ab omni mortis impetu tuum defende populum].*	The verse: *We ask creator [of all, In this joyous Easter From every attack of death, Defend your people].*
Versus: *Gloria tibi, domine, [qui surrexisti a mortuis, cum Patre et Sancto Spiritu in sempiterna secula].*	The verse: *Glory to thee, Lord, [Who has risen from the dead, With Father and Holy Spirit World without end].*
Et interim asportabit corpus dominicum de sepulcro incipiendo antiphonam: *Christus resurgens,*	And meanwhile he shall carry out the body of the Lord from the sepulchre, beginning the antiphon: *Christ rising,*
coram altari verso uultu ad populum tenendo corpus dominicum in manibus suis inclusum cristallo. deinde subiungat cantrix:	in front of the altar with his face turned to people, holding the body of the Lord enclosed in crystal.[333] Then the *cantrix* shall join in with:
Ex mortuis.	*From the dead.*
Et cum dicta antiphona faciant processionem ad altare sancte trinitatis cum solenni apparatu videlicet cum turibulis et cereis conuentus sequatur cantando predictam antiphonam cum versu: *Dicant nunc*	And with the said antiphon they shall make a procession to the altar of the Holy Trinity in solemn state, namely with censers and candles. The community shall follow singing the aforesaid antiphon with the verse: *Let them say now,*
et uersiculo:	and the versicle:
Dicite in nacionibus.	*Say to the nations.*
Oratio:	Prayer:
Deus qui pro nobis Filium tuum.	*God, who for us your son.*
Et hec processio figuratur per hoc quomodo christus procedit post resurexionem in galileam, sequentibus discipulis.	And this procession shall signify in what way Christ proceeded after the Resurrection into Galilee with his disciples following.

The Barking manuscript also contains a unique description of *Visitatio Sepulchri* (the only one preserved in England elsewhere than in *Regularis concordia*). Mary Magdalene dominates the performance, unlike in the Anglo-Saxon version. She is the first one to discover that Christ's body is not there. She also doubts Resurrection, and is the first person to be visited by Christ after He rose from the dead. Finally, she spreads the good news to other women and all gathered. In this way, Mary Magdalene humanizes the liturgy. Since the 12th century this figure often appears in continental rites, provoking the appearance of new, more realistic ges-

---

333 I.e. in the monstrance. Young supposes that *imago Crucifixi*, the image of the Crucified previously laid in the tomb, contained a hollow where the Host would be placed, and that *corpus Dominicum*, "enclosed in the crystal," is the Host.

tures and patterns of behaviour in the liturgy. In the Oriony-Sainte-Benoîte Abbey, located just outside St. Quentin, the nuns would stage a scene during which disciples, asking about the Resurrection, would pull Mary's sleeve.[334] Rubrics in *Ludus Paschalis*[335] ordered Mary Magdalene to clap, shout, lift her hands to the heavens, and even faint. Moreover, she had to sigh, just like later in Barking. In Braunschweig, on the other hand, Mary, seeking the Resurrected, wandered around the cathedral, sometimes stopping and singing. In her performance even static scenes acquired certain dynamism. Another interesting document from the 13th century contains a "scenario" of an unusual planctus performed in the cathedral in Cividale del Fiuri.[336] Main parts were sung by Mary Magdalene, who was accompanied by two other Marys, the Virgin and disciple John. All stood beneath the cross and gestured lively. *Planctus Mariae* contains 127 lines with music and rubrics containing a record number of seventy-nine instructions regarding recommended gestures. The instructions are provided in small script over the main text.

Continental practices may have probably inspired Katherine of Sutton to enrich the liturgy at Barking in the second half of the 14th century.

[VISITATIO SEPULCHRI][337]	THE VISIT TO THE SEPULCHRE
[...] procedant tres sorores a domina abbatissa preelecte et nigris vestibus in capella beate marie magdalene exute, nitidissimis superpellicijs induantur, niueis velis a domina abbatissa capitibus earum superpositis. sic igitur preparate et in manibus ampullas tenentes argenteas dicant *Confiteor*[338] ad abbatissam et ab ea absolute. in loco statuto cum candelbris consistant. Tunc illa que speciem pretendit marie magdalene canat hunc versum:	[...] three sisters selected by the lady abbess shall come forward, and, having taken off their black vestments in the chapel of the Blessed Mary Magdalene, they shall put on the most beautiful surplices, snow-white coverings being placed on their heads by the lady abbess. Thus prepared, therefore, and bearing silver jars in their hands, they shall say their confession to the abbess, and, absolved by her, they shall take their stand in the appointed place with candles. Then she who represents the person of Mary Magdalene shall sing this verse:

---

334 For Old French rubrics to this scene see: Young (1933, 1.418).
335 MS 927, Miscellanea Turonensia, fol. 1r-8v, Tours, Bibl. de la Ville. For Latin text of rubrics see: Young (1933, 1.442–444).
336 MS CI, Process. Cividalense, fol. 74r-76v, Cividale, Reale Museo Archeologico. For Latin text see: Young (1933, 1.507–512). For more on information on gestures in liturgical performances see: Ogden (2001).
337 University College, Oxford, MS 169, p. 169. For Latin text see: Young (1933, 1.381–384); Lipphardt 5, pp. 1458–1461, no. 770; Sheingorn (1987, 134–137).
338 The first word and name of the prayer beginning the general confession.

Quondam Dei […].[339]	*At one time of God.*
Quo finito, secunda que mariam iacobi prefigurat alterum respondeat versum: *Appropinquans ergo sola* […].	And when that is finished, the second who signifies Mary Jacobi shall reply with the second verse: *Drawing near, therefore, alone.*
Tercia maria vicem optinens salomee tercium canat versum: *Licet mihi vobiscum ire* […].	The third Mary, having the part of Salome, shall sing the third verse: *I am allowed to go with you.*
Post hec chorum incedentes flebili uoce et submissa hos pariter canant versus:	After proceeding to the quire, they shall sing the verse together, with weeping and humble voice:
Heu! nobis internas mentes [quanta pulsant gemitus Pro nostra consolatore, quo privamur misere; Quem crudelis Judeorum morti dedit populus].	*Alas [how many sighs beat on] the hearts within us [for our consoler, of whom we miserable ones are deprived; whom the cruel people of the Jews gave over to death.]*
Hijs versibus finitis, magdalena sola dicat hunc versum:	These verses ended, Magdalene alone shall say this verse:
Heu! misere, [cur contigit vider, mortem Salvatoris?]	*Alas, miserable one, [why has it happened that we see death of the saviour?]*
Iacobi respondeat:	Jacobi shall reply:
Heu! consolatio nostra, [ut quid mortem sustinuit.]	*Alas, our consolation, [why did he suffer death?]*
Salome:	Salome:
Heu! redempcio Israel [ut quit taliter agere voluit!]	*Alas, redemption of Israel, [why did he wish to undergo such things?]*
Quartum uero uersum omnes simul concinant, scilicet:	In the fourth verse they shall all join together thus:
Iam iam ecce [iam properemus ad tumulum, unguentes dilecti corpus sanctissimum].	*Now, now, lo, [now let us hasten to the tomb, The chosen ones anointing the most holy body].*
Tunc marie exeuntes a choro simul dicant:	Then the Maries going out from the choir together shall say:
Eya quis reuoluet [nobis lapidem ab ostio monumenti?]	*Alas, who has rolled away [the stone for us from the mouth of the monument?]*

---

339 According to Young, this line – and others whose further parts have not been found – was composed specially for the Barking abbey.

Cum autem uenerint ad sepulcrum, clericus alba stola indutus sedeat ante sepulcrum, illius angeli gerens figuram qui ab ostio monumenti lapidem reuoluit. et super eum sedit. Qui dicat illis:	When, however, they come to the sepulchre, a clerk dressed in a white stole shall be seated before the sepulchre, representing the angel who rolled the stone from the mouth of the monument and sat upon it, who shall say this:
Quem queritis in sepulcro o cristocole? Respondeant mulieres:	*Whom do you seek in the sepulchre, O companions of Christ?* The women shall reply:
Ihesum nazarenum querimus.	*We seek Jesus of Nazareth.*
Angelus uero subinferat:	The angel shall answer:
Non est hic, surrexit	*He is not here, he has risen*
Cumque dixerit *Venite et videte*, ingrediantur sepulcrum et deosculentur locum vbi positus erat crucifixus. Maria uero magdalene interim accipiat sudarium quod fuerat super caput eius, et secum deferat. Tunc alius clericus in Specie alterius angeli in sepulcro residens dicat ad magdalenam:	And when he has said, *Come and see*, they shall go into the sepulchre and kiss the place where the Crucified one was laid. Mary Magdalene meanwhile shall take the sudary [napkin] which was over his head, and shall carry it with her. Then another cleric in the person of the other angel sitting in the sepulchre shall say to Magdalene:
Mulier, quid ploras?	*Woman, why do you weep?*
Illa autem subiungat:	She shall answer:
Quia tulerunt Dominum meum.	*Because they have taken my Lord away.*
Deinde duo angeli simul concinentes dicant mulieribus:	Then the two angels joining together shall say to the women:
Quid queritis viuentem cum mortuis? etc.	*Why do you seek the living among the dead?* etc.
Tunc ille de resur[r]excione domini adhuc dubitantes plangendo dicant ad inuicem:	Then they, still doubting the Resurrection of the Lord, shall say mourning to each other:
Heu dolor etc.	*Alas, misery* etc.
Postea maria magdalene suspirando concinat[340]:	Then Mary Magdalene sighing shall join with them:
Te suspiro etc.	*I sigh for you* etc.
Tunc in sinistra parte altaris appareat persona dicens illi:	Then on the left-hand side of the altar the *Persona*[341] shall appear, saying to her:
Mulier, quid ploras? Quem queris?	*Woman why do you weep, whom do you seek?*
Illa uero putans eum esse [h]ortolanum respondeat:	She, thinking him to be a gardener, shall reply:

---

340 Young: *concinat*. MS: *concinant*.
341 Perhaps a performer wearing a "mask" of Christ.

Domine si tu sustulisti eum etc.	*Lord, if you have carried him away* etc.
persona subiungat:	The *Persona* shall answer:
maria!	*Maria!*
Tunc illa agnoscens eum pedibus eius prosternatur dicens:	Then she, recognizing him, shall prostrate herself at his feet saying:
Raboni!	*Raboni!*
Persona autem se subtrahens dicat:	The *Persona*, however, drawing back shall say:
noli me tangere etc.	*Do not touch me* etc.
Cum persona disparuerit, maria gaudium suum consociabus communicet uoce letabunda hos concinendo versus:	When the *Persona* has disappeared, Mary shall communicate her joy to her companions with joyful voice singing these verses:
Gratulari et letari etc.	*Rejoice and be happy* etc.
Quibus finitis, persona in dextera parte altaris tribus simul occurrat mulieribus dicens:	When these are ended the *Persona* shall appear to the three women together on the right of the altar saying:
Auete nolite timere etc.	*Hail, do not be afraid* etc.
Tunc ille humi prostrate teneant pedes eius et deosculentur. Quo facto, alternis modulacionibus hos versus decantent, maria magdalene incipiente:	Then, prostrate on the ground, they shall hold his feet and kiss them. Which done, one after another they shall sing these verses, Mary Magdalene beginning:
Ihesu ille nazarenus etc.	*Jesus the Nazarene* etc.
ffinitis hijs versibus, tunc marie stantes super gradus ante altare uertentes se ad populum canant hoc Responsum:	These verses being finished, the Maries standing on the step before the altar turning to the people shall sing this response:
alleluia surrexit dominus de sepulcro [...], choro eis respondente. ffinitis hijs, sacerdotes et clerici in figuram discipulorum christi procedant dicentes:	*Alleluia, the Lord has risen form the sepulchre*, with the choir replying to them. When these are ended, priests and clerks representing the disciples of Christ shall come forward saying:
O gens dira [...].	*O people hard-hearted.*
Tunc vnus illorum accedat et dicat marie magdalene:	Then one of them shall approach and say to Mary Magdalene:
Di[c] nobis maria etc.	*Tell us Mary* etc.
Illa autem respondeat:	She shall reply:
Sepulcrum christi [*viventis, et gloriam vidi resurgentis*].	*The sepulchre of Christ* [*living and the glory of the risen one I have seen.*]
angelicos testes, [*sudarium et vestes*].	*Angelic witnesses,* [*the sudary and the clothes.*]
digito indicet locum vbi angelus sedebat, et sudarium probeat illis ad deosculandum, hunc adicientes versum:	With her finger she shall point out the place where the angel was sitting, and shall hold out the sudary for them to kiss, adding the verse:
Surrexit christus spes nostra; [*praecedet suos in Galilea*].	*Christ our hope has risen,* [*he has preceded us into Galilee.*]

Tunc subiunga[n]tur a discipulis et a choro hij ultimi versus: *Credendum est [magis soli Marie veraci quam Judeorum turbe fallaci],* et *Scimus christum [surrexisse a mortuis vere; tu nobis, victor rex, miserere].* Postea incipiat magdalena: *Christus resurgens,* clero et choro pariter succinente. Hijs itaque peractis, solenniter decantetur a sacerdote incipiente ymnus Te Deum laudamus. Et interim predicti sacerdotes in capellam proprijs vestibus reinduentes cum candelabris per chorum transeuntes orandi gratia sepulcrum adeant, et ibi breuem orationem faciant. tunc redeant in stacionem suam usque abbatissa eas iubeat exire ad quiescendum.	Then these final verses shall be added by the disciples and choir: *It is to be believed [rather by the truth of Mary alone than by a crowd of Jews.]* and *We know Christ [has truly risen from the dead: pity us, victorious king.]* Then Magdalene shall begin: *Christ rising,* with the clergy and choir joining in at the same time. These ended, the hymn O God, we praise thee shall be solemnly chanted, the priest beginning. And meanwhile the aforementioned priests putting their ordinary clothes on again in the chapel, crossing through the quire with candles, shall approach the sepulchre to give thanks and make a short prayer there. Then they shall return to their station until the abbess shall order them to go out to rest.

An equally dramatic performance, also mature in literary terms, was delivered ca. 1400 in St. John the Evangelist Church in Dublin. Both manuscripts also contain music in four-line staff.[342] Detailed rubrics contain numerous instructions for performers. The ceremony would begin after the third responsory of the morning Mass. Three Marys would enter the church, walking in veils along the nave, dressed in surplice and silk coats. Each carried a can (*pyxis* in Latin) with oils. They would approach the Tomb, lamenting the loss of Jesus. Later, they would answer the key question posed by the angel – *Quem quaeritis?* – and enter the empty Tomb. On their way back, they would meet two Apostles, barefoot and carrying appropriate accessories: John, in a white tunic and carrying a palm, and Peter, in a red tunic and carrying keys. During the finale, the choir would sing in full voice *Scimus Christum surrexisse a mortuis*. Then, the service would continue with *Te Deum*. A similar structure might have also been used in Easter performances at a small convent in Eynsham, Oxfordshire, and in the St. Edith Convent in Wilton.[343]

---

342 Dublin, Marsh's Library, MS Z.4.2.20, fol. 59r-61r; Oxford, Bodleian Library, MS Rawlison liturg. D.4, fol. 130r-132r. For Latin text see: Chambers (1903, 2.315–318); Young (1933, 1.347–350). For reconstruction of music and full commentary see: Fletcher & Egan-Buffet (1990). Cf. Davidson (2007, 27).

343 Eynsham: Easting (2002, 26–27) (source text); Woolf (1972, 18); Davidson (2007, 28). Wilton: Rankin (1981).

4. These immensely elaborate and spectacular performances must have certainly offered an intense experience for all participants. In Barking they must have been successful in overcoming the spiritual slumber in the convent, and perhaps even pacified rebellious moods, as was intended by their wealthy author, abbess Katherine of Sutton. The "spectacular" character of certain solutions is particularly striking, especially upon comparison with the more austere versions preserved in *Regularis concordia*. In Barking, the entire convent represented the Old Testament patriarchs. Christ ceased to be present by way of His "absence." He revealed himself to the faithful in the form of the Host, and was represented by celebrants and performers. In the 14th and 15th century, when the theatre of artisans and artists celebrated its first triumphs, the form of liturgical performances must have been heavily influenced by popular shows staged in front of churches, on squares or in the streets of towns and villages.

Many elements seem to suggest that the main audience of the three performances were the parishioners. The date of the celebration was moved from before matins to a later time after the morning Mass, probably in order to encourage more local people to come and participate. The elaborate and spectacular character of the rite was probably meant to enchant and humble the lay audience. Ordinary people would not participate actively in the ceremonies, but only look from a distance and pray. The aim of this approach was to reinforce the authority of both abbess and abbey in the face of religious unrest. All three performances conveyed a triumphal message: they confirmed belief in the Resurrection of Christ as the ultimate victory over death, humanity's greatest weakness. If the performance enlivened the apathetic nuns, it would also create distance between the convent and the parishioners. The show dominated over the liturgy. Rapid urbanization and population growth imposed new requirements on liturgical performances. Austere and ascetic celebrations of the early Middle Ages lost their efficacy. New performative strategies were developed by members of the mendicant orders, primarily the Franciscans, who would leave monasteries and spread the gospel among the people.

In Barking, performances continued to function as an organic part of cultic practice. However, the liturgy came under the overwhelming influence of new cultural transformations. In eastern England, parishioners staged huge performances on squares in front of churches.[344] In northern parts, craftsmen staged religious plays on pageant wagons, which travelled through cities. In the years 1417–1418, during the Easter performance (*ludus*) in the Wells cathedral (Somerset) three

---

344   Kocur (2012).

Marys would appear in regular theatrical costumes: a receipt for making three buckram coats has been preserved.[345] In the years 1494–1495, the St. Saviour's Church in Dartmouth (Devon) paid eight pence to a painter named George "for painting costumes for an Easter play" (*for payntyng of the clothes for the play on Ester day*). In her will, made in 1504, Dame Agnes Burton left "a red, damask mantel" (*my rede damaske matell*) for the "Sepulchre service" in St. Mary Magdalene's Church in Taunton (Somerset), and a "silk-lined mantel" (*my mantell lyned with silke*) for a "play with Mary Magdalene" (*Mary Magdalen play*).[346]

Performances in Barking were also distinguished by their specific realism. Deacons would take Christ's "body" from the cross and wash it. The celebrant would knock on the chapel's closed doors thrice using the cross; then, he would lead the patriarchs out in a procession carrying unlit candles. Marys would be played by three nuns. The description of the nuns' transformation into Marys is particularly intriguing as it is unprecedented among available versions of *Visitatio*. First, the abbess would help the nuns dress in "the most beautiful" costumes, after which they would ceremoniously confess their sins before her. Although spectacular, representing Marys was chiefly a liturgical act. The performance itself was equally fascinating. The Marys would deny Resurrection for a long time. Their doubts not only made the story dynamic, but also indicated a profound religious message: God incarnated himself not because people are infallible, but precisely because they err.

5. The example of Benedictine Easter performances was also followed by the Cluniacs, Augustinians, Carmelites, Dominicans and Franciscans. A Carthusian monk from Yorkshire probably authored two English plays meant for Easter, dated to the second decade of the 16th century: *Burial* (864 lines) and *Resurrection* (767 lines).[347] This document offers unique insight into the "dramatist's workshop."[348] At the top of the first leaf (fol. 140r), over the Prologue, the author does not call his work a "play," but claims it to be a "treatise or meditation on the Burial of Christ and the mourning that followed" (*treyte or meditation off the buryalle of Criste and mowrnyng þerat*). In the Prologue he advises the reader to "read this

---

345   *REED Somerset* 1.243.
346   *REED Devon* 62; *REED Somerset* 1.227.
347   MS *e Museo 160*, Bodleian Library, Oxford. In the manuscript the plays are not separated. For full text see: *The Digby Plays*, eds. Baker, Murphy & Hall (1982, 141–193); for information on relations with the Carthusian convent see: Baker, Murphy & Hall (1982, lxxxi–lxxxiii). For more commentary see: Rowntree (1990); Davidson (2007, 171–177).
348   Baker (1989, 35–37).

treatise" (line 3: *Rede this treyte*). On the reverse of the same leaf (fol. 140v), at the beginning, he also managed to squeeze in a remark, written in the same hand as the rest of the text, but in red ink (after line 55)[349]:

> This is a play to be played, on part on Gud Friday afternone, and þe other part opon Ester Day after the resurrection in the morowe, but at [the] begynnynge ar certen lynes which [should] not be said if it be plaied, which… [remaining words cut off at the bottom].

Finally, the author decided to compose a play, although meditative passages disappear only after folio 147 (verso). *Burial* is filled with lamentations. Joseph of Arimathea begins the series alone (lines 16–55), but is soon joined in mourning by the three Marys, and later by others: Nicodemus (after line 391), Virgin Mary (after line 439), and John the Evangelist (after line 450). An important role in the performance was also played by a wooden figure of Christ, which had moveable limbs. Virgin Mary asks Joseph to allow her to "hold my son for a moment" (line 605: *holde my son a space*). Nicodemus and Joseph agree. The mother sits under the cross, takes her son into her arms and, after assuming the traditional pieta position, performs an elaborate mourning lament – planctus (lines 612–791). Only towards the end of the play, after line 832 and the departure of Virgin Mary, Christ is laid in the Sepulchre. *Resurrectio*, which is also filled with lamentations, begins with the traditional scene of *Visitatio Sepulchri*; in the finale, which occurs after line 692, the three Marys intone a Latin hymn and partake in a sung dialogue with Apostles Peter, Andrew and John, also conducted in Latin. At the end, all perform together the song *Scimus Christum*, which has not been identified yet by scholars in any of the preserved liturgical books.

All Latin texts in both plays are borrowed from the Easter liturgy. Moreover, many monologues are in fact quotations from meditative writings such as *Meditationes vitae Christi* by Pseudo-Bonaventura, and from traditional plancti.[350] Therefore, certain scholars assumed these texts to be scenarios of liturgical performances. Meg Twycross argued, for example, that they might have been easily added to Easter celebrations, because the performance of each play would not exceed one hour; however, she also noted that professional singers would be needed to stage *Resurrection*.[351] Richard Rastall advised caution in linking the plays to the liturgy, because both *Burial* and *Resurrection* omit many key elements of the Easter liturgy, which suggests that these plays were performed indepen-

---

349 *The Digby Plays*, eds. Baker, Murphy & Hall (1982, 142).
350 *The Digby Plays*, eds. Baker, Murphy & Hall (1982, lxxv–xcv).
351 Twycross (1994, 65); (2008, 55). This opinion is also shared by Peter Meredith (1997).

dently of official celebrations, and perhaps at a different time. Clifford Davidson, on the other hand, tends to consider these texts as unique proof of incorporating acting practices developed in Latin liturgical performances into English-language folk theatre.[352] However, the monastic context has fundamentally determined the form of both plays. Carthusian genealogy certainly shaped the meditative character of the work. Carthusian monasteries were famous for their great rigour and long, silent meditations. Mute prayer could last from 10 pm till 2 am. Intense spiritual experiences were also augmented by contemplation of images depicting Passion.[353] Lamentations from both plays abound in vivid descriptions of Christ's wounds and suffering, which was probably meant to provoke an equally intense emotional reaction in the audience. In *Burial*, Mary Magdalene laments under the Cross (lines 321–322):

Who saw euer a spektacle more pitevs?
A more lamentable sight and dolorus?

The said spectacle, however, was presented to the public not through vivid images, but primarily through the words of subsequent plancti.

In contrast to the celebrations in Barking, Carthusian performances stimulated the parishioners to participate and empathize, to meditate on one's guilt and lament Christ's Passion.

6. In cathedrals, liturgy was supervised by the clergy, but in parish churches many duties were assigned to lay people. Liturgical performances were also realized with the help of puppets. The earliest examples of English puppet shows date back to the first half of the 15th century. Court archives in Grimsby (today's Humberside in Lincolnshire) contain a complaint, registered in court records (*Court Rolls*) on 3 September 1431, regarding the matter of not having provided on time the *instrumenta joci*, i.e. "certain instruments of play" necessary to stage a puppet show titled *Ioly Walte and Malkyng*.[354] In the years 1465–1467, the Czech aristocrat Leon von Rozmital wandered around Europe looking for support for the Czech king. Two people from his retinue left descriptions of

---

352 Rastall (1996, 13–14); Davidson (2007, 170).
353 Davidson (2007, 171–177 & 183).
354 Mention of "Ioly Walte and Malkyng" has been preserved also in the *City Chamberlain's Book* in York. Records from 1447 and 1448 refer to payments made to "players from (*ludenti cum*) 'Ioly Wat and Malkyn'"; in the first mention only one "player" is indicated, but in the second – two (*REED York* 70 & 72). Cf. Lancashire (1979); Butterworth (2005, 127–128). See also: *OED*, entry: *malkin* (4): "A scarecrow; a ragged puppet or grotesque effigy."

incredible performances they saw in 1466 in the Salisbury Cathedral. Beautiful carved figures representing the Three Magi, moved with weights, would bring gifts to Mary and the Child. "Our Lady and Joseph bowed and did obeisance to the Three Kings," recalls Gabriel Tetzel from Nuremberg, praising the masterful staging. Schaseck, Rozmital's squire, wrote with great admiration for the elegance of the dolls. Both emphasized that the figures seemed to be alive. A similar puppet show would be performed in Salisbury during Easter. Schaseck recalls that the angels would open the Sepulchre, while Christ would rise from the dead wielding a banner.[355]

Puppets would be also used to stage the "Whole Action of the Resurrection," performed each year in Witney (Oxfordshire), as reported by William Lambarde (1536–1601) in his work *Dictionarium Angliæ Topographicum et Historicum*, written in the 16th century, but published only after 1730. Little puppets (*certein smalle Puppets*) would represent such figures as Christ, the watchman, and Mary: "one bare the Parte of a wakinge Watcheman, who (espiinge Christ to arise) made a continual Noyce, like to the Sound that is caused by the Metinge of two Styckes, and was therof commonly called Jack Snacker of Wytney."[356]

Liturgical performances in parishes were naturally much more modest, but a significant number of sources mention staging of plays inspired by Easter, although they offer incomplete information from later times. Scholarly research on this matter is still carried out in parish archives. Alexandra F. Johnston, director of the international project Records of Early English Drama, quotes for example preliminary results of surveys conducted in southern England, in the Thames Valley. It turns out that Resurrection plays were performed in such places as Kingston-upon-Thames (1520), Thame (1522–1538), Reading (1506–1534) and Henley (1511). In the St. Laurence parish in Reading, archived receipts contain records of a payment made to a priest named Laborne for writing down one such play.[357]

7. Easter sepulchres constitute a telling piece of evidence of liturgical performances. In England they were created between the 10th and 16th century. Their symbolism expressed the fundamental message of Christianity: they not only commemorated death, but also promised resurrection, following the example of

---

355 Letts (1957, 57 & 61); Butterworth (2005, 120); Rogers (2005). Cf. Davidson (2007, viii).
356 Lambarde (1730, 459); Young (1933, 2.542–543). Cf. DTRB no. 1520; Davidson (2007, vii).
357 Berkshire Record Office, D/P 97 5/1, p. 194 & 202. Cf. Johnston (1996, 98–99); Davidson (2007, 28).

Christ.[358] *Regularis concordia* recommended placing the sepulchre (*sepulchrum Domini*) on the altar. It was a temporary construction. When the custom of erecting stone graves became firmly established in the 14th century, they were built at the northern wall of the presbyterium. However, makeshift constructions, or partly temporary ones, remained in use until the 16th century, with some elements of their construction – such as wooden frames and richly embroidered curtains – stored in magazines, which is confirmed both by numerous surviving archival records and preserved monuments. St. Michael's church in Cowthorpe (Yorkshire) hosts a wooden sepulchre topped with a gabled roof from the 14th century (1.5 m long, 0.7 m wide and 2.1 m high). Outside the monasteries, liturgical duties were performed by the parishioners. In Canterbury, in the spring of 1556, two people named Absle and Bekerstaffe were paid eight pence for guarding the sepulchre in St. Andrew's church. Beyond the liturgical dimension, the watch at the sepulchre was also practical because it made sure that candles did not set fire to the parish church.

The earliest stone sepulchres were created probably when the new Corpus Christi celebrations gained popularity. This holiday was established in reaction to intensified interest in the visible dimension of the liturgy, particularly the obsession with the Sacrament. The Easter sepulchre would be often merged with the founder's grave, reinforcing the symbolic triumph of Christ over death. One of the first and simultaneously most beautiful monuments of this kind was erected in the Lincoln cathedral towards the end of the 13th century. The eastern, liturgical half of the building was embellished with bas-reliefs depicting three sleeping soldiers. The western half is occupied by a grave, probably belonging to St. Remigius, the cathedral's founder. The entire structure is made coherent by uniform architectural design. In Lincoln, liturgical performances were entrusted to the Resurrection Guild. Preserved receipts suggest that the celebrations were lavish. Twenty candles burned before the sepulchre on Easter Eve. The silver sculpture of Christ was gold-plated, and silk cloth was used to line the sepulchre. According to certain sources, guilds that tended the Easter sepulchres were particularly numerous in Northumbria (source dates in parenthesis): *Gilde sepulchri Domini* (1496), *fraternitas resurrectionis* (1496), *fraternitas sepulchri* (1521), *gyld of the sepulcr lyght* (1522), *sepulkr gyld* (ca. 1522), and *bretherhed of the sepulcre* (1530).

8. According to surviving documents from the 15th and 16th century, the main liturgical performance in the Easter cycle was the Elevation (*Elevatio*), which

---

358 All information on Easter sepulchres in England after: Sheingorn (1987).

was celebrated in public. The key "performers" – the Cross and the Host – would be revealed to the faithful who yearned for that sight. Sometimes the liturgy would transform into a show. In 1511, the church of St. Mary the Great was in possession of an "ymage of Jhesus for the Resurreccion," and in 1535 paid for "mendyng of the vice for the Resurrexcion." The repaired mechanism probably lifted a wooden figure of Jesus from the sepulchre. No such sculpture survives, but documents confirm that they were used in such places as Bristol, Ludlow (Shropshire), Witney (Oxfordshire) and Patrington (Yorkshire). In Durham, a giant Crucifix, "all gold," would be placed in the sepulchre during *Depositio*, while at the time of *Elevatio*, between 2 am and 3 am, a wooden cross would be lifted, with the image of resurrected Christ nailed to it.[359] The most famous "moving" crucifix was held in the Cistercian abbey in Boxley (Kent). When Henry VIII ascended to the throne, he donated half a mark to this Rood of Grace; in 1518 it was admired by the papal legate Lorenzo Capeggio, who spent the night in Boxley on his way to London. The miraculous figure of Christ reacted to the calls of the sick with movement of eyes, lips and even limbs, just like a puppet. When proponents of Reformation wanted to destroy the Rood, they diminished this wondrous object by calling it a theatrical prop, thus demeaning it. First, they brought the crucifix to the royal court, where courtiers laughed and greeted it with derision, ridiculing the puppet's movements. Several days later, on 24 February 1538, the Bishop of Rochester publicly revealed the scam, demonstrating to the faithful gathered in London's cathedral of St. Paul how the hidden strings and springs worked.[360]

The height of popularity of spectacular Easter liturgies coincided with the period directly preceding the Reformation, which led to the dissolution of monasteries and severing of ties between England and the Catholic Church in the 1530s. In 1547, doctor Barlow demonstrated one "idolatrous" figure of Christ to the people gathered to hear his sermon in London, after which some boys smashed the "idol" into little pieces. Earlier, the same end was met by the Boxley Rood of Grace. During the same year, John Hooper, Bishop of Gloucester, thundered against the performance of *Elevatio*: "à ded post caryd à prosession as mouch resemblyth the resurrextion of Christ As uery deathe resemblyth lief."[361] In the 16th century, the term "puppetry" became the favourite insult, due to the fact that it was also reminiscent of the word "pope." Sermon

---

359 Raine (1842, 9–11); Davidson (2007, 29–31).
360 Butterworth (2005, 123–127). Cf. Aston (1993, 267–268).
361 John Hooper, *A Declaration of Christe and his offyce* (A. Fries, Zurich 1547), sig. EiV; after: Sheingorn (1987, 62).

writers indulged in such wordplay, coining for example the word "popetry" denoting "papal puppetry." The eponymous hero of John Bale's 1538 play *King Johan* sneers at the Catholic clergy, referring to church performances using the phrase "popetly plays" in the sense of "papal puppet theatre" (line 415). In 1548, ten years after the dissolution of monasteries, performing of *Depositio* was officially banned.[362] Thus, the age of English liturgical performances drew to a definite close.

---

362   Sheingorn (1989, 150–155).

Performance Art of Anglo-Saxon Monks

A performative perspective allows to clearly discern in monastic practices a revolutionary artistic programme, without vulgarizing or banalizing the phenomenon of vocation. This also finds historical grounding. In the Middle Ages, monks would be called "actors" or "artists" only when they betrayed clerical solemnity by behaving in a contemptible or immoral way, which was then stereotypically identified with pagan ancient times, especially theatre, known almost solely from literature, usually Roman and hence deemed dissolute. Rarely could anybody read Greek in the monasteries. Performative practices developed in Anglo-Saxon churches under the influence of continental monastic reforms expressed a new, revolutionary concept of art. However, the practices themselves should not be reduced to merely artistic activities, because they were not intended as such by those who adhered to the strict principles of monastic life. Monks would perceive and practice their performances in the context of serving God as testimony to deep faith. Such proof had a sensual dimension as it was realized in and through the body, communicating the religious message through "living images." Monks invented and partially codified Christian performativity, making it possible for future performers and lay artists to treat it as a point of reference.[363]

These are the foundations of the programme for Christian art which can be discerned in the practices of Anglo-Saxon monks:

- TESTIMONY is the main task and calling of any Christian. Christian artists reject ancient masks and reveal to the audience their own bare face. Traces of God can be discerned in the human face, which also bears testimony to "the interior man." In Greece, on the other hand, "the exterior man" would dominate. Identity was a construct, a mask, and would not necessarily have to have any connection with the internal essence of the human being. Ancient Greeks could have many different identities and only needed to switch masks, as in theatre. In contrast to this, Christians would have one face only and one "internal man," also in theatre.
- TRUTH would have to be present in the work of art; hence, every artistic endeavour should testify to the truth. Greek artists would locate truth not on the stage, but in the audience. In order to make spectators cry or laugh at the right moment, ancient craftsmen had to be very skilful in creating perfect illusions which were powerfully and efficiently seductive. When Romans experimented with placing truth on the theatrical stage, they performed mass killings of

---

363 Kocur (2009).

animals, or undressed women. In Christian art, only the artist's face would be bared and revealed for everyone to see. The artist would seek the truth, counting on the support and intervention of higher powers.
- CONFESSION is the duty of every artist and the expression of highest professionalism. It also comprises an ambitious artistic project, successfully realized for the first time by St. Augustine. His *Confessions*, a major literary work, offer a shocking account of a life full of doubting, erring, and striving towards God. Ancient artists were primarily skilled craftsmen, who could wilfully make the audience cry or laugh. The scale of influence achieved by a work of art, or its value, depended more on the level of craftsmanship and the efficiency of performance rather than on the story itself or the names of the protagonists. Would anyone living in 5th-century Athens be bothered with Antigone or Oedipus if Sophocles had not composed his marvellous tragedies? In Christian art content dominated over form. This is why the story of Jesus could inspire the development of a new language in art. Confession could be made everywhere: in church, on the street, on a cart, in a private house, in a palace, on a scaffolding. No Christian should be indifferent to Jesus, who could reveal himself everywhere and in everyone. Participation in a liturgical performance or a religious play was a declaration of faith. Artists confessed in public, and the impact of their message depended on the honesty, zeal and authenticity of expression rather than craftsmanship. This does not entail, however, that Christian poetry was less valuable than ancient one. Elevated content stimulated the development of ambitious forms.
- PERFORMATIVE SPACE provoked artists to engage in dialogue, and suggested the possibility to transform the performer and the audience. It should be emphasized at this point that in contrast to ancient times or the Renaissance, during the Middle Ages there existed nothing that could be defined as a typical "theatrical space."[364] However, analysis of monks' spatial practices allows to discern *locus* and *platea*. These terms accurately describe the strategies of "using" and "producing" space by mediaeval performers. *Platea* is the inside of the church or abbey, a road or a square. Basically, *platea* does not represent anything and generally constitutes a space where the liturgical or theatrical performance takes place. It is a neutral, indefinable term that acquires meaning as a result of the actors' performance.[365] *Locus*, on the other hand, is a meaningful place, e.g. altar, sepulchre, crypt, chapel, scaffolding or mansion.

---

364 Konigson (1975, 77).
365 Rey-Flaud (1980, 23–47).

Locus always represents something, and can acquire special meanings during the performance, sometimes modified by the actions of the performers. There is usually one *platea* and many *loci*. During the Easter liturgy in Barking, the isolated part of the church's interior is *platea*, while *loci* include the chapel, sepulchre, the left- and right-hand sides of the altar, as well as the steps to the altar and the choir. The terms *locus* and *platea* appear already in stage directions to *Ordo representacionis Ade*, the first drama written in a non-sacral language.

- LIVING IMAGE is the main mode of staging in the Christian "theatre of memory." Performances realized in daily, weekly and annual cycles allowed to re-enact again and again the key event in the life of Jesus and the Christian community. Living images affected both the performers and the faithful gathered in the audience, thus having a greater impact than words said in Latin, which was a foreign language. In the great biblical cycles performed on the streets (*platea*) of York or Chester, every pageant wagon (*locus*) with performers would stage for the audience a different living image from the biblical history of the world. In eastern England, scaffoldings (*loci*) would be put in a circle on a square (*platea*) outside the town, where living images would be staged as part of polyphonic spectacles like *The Castle of Perseverance*. On the other hand, Globe and other professional theatres would transform the one and the same stage (*platea*) into different places of the action (*loci*), usually without changing the stage design.
- Being a PERFORMER is a permanent condition: one is an artist the way one is a monk. Performer is an ethical model to follow. By participating in the life of the community and adhering to the Rule, monks were natural performers. Lay performers, on the other hand, could not function outside a Christian community. The work of art was indivisible from religious reality. In the performance *Ordo representacionis Ade*, the role of Figure, or God, was probably played by an actual priest, who would enter and leave the real church during the play. In the finale of the performance, the audience was encouraged to somewhat "complete the play" by taking specific actions.[366] The call to "imitate Christ" posed a performative challenge for every Christian: "imitating" meant being a performer in the right performances.
- PERFORMANCE is a way of life. The world in the work of art was real. Christ could be present in every man. Lack of a clear boundary between the world of

---

366 For more information on this subject see below, the chapter on *Ordo representacionis Ade*.

the liturgical performance and the real world made artistic practice belong in equal measure to the cult and to everyday reality.
- TRANSFORMATION was the goal of all performative practices. Serving Christ meant imitating him and striving towards complete unity with God. One would become him- or herself only after entrusting oneself to the operation of higher powers. In ancient theatre, being Other boiled down to skilful affecting of the audience. A performance would be successful if spectators were convinced or manipulated. Judges would then award prizes. Christian artists, on the other hand, stood before the audience naked, not armed with any tricks, and would attempt to testify to the truth. In case of success, they would experience internal transformation and stimulate such change in others. Actual Christian performances would take place in the spiritual dimension, where Christ's presence could become real.
- BODY was the foundation and vehicle of spiritual transformation. Christian artists could testify to their faith only through the body. The body would imitate Christ, the God who was incarnated in order to redeem ordinary people: the miserable, the doubtful and the lost. Incarnation lent human corporeality special status, thus legitimizing liturgical and theatrical performances.
- SONG was monotonous, single-voiced, prolonged with never-ending melismas and ornaments, not only allowing one to meditate the meaning of words, but also inducing a state of trance both in performers and members of the audience. Singing is also a transformative technique, and perhaps the first language of humankind.[367] In ancient theatre singing was limited by strict metric rules. It was supposed to delight and evoke associations, mainly through rhythm; primarily, however, it attacked the audience's emotions, aiming particularly at its most important members, i.e. the judges who awarded prizes. The singing of a Christian artist evoked angels, and was possible only thanks to the divine grace inspiring the artist: beauty and purity of sound testified to the truth of the message and the song's extraterrestrial origins.
- PRESENCE was also the task of the audience. It constituted the chief means of communication and artistic expression for the Christian artist. Education and edification were an important dimension of art, which reinforced faith in all people, including those who did not belong to the monastic community. Every message communicated on the stage had to be understandable, because it testified to a truth independent of the performer. In Greek theatre, actors-heroes addressed the audience usually by turning to the choir. In tragedies by

---

[367] Kocur (2013, 141–148).

Aeschylus, characters would more frequently dialogue with the choir rather than with each other. The world of Greek tragedy was separated from that of the audience. In comedies, on the other hand, especially in those written by Aristophanes, the presented world was distorted, and parodied reality. Although this author sometimes gave portraits of real people in his works, the actors would address the audience mainly to insult or bribe its members. Greek artists would take their audience to mythological or fictional worlds, whereas Christian performers would situate the presented world in the world of the audience so that everyone could experience the performance "here and now," which strengthened their faith.

Part three: Church and Theatre

Liturgical performances in monasteries required the presence of ordained priests and clerics. Monks could not conduct services themselves. Moreover, the clergy played a key role in the religious life of lay people. Cathedrals and churches needed professional support, while pastoral work in parishes posed an even greater challenge. Just like monks living in monasteries, the clergy from cities and villages faced many difficult tasks, which were often far removed from the ideals of monastic life and demanded different performances. Priests and parishioners were also performers, but they donned different costumes than the monks, and moved in the real world, which was much more dangerous and less predictable than the enclosed, self-sufficient and unchanging cosmos of the abbey. Performances delivered by the clergy, however, did not lose their ties to the liturgy despite being increasingly often performed in the local language. Although the celebration of *Ordo representacionis Ade* could be considered a non-liturgical performance, its main goal was nevertheless to promote the Church.

The Clergy

1. Christian clergy was strictly hierarchized since its early days. Each office required ordaining. Greater vows were taken by:

- bishop (*episcopus* in Latin, *epískopos* in Greek: "overseer," "guardian," "protector"), who led the local church;
- priest or presbyter (from Greek *presbýteros*, "elder"), who conducted the services and administered sacraments;
- deacon (from Greek *diákonos*, "servant"), who read from the Gospels during Mass.

Lesser vows were taken by:

- subdeacon, who read aloud letters from the New Testament and ministered at the altar;
- lector (*lector*), who read aloud letters and passages from the Prophetic Books of the Old Testament;
- exorcist (*exorcista*), who knew the prayers and incantation driving out evil spirits;
- acolyte (from Greek *akólythos*, "companion," "one walking after or with somebody"), who ministered at the altar and during the celebration of the Eucharist;
- porter (*ostiarius* in Latin), who served the role of today's sacristan.

From the 4th century, only people above thirty years of age were admitted into the clergy.

Solemn celebrations were usually led by the bishop, although lesser vows in the Roman Rite could have been conferred by a committee. The key part of the ordaining ceremony was the performance that involved the "transferring of instruments" (*traditio instrumentorum*), i.e. the awarding of symbolic representations of the office:

- deacon would receive the Gospels;
- subdeacon – an empty cup, a wine flask and a book with letters;
- porter – keys;
- lector – the Bible;
- exorcist – a collection of exorcisms;
- acolyte – a candlestick (*ceroferarium*) and a jug (*urceolus*).

These objects not only expressed the essence of each office, but also constituted the intrinsic "accessories" necessary to conduct services. In the light of theology, the transferring of instruments during the vows also transformed a private person into a member of the ecclesiastical hierarchy. Acquiring a new identity, symbolized by accessories and costumes, also entailed obtaining special competences. Only an ordained person could be entrusted with particular liturgical duties during celebrations.[368] Ordaining is a transformative performance that changes a private person into a professional employee of the Church.

2. Initially, monks were not considered to belong to the clergy. However, since it was ruled that entering the monastery should entail ordaining, monks began to be perceived as members of the clergy. In continental Europe, attempts were made to differentiate between *ordo monasticus* and *ordo canonicus* already since the times of Chrodegang (d. 766), the Bishop of Metz. The division between two orders was finally institutionalized by Louis the Pious (778–840). Out of the initiative of his advisor, the famous promoter of monasticism Benedict of Aniane (d. 821), the Emperor ordered to develop a complex reform programme for religious communities, which was presented for consideration at synods that assembled in Aachen in the years 816, 817 and 818–819. Legislation adopted during these gatherings ordered monks to follow Benedict's rule, while the clergy was to follow canon law.[369]

At the beginning of the 7th century, Roman monks in England attempted to establish proper relations with the clergy. Efficient missionary activities demanded the regulation of the relationship between bishop-monk and the cathedral clergy who accompanied the first evangelical mission. Augustine asked Pope Gregory for advice, and was instructed to recall his own monastic experiences and avoid separating himself from the clergy: "you ought to institute that manner of life which our fathers followed in the earliest beginnings of the church: none of them said that anything he possessed was his own, but they had all things in common."[370] Thus, monasteries were supposed to define models of life for both the clergy and the monks. However, social roles played by priests and monks differed, although the expectation was that they would all live together. Abbeys in Whitby, Melrose (Northumbria) or Breedon-on-the-Hill (Mercia), educated future bishops.[371] In 900 almost the entire English clergy lived in monastic communities, or was strongly associated with them. It was only in the 10th century, when monasticism was reformed, that priests began to move on a large scale to farms and local churches.

---

368   Palazzo (2008, 479–482).
369   Semmler (1980).
370   Bede, *HE* 1.27, p. 80: "hanc debet conuersationem instituere, quae initio nascentis ecclesiae fuit patribus nostris; in quibus nullus eorum ex his quae possidebant aliquid suum esse dicebat, sed erant eis omnia communia." Cf. Acts 4:32.
371   J. Barrow, *Cathedral clergy*, in: Lapidge (1999, 84–87).

Final regulations regarding lay canons were introduced in the 970s during the Synod of Winchester, which is discussed in greater detail in the first chapter.

Although the monastic clergy was still strong in numbers in 1100, many more priests lived in local parishes. The rift between monks and lay (i.e. non-monastic) clergy deepened. As long as they were not Benedictines, the latter could marry and hold property. Priests living in cities began to be accused by monks of all possible depravities. Æthelwold, one of the key reformers of the monastic movement, called them "unclean." The loosening of ties with monastic communities actually lowered the standards and slackened the rigour of the performance of offices, especially in countryside parishes. Many parish priests were able to support their churches thanks to trading – not as a result of their deep piety. Priests often had no knowledge of Latin, did not shave, and got drunk, starting fights and wielding weapons in church. Despite calls for retaining purity, they would not renounce their wives. However, outstanding intellectuals such as the great scholar Ælfric, the influential Archbishop Wulfstan, or the anonymous author of the *Northumbrian Priests' Law* imagined priests to be "the moral leaders of local communities."[372]

3. A thorough reform of ecclesiastical institutions and religious life was initiated by Pope Gregory VII (1073–1085). From that time, the Church promoted monastic poverty, purity and manual labour as the cornerstones of the model to be followed in everyday life by all Christians. The Pope also desired to strengthen the role of church hierarchy, including his own position, by imposing monastic ideals on people leading lay lives, thus bringing them under the control of the Church. The clergy was supposed to provide a model to follow, especially in parishes. Its members could not have wives and children; they were expected to abandon lavish lifestyles, as well as promote virtue and poverty. Radical ideas met with a favourable response. In the 12th century, Europe's population probably doubled. Thousands of new cities were founded, especially ones specializing in trade.[373] Charismatic preachers who travelled across Europe praised evangelical simplicity and lived solely on alms, just like the mendicant orders would in the next century. Their teachings, sometimes quite spectacular, attracted crowds everywhere.[374] In 813, the Council of Tours ordered that sermons be delivered in plain language understandable to all people; however, Carolingian decrees came into life in England as late as at the turn of the 10th and 11th century, in the circle of Archbishop Wulfstan. From that time priests would have to teach on Sundays and during holidays, explicating the meaning of the Gospels to the parishioners in English. From its

---

372 Blair (2005, 497); for a review of sources and commentary see pp. 489–497.
373 Rubin & Simons, in: *CHC* 4.2.
374 Kienzle (2002); (2009, 41–42).

beginnings, the mediaeval art of preaching stimulated the development of local languages, although most sermons preserved from that period are in Latin.[375] This telling rift between the oral tradition and archival documents indicates the kinds of obstacles modern scholars face in reconstructing mediaeval performances.

The four Lateran councils (1123, 1139, 1179 and 1215) and two held in Lyon (1245 and 1274) sanctioned the reforms and coined a new definition of Christianity.[376] All four Lateran councils recommended celibacy to all members of the clergy. The second one forbade listening to Mass if said by priests holding wives or cohabiting with a woman (Lateran II, c. 4). The third and especially fourth imposed the regulation ordering the clergy to expand knowledge alongside practicing poverty and chastity. "The decrees of Lateran IV in effect secured the monasticisation of the clergy."[377]

Common people also needed educating. The Fourth Council of the Lateran ordered the faithful "of both sexes" to confess sins to the parish priest at least once a year after coming of age, i.e. since the age of seven (Lateran IV, c. 21.1). Confession was supposed to be made in accordance with strictly defined rules, which in turn entailed that parishioners be properly prepared. Church in England developed instructions for religious education of lay people as early as in 1281, during the Lambeth Conference, which was called by John Pecham, a Franciscan and Archbishop of Canterbury. From that time on, parishioners were supposed to be educated on religious matters through listening, four times a year, to a text phrased in their local language, known as *Ignorantia sacerdotum* (*The ignorance of Priests*).[378] The six key doctrines explained to the faithful included: Articles of Faith, Commandments, Works of Grace, Seven Deadly Sins, Seven Virtues and the Holy Sacraments. The document was initially addressed to the Canterbury province, but it spread rapidly, gaining popularity in entire England. It was imitated and used in all dioceses until the Reformation. By teaching the religion's basics to the faithful, local priests would also efficiently revise the teachings of the Church themselves. A huge didactic role was also played by religious performances, which affected the imagination of the faithful with the mighty "living images." First such shows date back in England to the middle of the 12th century.

---

375 Jansen (2009, 115).
376 Cf. Perron (2009, 23–25).
377 Leyser, in: *CHC* 4.17.
378 The work's first publisher – D. Wilkins (*Concilia Magnae Britanniae et Hiberniae*, London, 1737, vol. 2, pp. 54–56) – titled the text *De informacione simplicium*, but it was the name derived from the treatise's first words that became more recognizable (*Ignorantia sacerdotum*).

Mass

1. Since the beginning of Christianity, the Eucharistic supper has been the crucial and most celebrated ritual. Its fundamental structure, laid down by Jesus during the Last Supper, has remained unchanged for centuries. First, the faithful would listen to the Word of God; then, those taking the Communion would participate together in contemplating the death of Jesus Christ. Also, efforts were made to collect alms for the poorest. In this way, Christians would thank Jesus for His sacrifice, which they believed was bound to secure their redemption. That is why this crucial ritual began to be called the Eucharist as early as in the 1st century – *eucharistía* means "thanksgiving" in Greek.[379] However, this thanksgiving ritual served not only to praise God and His deeds, but also made the past present. From the 2nd century, the Eucharist also referred to the gifts brought by the faithful to the festive supper.

Christ was actually present in the Eucharist – not in a symbolic or metaphorical way. This is exactly how Paul interpreted in I Corinthians (11:24–27) what Jesus said during the Last Supper when he handed pieces of bread to the Apostles: "This is my body…" This letter is also the earliest evidence of words that led to the establishing of the tradition of the Eucharistic meal (11:24): "do this in remembrance of me!" This instruction was also recalled later, probably after Paul, by only one out of four evangelists, namely Luke (22:19). Paul emphasizes that all of these teachings had been "given by the Lord."[380] Some highly critical scholars claim, however, that Paul did not receive the Eucharist, but rather invented it.[381] The pagans' Apostle taught the Corinthians in the first letter (11:27) that "[w]hoever, therefore, eats the bread or drinks the cup of the Lord in an unworthy manner will be answerable for the body and blood of the Lord." The Eucharist is a particularly dramatic performance, because its every repetition stimulated the faithful to once again experience the martyr's death of God and His resurrection.

2. Due to lack of evidence, it is barely possible to reconstruct the earliest Christian rituals. Some rare documents suggest that the first church services were surprisingly diverse. The apocryphal *Acts of John* (94–96) contains a description of an extraordinary performance. After the Last Supper, Jesus rose from the table and asked the Apostles to stand around him, forming "a circle" (*gŷron* in Greek) and

---

379 Cf. Luke 22:19; 1 Corinthians 11:24. For more information on the evolution of Mass names see: Jungmann (1992, 1.169–175).
380 In some manuscripts the phrase "from God" is preserved. Cf. Page (2010, 57).
381 Cf. Maccoby (1991).

holding hands. Then, he intoned a hymn praising God, while others danced in the circle and responded in chorus: "Amen!" Perhaps such performances were practiced in some early Christian communities. Eric Junod and Jean-Daniel Kaestli, authors of the latest edition of *Acts of John*, argue that the hymn's choreography might echo one of many ancient liturgical practices.[382]

Acts of John is now available only in modern, reconstructed versions. The text dates back to the end of the 2nd century. In this unusual document, Christ reveals Himself to John during the Crucifixion and claims that He does not actually hang on the cross. He laughs at the people gathered at the Golgotha. His corporeality is an illusion. John even puts a hand into Christ's "body." It is an intriguing paradox that the account of the dancing Jesus is contained in the same text that questions his bodily nature. The four canonical Gospels, which all underline the human dimension of Christ's body, do not mention dancing at all.[383]

3. The 10th-century Mass celebrated according to the Roman Rite did not differ substantially from contemporary Mass.[384] The key figure in the service was the celebrant (*celebrans* in Latin). He was the one who uttered the formula of the Consecration; thus, it was through him that the sacrifice would be made. In bigger churches, the celebrant would be assisted by two ministrants (*ministri* in Latin); a deacon and a subdeacon; the master of the ceremony (*cæremoniarius* in Latin) conducting the celebrants' movements; an assistant wielding a thurible; and finally, acolytes and people holding torches. The celebrant would be supported by the choir, with four featured singers called cantors, who performed the leading parts and sung selected liturgical passages solo.

In the Middle Ages, a wide range of specialized liturgical books would be used to conduct the service properly, the key ones being:

- a sacramentary (*sacramentarium* in Latin) containing the parts of the celebrant;
- a gradual (*graduale* in Latin) – a songbook for the choir, with music;
- a gospel-book (*evangeliarium* in Latin) with passages from the Gospels, to be read by the deacon;
- an epistle-book (*epistolarium* in Latin) with passages read by the subdeacon.

In late Middle Ages, the English Church recommended that each parish hold eight different liturgical books, including the missal, gradual, a collection of antiphons,

---

382 *Acta Johannis*, eds. Junod & Kaestli, 1.198–207 (Greek text and French translation), 2.632–644 (commentary). Cf. Page (2010, 30–32 & 78–79).
383 Page (2010, 31).
384 Young (1933, 1.20).

the psalter, special service instructions book (for baptism, marriage or extreme unction), and a breviary with words and music for the Liturgy of the Hours.[385]

4. The first part of the Eucharist – the Liturgy of the Word – consists of reading the Scriptures (*lectio*) and praying (*oratio*). "God spoke and humanity answered"[386]: when read aloud, the Word of God was theoretically meant to be soaked up by the minds of the faithful, who would respond with prayer. Since the very beginning, appropriate passages from the Old and New Testament were carefully selected to match the liturgical year and the current holiday, which quickly led to the development of a rigorous canon of readings for every occasion, recorded in books known as lectionaries. Homilies or sermons explaining biblical texts were in turn supposed to aid the faithful in understanding and interiorizing the passages read earlier. These were usually the most elastic parts of the liturgy – although sermons would be derived in their entirety from the Word of God, their delivery was not limited by any predefined verbal formulas or gestures. A talented bishop or Pope, like Gregory the Great, could turn a homily into a breathtaking performance. The Liturgy of the Word – in which everyone could participate, including those who have not been baptized – transformed Christianity into a religion of the book, and initiated cultural changes[387] by stimulating reading and writing, production of books, new techniques of text analysis, as well as the creation and development of modern theatre.

The second part of the Eucharist – the offertory – was perceived in early church as a spiritual experience, making it fundamentally different from pagan or Jewish sacrificial practices, in which a major role was assigned to material offering. Christian performances, such as thanksgiving for redemption and participating in the martyr's death of Christ, were staged in the minds of the faithful, who would follow Paul's instructions and become like Christ, sacrificing themselves in the mind, offering "your bodies as a living sacrifice, holy and acceptable to God."[388] Such self-sacrifice depended primarily on the intensity and truthfulness of one's internal experience. In this performance material objects played a secondary part. Bread and wine brought by those participating in the ceremony acquired religious meaning only as gifts to the poor, who were also "God's friends." The spiritual concept of the Eucharist survived until the end of the ancient era; the mediaeval turn towards realism enforced a new interpretation of Eucharistic paraphernalia

---

385　Duffy (1992, 133); French (2001, 182–183).
386　Angenendt (2008, 454).
387　Angenendt (2008, 455).
388　Romans 12:1.

and led to the creation of a new holiday – Corpus Christi – in the 14th century. This, in turn, provided an excuse for wealthy craft guilds to stage many-hour-long theatrical performances.

5. In early Christianity, bread and wine necessary to conduct the Eucharistic service were chosen from among gifts brought by the faithful. They were laid on the table without any additional rituals or liturgical formulas. The sacrificial ritual boiled down to – as its early name suggests – "the breaking of bread"[389] and the repetition of the gesture made by Jesus during the Last Supper. In some places, as Paul seems to suggest in 1 Corinthians 11:21, brotherly meals were practiced, known as agapes or "love-feasts" (from Greek *agápē* meaning "love").[390] All, including the bishop, would sit at the same table. According to the report of Pliny the Younger, contained in a letter to Emperor Trajan from the beginning of the 2nd century, they would gather "to take food of an ordinary, harmless kind."[391] Nevertheless, the relationship between agapes and modern Eucharistic celebrations is problematic. In the same letter, Pliny seems to suggest that proper Eucharist was celebrated during other meetings, "before dawn on a fixed day" (*stato die ante lucem*). The beginning of the Eucharist as ritual was related to the supper, but focusing on prayer made the faithful assume a standing position, which quickly displaced sitting at a table together.[392]

Since the end of the 8th century, the Western Church would issue directives ordering that the objects used for the Eucharist be undefiled. According to the advice given by Alcuin (ca. 735–804), "the consecrated bread, turned into Body of Christ, cannot contain any additives and must be entirely uncontaminated; similarly, the water cannot be stained, and must be as pure as possible; also, the wine cannot be mixed with anything else, and must be thoroughly purified."[393] These criteria

---

389 Acts 2:42, 46; 20:7.
390 Cf. 2 Peter 2:13 ("love-feasts" is the translation suggested in footnotes to NRSV); Jude 12; Ignatius of Antioch, *Ad Smyrnaeos* 8.2 (in a letter to the people of Smyrna, Ignatius wrote that an agape cannot be held without a bishop); Tertullian, *Apologeticus* 39.16.
391 Pliny, *Ep.* 10.96.7: "coeundi ad capiendum cibum, promiscuum tamen et innoxium." Trans. B. Radice (Loeb).
392 Jungmann (1992, 1.7–22); McGowan (1997); Bradshaw (2004, 29–30).
393 Alcuin, *Ep.* 137, ed. Dümmler, pp. 211–212: "Scilicet panis, qui in corpus Christi consecratur, absque fermento ullius alterius infectionis debet esse mundissimus; et aqua absque omni sorde purissima; et vinum absque omni commixtione alterius liquoris nisi aquae purgatissimum." Cf. Rabanus Maurus, *De instututione clericorum* 1.31 (*PL* 107.318d): "panem infermentatum" (unleavened bread).

could not be met by products made at home. In the West, since the middle of the 11th century, only unleavened bread was used for the Eucharist, formed in a round shape and baked with great care.[394] However, many Eastern Churches continued to use leavened bread, because it was the kind that Christ used.

6. Granting such special meaning to objects used for the Eucharist entailed radical transformation of the liturgy. Members of the Christian community lost the ability to directly participate in the celebrations. From that point on, holy objects were supposed to be touched only with the untainted hands of an ordained person – a priest. The faithful taking the Communion ought to refrain from tainting consecrated objects; thus, the priest would put the Host directly on their tongues. Also, not everyone could take the Communion as the Church excluded all those who have "soiled themselves" with sexual contacts, even in marriage.[395] As a result, the faithful would take the Communion rarely, usually once a year. The concept of "pure hands"[396] enforced celibacy and reinforced the position of the clergy, relegating community members to the rank of audience rather than participants in liturgical performances. In early church, the priest would pray together with the faithful, who formed a circle (*circumstantes*) and repeated the priest's gestures.[397] After the year 800, however, the faithful were moved away from the altar, with the priest now praying for and to them.

The ritual of the Eucharist was strongly codified as early as in the 5th century since it had a predefined performative structure described in liturgical books. By turning into the Holy Mass[398], the Eucharist metamorphosed from a thanksgiving celebration into an act of supplication. In early Middle Ages, spiritual self-sacrifice was displaced by material offering. The faithful increasingly believed that their participation in the service constituted sound means of securing divine support. The offering was accordingly perceived as a gift made by humans, one that was meant to encourage God to show gratitude and reciprocate. Freed from the duty to provide objects for the Eucharist such as bread and wine, the faithful started to shower the church with generous gifts. They all needed to be presented to the priest, for he was the only one with "pure hands," i.e. had the competences necessary to make the offering. In parish churches some of the gifts were adopted as salary for parish

---

394 Angenendt (2008, 459); Jungmann (1992, 2.33–34). Unleavened bread was used in Armenia already from the 6th century.
395 Lutterbach (1999, 80–96); Angenendt (2008, 460).
396 Angenendt (2004); (2008, 458–460).
397 Angenendt (2008, 457); Jungmann (1992, 1.239).
398 The word "mass" (from Latin *missa*) is used to refer to this ceremony since the end of the 4th century.

priests and other members of the clergy. Thus, the Eucharist began to be a complex transaction between the faithful, their priest, and God, from whom everyone expected blessings. The name of the liturgy – "Mass" – refers to the last words of the final blessing of the Eucharist: *Ite, missa est*, meaning: "Go, it is the dismissal."

The number of Masses rose astronomically, the initial reason for their popularity being the concern for the dead. It was believed that the Mass can greatly contribute to the expiation of the sins of souls staying in the Purgatory for diverse reasons. Special brotherhoods were even founded to pray for the souls of the poor. The Mass had to meet the increasing expectations of the faithful. The oldest manuscript of the so-called *Gelasian Sacramentary*[399] – a collection of liturgical texts from the 8th century – contains instructions for services conducted on numerous occasions: for travellers; for love; for harmony; for converting non-believers; for the time of death and plague; and even against evil princes. If need be, the priest could say Mass twenty times a day.[400]

7. It was the 9th century that provided a breakthrough in the development of the liturgy. New interpretations of the Mass emerged alongside first debates on the nature of the Eucharist. Amalarius, the Bishop of Metz (d. ca. 850), explained the meaning of the Mass using an allegory. Developing the concept of Gregory the Great, who wanted the liturgy to combine the "visible" and the "invisible," Amalarius decided that there must exist a "secret meaning" of the Mass conveyed by God; thus, he dedicated himself to explicating it. Subsequent parts of the liturgy were supposed to reflect the life and passion of Jesus, from the beginning till the end. Accordingly, the introit would represent the prophets' predictions about the coming of Christ; the canon would refer to the Passion; and lastly, the blessing at the end would reiterate the blessing of the Apostles during the Assumption. The allegorical method, which was immensely popular in the Middle Ages, initially reduced the Mass to text, interpreting each performance as if it belonged to the Scriptures.

Later authors also developed performative interpretations. The most famous example of a "theatrical" allegory is the 1100 description of the Mass made by Honorius of Autun, a Regensburg monk. In "De tragoediis," the seventy-third chapter of the philosophical and moral treatise *Gemma animae* (*The Gem of the Soul*), he writes[401]:

---

399 *Sacramentarium Gelasianum*, The Vatican, Biblioteca Apostolica Vaticana (BAV), MS Reginensis latinus 316. For the text see: Mohlberg (1981).
400 *Paenitentiale Merseburgense A* (Vienna, National Library, Cod. Lat. 2225), art. 49, ed. Kottje, p. 138. Cf. Angenendt (2008, 457).
401 Latin text after: *PL* 172.570B-C. Trans. *MES* 58–59 (B1b).

| Sciendum quod hi qui tragoedias in theatris recitabant, actus pugnantium gestibus populo repraesentabant. Sic tragicus noster pugnam Christi populo Christiano in theatro Ecclesiae gestibus suis repraesentat, eique victoriam redemptionis suae inculcat. Itaque cum presbyter *Orate* dicit, Christum pro nobis in agonia positum exprimit, cum apostolos orare monuit. Per secretum silentium, significat Christum velut agnum sine voce ad victimam ductum. Per manuum expansionem, designat Christi in cruce extensionem. Per cantum praefationis, exprimit clamorem Christi in cruce pendentis. Decem namque psalmos, scilicet a *Deus meus respice* usque *In manus tuas commendo spiritum meum* cantavit, et sic exspiravit. Per Canonis secretum innuit Sabbati silentium. Per pacem, et communicationem designat pacem datam post Christi resurrectionem et gaudii communicationem. Confecto sacramento, pax et communio populo a sacerdote datur, quia accusatore nostro ab agonotheta nostro per duellum prostrato, pax a judice populo denuntiatur, ad convivium invitatur. Deinde ad propria redire cum gaudio per *Ite missa est* imperator. Qui gratias Deo jubilat et gaudens domum remeat. | It should be realised that those who recite tragedies in theatres were representing to the people by their actions the acts of those in conflict. Thus our tragic actor represents to Christian people by his actions in the theatre of the church the conflict of Christ and demonstrates the victory of his redemption to them. So when the priest says, *Pray*, he expresses for us Christ in his agony when he advised the apostles to pray. Through the silence of the Secret [prayer], he signifies Christ as a lamb led in silence to the slaughter. Through the stretching out of his hands he depicts the stretching of Christ on the cross. Through the singing of the Preface, he expresses the cries of Christ hanging on the cross. For he sang ten psalms, that is *My God, look upon me* to *Into thy hands I entrust my spirit*, and so died. Through the Secret [prayer] of the Canon [of the Mass] he indicates the silence of [Easter] Saturday. Through the kiss and the exchanging [of it] he shows the peace given after the resurrection of Christ and the communication of joy. The sacrament completed, peace and communion are given to the people by the priest, because, [with] our accuser [i.e. Satan] prostrate through the fight with our champion, peace is announced by the judge to the people invited to the feast. Then he tells them with *Go, the Mass is ended* to return with joy to their own business, and they happily give thanks to God and joyously return to their homes. |

8. Employing "theatrical" terms, Honorius attempted to conceive of the Mass as a dynamic performance delivered in time and space, realized with the priest's gestures and bodily movements. It was an objective rendering, which nevertheless did not – as many contemporary commentators point out[402] – reduce Church to theatre, and Mass to drama. It was rather the other way round. Lawrence Clopper

---

402 Analyses by Hardison became the most influential ones, especially those offered in his well-known programmatic work *The Mass as Sacred Drama* (1965, 35–79); for more information on Honorius see pp. 39–40.

has drawn attention to Honorius's liturgical language. The verb *repraesentare*, used at the beginning of the text to introduce the theatrical analogy, has roots in religious terminology. The *populo repraesentabant* performers would show the people real images, not mimetic approximations. The Latin verb *repraesentare* literally meant to "again" (*re*) "make present" (*praesentare*). The essence of the strategy, therefore, was not to imitate (*mimesis*) and construct illusions, but to restore a real presence. This is also probably the way in which the priests and clerics would render some liturgical passages from the performance *Ordo representacionis Ade* (*The Service for Representing Adam*).

Honorius could not watch *Adam* performed outside the church because he died ca. 1151, while the text is believed to have been created in the 1160s.[403] Moreover, he could not see any theatrical performance. Thus, he traces parallels from the perspective of early 12th century, and describes ancient theatre, which he knew only from literature, with the help of mediaeval categories. He surely read *Etymologies* by Isidore, where tragedians are defined (in 18.45) as:

qui antiqua gesta atque facinora	those who would sing for the audience
sceleratorum regum luctuosa carmine	in poetry about the ancient deeds and
spectante populo concinebant.	lamentable crimes of wicked kings.

Another problem regarding the Middle Ages is the way mediaeval people understood, or rather misunderstood, the concept of *tragoedia*. Isidore did not know it. It was introduced into English for good later by Chaucer.[404] Honorius attributed singing and elaborate gesticulations to ancient actors because this is how a contemporary priest would behave during Mass in a local church. The faithful could not always unravel the deeper meanings of the celebrant's words and gestures, but they could admire music and images. Although services in parish churches were a certain kind of spectacle, they were quite unlike ancient theatrical performances, or those from the late Middle Ages. It did not take much time for the clergy to introduce additional performances that explicated the mysteries of the faith to the congregation, explaining the contexts of certain ritual practices. Just like other liturgical performances, the Mass remained the model of all communication between the clergy and the faithful on matters of religion. Thus, it was monks and priests who provided future theatre artists with tools necessary for composing their shows.

---

403 This dating bases on analyses of language and versification. The only surviving manuscript of *Adam* was made in the 13th century in southern France.
404 Kelly (2000).

Transubstantiation

The Church struggled with explaining Christ's bodily presence in the Host for several centuries. The debate on the Eucharist first began in the 9th century. According to the "realists," Jesus was "really" present in the Eucharist because consecration turned bread and wine into the "real" body and blood of Christ. On the other hand, the so-called "symbolists" claimed that transubstantiation was merely an "image" evoking Christ's original sacrifice at the foundation of the Church; thus, they would argue that there is no need to reconstruct this act "in reality." "Realists" focused on spoken word and performance, while the "symbolists" – on writing and hidden meanings. In the end, "realists" triumphed. The cult of the Host favoured the realists, because it spread rapidly in northern Europe in the 13th century, ultimately giving rise to the Corpus Christi holiday. In consequence, the faithful would deepen their experience of Christ's real presence during the liturgy. The truth would reveal itself to the senses. Broadened awareness of the performative dimension of the Eucharist inspired the clergy to develop theatre.

1. The controversy around the Eucharist stimulated Christians to make passionate addresses. The debate was also partially provoked by the above-mentioned Romanization of the Gallican liturgy. The Gallican Rite emphasized Christ's real presence in bread and wine, while the new rite imported from Rome underlined God's symbolic presence. A particularly problematic case of interpreting the liturgy emerged in relation to monks converting the Saxons. Placidus Varinus, abbot of the new Corvey monastery in Germania (*Corbeia nova* in Latin), the evangelical heart of Saxony, found himself in a quandary and pleaded for help with his former teacher, abbot of the famous Benedictine monastery in Corbie, Amiens (in northern France; *Corbeia aurea* or *vetus* in Latin). Abbot Paschasius Radbertus (ca. 790 – ca. 860) responded in 832 by furnishing for his student a treatise, the first one in a series under the same title: *De corpore et sanguine domini* (*On the Body and Blood of our Lord*).[405] In 844, a revised version of the text was sent as a

---

405 Paschasius Radbertus Corbeiensis, *De corpore et sanguine domini* (PL 120.1255–1350D; a critical edition of the text was published by Bede Paulus in 1969). Ratramnus Corbeiensis, *De corpore et sanguine domini* (PL 121.125–170C; a critical edition of the text was published by Jan Nicolaas Bakhuizen van den Brink in 1954, 1974). Cf. also, among other works: Durandus Troarnensis Abbas, *De corpore et sanguine Christi* (PL 149.1375–11424B); Guitmundus Aversanus Archiepiscopus, *De corpore et sanguine Christi* (PL 149.1427–1494D); Lanfrancus Cantuariensis Archiepiscopus, *De corpore et sanguine domini* (PL 150.407–441).

Christmas gift to Charles the Bald. The king sent the document back to Corbie, asking a younger monk named Ratramnus (d. ca. 870) to clarify some of the abbot's problematic phrases. Ratramnus questioned the views of his superior, as a result of which both Benedictines set out the two major directions followed by later interpretations.

Paschasius conceived of the Eucharist as food for the senses. He claimed that the Eucharistic body (*caro*) was "in no way distinct from that which was born of Mary, and suffered on the cross and knew the resurrection from the grave."[406] In response, Ratramnus argued that the Eucharistic body, though identical with the historical body of Jesus, had only spiritual existence as an "invisible substance."[407] A similar position was assumed by John Scotus Eriugena (ca. 810–877). It was even assumed that he wrote the treatise authored by Ratramnus. Eriugena's own commentary on the Eucharist was written at the request of Hinkmar of Rheims (806–882). Although it did not survive to this day, traces of the theory outlined in it can be found in his other writings. For example, in the lengthy commentary to the *Celestial Hierarchies* by Pseudo-Dionysius Eriugena claims that the visible Eucharist "is the symbolic similitude of spiritual participation."[408]

2. The position of most monks in the debate over the Eucharist was fundamentally different from that of the clergy. In the context of monastic routine, this issue did not seem to demand an urgent and robust solution.[409] However, the debate carried on and for the next two hundred years arguments seem to have turned the scales in favour of those supporting real presence. The realism of the experience of the Eucharist was meant to balance the exclusion of the faithful from direct participation in the liturgy and their distance from the altar during services. In 1073 Pope Gregory VII canonized Paschasius. Earlier on, in the middle of the 11th century, the position of the "realists" was attacked with great accuracy and efficiency. Berengar of Tours (ca. 999–1088), a well-educated biblical exegete, employed scientific tools like dialectic and grammar to disprove claims made by Paschasius. The Church considered this attack with great attention.

---

406 Paschasius, *De corpore et sanguine domini* 1.2: "non alia plane quam quae nata est de Maria et passa in cruce et resurrexit de sepulchro" (*PL* 120.1269B). Trans. *CHC* 3.503 (Boureau).

407 Ratramnus, *De corpore et sanguine domini* 48 (*PL* 121.147A): "secundum invisibilem substantiam […] uere corpus et sanguis Christi existunt." Cf. Boureau (2008, 503).

408 Eriugena, *Expositiones in hierarchiam coelestem* 1.3.17: "typicam esse similitudinem spiritualis participationem." Trans. *CHC* 3.503 (Boureau).

409 Rubin (1991, 16).

During the four decades spanning Berengar's first condemnation in 1050 and his death in 1088, his views were stigmatized as many as fourteen times during synods and councils. On the order of his superiors, Berengar first renounced his views, but later ostentatiously took his words back, thus exacerbating the dispute.[410]

Berengar's chief strength lay in his great ability to combine lucid scientific argumentation with polemical commitment. During his lectures, he would thrill the audience with dignified gesticulations and surprising renderings of well-known words. Moreover, he would not shy away from commenting on political life in Anjou. He wrote letters to Prince Geoffrey II Martel and even tried to justify the highly controversial imprisonment of bishop Gervais. He would also severely criticize his adversaries, calling Paschasius's views the "madness of the crowd."[411] This natural born "performer" elevated the dispute on the Eucharist to dazzling heights of abstract intellectualism. Berengar did not question the presence of Christ in the Eucharist, but attempted to engage in the debate using arguments derived from semiology and linguistics. In a letter to Adelmann of Liège (d. 1061) – his colleague from studies at Chartres, and Bishop of Brescia since 1048 – Berengar argued, quoting St. Augustine, that the sacrament would have to be understood as a "sign" (*sacrum signum*) that is different from the denoted object (*res*).[412] The real presence of Christ's body in the Eucharist did not really amount to annulling the reality of the "sign," i.e. the reality of bread and wine. Berengar emphasized God's crucial role in establishing the "sign": it was Christ himself who used bread during the Last Supper. Additionally, Jesus imposed the Eucharistic offering of bread to express the gift of His saving grace. God's presence in the sacrament, therefore, ought to be interpreted in the categories of a real relation, not matter. Bread and wine were not transformed into Christ's body and blood in sensual terms (*sensualiter*), but intellectual ones (*intellectualiter*). The body was not "consumed" but "assumed."[413] In this way, Berengar diminished the priest's role in the Eucharist by depriving him of the ability to transform bread into body, and stripping the spoken word of performative power.

---

410   Boureau (2008, 504).
411   Gibson (1978, 63–97); Chadwick (1989); Cowdrey (2003, 59–74). Berengar's phrase is quoted by Lanfranc in *De corpore et sanguine domini* 4 (text in: *PL* 150.412D: "vecordia vulgi").
412   Letter quoted after: Montclos (1971, 533).
413   Montclos (1971, 534); Stock (1983, 276); Boureau (2008, 504).

3. Berengar's speeches and letters provoked numerous reactions, usually negative ones.[414] One of his main opponents was (on request of Pope Leon IX, among others) Lanfranc of Bec (ca. 1010–1089), grammarian and later Archbishop of Canterbury (since 1070). Lanfranc's writings paradoxically offer testimony to Berengar's success, which meant that the language of Aristotelian ontology found its permanent place in theological disputes. From that time, matters pertaining to the Eucharist were discussed almost solely by learned theologians and scholastics. Lanfranc rejected Berengar's view that the Eucharist is merely a sign of Christ's body, even if it were only material and took the form of bread and wine. He decidedly rejected the claim that accidents – properties perceived externally, such as colour, hue or taste – cannot exist without the substance they refer to. Although he was unable to precisely define the relation between separated accidents and substance, he indicated the general direction in which reflection would proceed next, finally taking the shape of the doctrine of transubstantiation.

The term "transubstantiation" is a neologism of unclear origin. Its introduction has been attributed to many authors: Peter Damian (1007–1072), Hubert of Lavardin, and even Roland Bandinelli, future Pope Alexander III (d. 1181). The coinage constitutes proof of the desperation with which theology sought a concept that would join radical opposites: the visible and the invisible, the spiritual and the material. The idea of transforming bread into Christ's real body was highly abstract. That is why attempts were made to rescue the sensual dimension of the Eucharist by developing arguments similar to those used by Berengar. According to the doctrine of transubstantiation, during the consecration brought about by God's power, a transformation would occur, changing the substances of bread and wine into the substances of Christ's body and blood without changing the formers' accidents, i.e. the sensually accessible forms of bread and wine. The new substance would reveal itself to the empirical world with accidents characteristic for the previous substance. To employ the language of Aquinas's metaphysics, it is the matter that undergoes transformation, but not the form. It was not a "natural mutation" and hence – as many theologians claimed in the 13th century, including Bonaventura – if this "miracle" were to happen, it would be necessary for God to intervene. This view, however, seemed to engage God in particular action during the ritual of the Eucharist, which was unacceptable for Franciscan theologians. Thus, the dispute carried on.[415]

---

414 Stock (1983, 281–295).
415 Rubin (1991, 24–35).

4. Additionally, the doctrine of transubstantiation indirectly offered an intriguing vision of performance art. By using words and gestures, the artist caused his bodily substance to transform into the substance of the dramatic figure, albeit retaining his outside features. In this way, the performer could become witness to the truth. The only condition would be to "shed the mask" and bare one's face. In this new theatre, "acting" was the complete opposite of classical craftsmanship: the actor would not pretend to be anyone and did not wear any costume to cover himself. Quite on the contrary: his playing would boil down to revealing himself in the act of confession, exposing his corporeality and becoming susceptible to wounding. By incarnating as an ordinary man, Christ called the human body – imperfect, frail, frequently diseased, or even ugly – onto the stage of the grand cosmic drama in which God "emptied himself" of His Divinity in order to suffer and die scorned, like a human being. The triumph of those supporting Christ's real bodily presence in the Eucharist profoundly impacted the development of Christian theatre. An unmasked artist entered the stage.

The 12th century played a key role in this. In that period, religious practices and models of piety underwent fundamental changes. An increasingly important role was played in monasteries by visual stimuli. The learned Benedictine monk Rupert of Deutz (ca. 1075–1129) attempted to follow the monastic ideal of imitating Christ through intense staring at the crucifix. Others, like Anselm of Canterbury (d. 1109), wrote handbooks instructing the pious, including lay people, how to meditate the crucifix.[416] The way of presenting the Crucified also began to change fundamentally. The image of the triumphant Christ was more and more often displaced by that of the dying Christ – human and provoking a strong emotional reaction among the onlookers. Thus, a frail and sinful man could become the icon of Jesus. The usefulness of images was finally recognized and acknowledged. After a lapse of two hundred years, manuscripts with full-page illustrations began to appear in England. The oldest document of this type, *St. Alban's Psalter* – composed probably in the years 1119–1145[417] – preserves an entire programme of defending Christian art, presented in the form of a French version of a letter ascribed to Gregory the Great[418]:

---

416 Fulton (2002, 336–341); Lipton (2005). Cf. Lipton (2009, 260).
417 Dating by Jane Geddes (2005, 126). Earlier commentators used different estimates.
418 *St. Alban's Psalter*, p. 68, St. Godehard, Hildesheim. The same page contains a Latin version of the letter over the French text: "Aliud est picturam adorare, aliud // ratione[m] de pict[ur]is int[er]roganti / per picture historia[m] quid sit adorandu[m] addiscere. Nam quod legentib[us] / scriptura hoc ignotis prestat pictura." Trans. P. Edwards (www.abdn.ac.uk). Cf. Lipton (2009, 254).

| Altra cóse est aurier la painture / e altra cose est par le histoire de la painture ap[re]ndre / quela cóse seit ad aurier, kar ico que la scripture aprestet / as lisanz, icó aprestet la painture as ignoranz. | It is one thing to worship a picture; another to learn, through the story of a picture, what is to be worshipped. For the thing that writing conveys to those who read, that is what a picture shows to the illiterate. |

The programme of art as a "lesson for the people" (*leceun as genz*) was also realized through spectacles. The first such performance was staged in England in the 12th century in Old French.

Ordo Representacionis Ade

The 12th-century text titled, in manuscript, *Ordo representacionis Ade* is one of the first performance scripts written in a vernacular language.[419] Although it does not originate in the liturgy, the document offers an astonishing synthesis, developing performative strategies adopted by the Church for ritual purposes. There are two different traditions of interpreting this work. Since the main dialogues and monologues were composed in the Anglo-Norman dialect, French scholars consider it as a representative of early French literature. British scholars, on the other hand, consider it as belonging to the prehistory of British theatre, which also has some justification. In the middle of the 12th century, Anglo-Norman was the official language of the court and aristocracy in England. It was also used by numerous clerics and settlers, who populated the island after the Norman Invasion. The text was probably created in England around 1160, but it survived only in one manuscript, which was made later, in the 13th century, not in England but in southern France. An anonymous writer, who would use the Occitan language on everyday basis and knew only some Latin, copied the text on paper coming from Mauritian Spain. It was the oldest type of paper used in France. In the 16th and 17th century the manuscript belonged to an aristocratic family, and was later kept in Benedictine abbeys – first in St. Maur and then in Marmoutier. Finally, in 1791 it was acquired by Bibliothèque Municipale in Tours, where it is currently stored.[420] Its peregrinations prove that the proper addressee of *Ordo representacionis Ade* was an Anglo-Norman aristocratic audience. The text was also probably performed and studied in affluent abbeys which could afford lavish staging.[421] Historians have proposed different reconstructions of the original stage adaptation. A performative perspective, however, can shed new light on the question of artistic practices in the 12th century.

1. It was an immensely complex and costly effort to stage *Ordo representacionis Ade*, which seems to indicate that this work, addressed to the new Norman elites, was originally meant to be performed by a wealthy cathedral rather than a poor parish. In the first part, God would reveal Himself to the audience in episcopal

---

419 In *Ordo representacionis Ade* an important role is played also by Latin texts. In 12th-century Catalonia, a scenario written entirely in the vernacular was created under the title *Auto de los reyes magos*.
420 Bibliothèque Municipale de Tours, MS 927. Other works have been also preserved in this manuscript, e.g. Latin liturgical performances with music, hymns, sibyl prophecies and the lives of saints in French. Cf. *Le mystère d'Adam*, ed. Aebischer, pp. 14–18.
421 Muir (1995, 30).

*11. The Expulsion from Paradise, on the left the cherub with the flaming sword.
St Albans Psalter, p. 18. Dombibliothek Hildesheim, Hs St God. 1 (Property of the Basilika
of St Godehard, Hildesheim)*

attire, i.e. as a bishop. Latin played an important role in the performance. Anglo-Norman dialogues, interspersed with Latin phrases, are framed with two *lectio* and eight *responsoria* performed in Latin. Quotations from the liturgy and Bible open the scenes, determining the main subjects, which are later developed and explicated in Anglo-Norman dialogues and monologues. Therefore, the script clearly realizes an educational task. All directions for performers, called "rubrics," are also provided in Latin, and are as detailed as those in liturgical texts. Thus, performers would have to know Latin, which in turn suggests that they hailed from the clergy, probably of lower rank, although surely not all, because the use of a bishop's stole, worn by God, might have been restricted for priests of higher rank.

The Service for Representing Adam consists of three separate parts of different length, which are only loosely connected in thematic terms[422]: Adam and Eve (lines 1–590)[423], Abel and Cain (lines 591–744), and "the procession of prophets" (lines 745–944). Unfortunately, the manuscript is incomplete: only the first two parts are preserved in their entirety, while the last one survives only in the form of a large excerpt with a problematic ending. "The procession of prophets" was inspired – just like many similar works called *Ordo prophetarum* – by the sermon *Contra Judaeos, Paganos et Arianos*[424] ascribed in the Middle Ages to St. Augustine. A reading from this sermon opens the third part of *Ordo representacionis Ade*: *Vos, inquam, convenio, o Judaei* ("You, I say, I do summon before a tribunal, O Jews"). The main idea of the sermon is preserved here: prophets accuse Jews of not being able to discern clear signs heralding the coming of Christ. Among the speakers we find prophets from the Old and New Testament, as well as pagans. In *Ordo representacionis Ade*, however, only Old Testament Fathers speak, and not even all of them. At the end, Nebuchadnezzar, King of Babylonia, quotes the sermon verbatim. The text breaks off abruptly during his monologue: probably one or several leaves of the manuscript are missing. The next work contained in the manuscript is the Sibyl prophecy titled *Quinze signes du Jugement*. In a sermon ascribed to St. Augustine, Sibyl is also quoted after Nebuchadnezzar. Consequently, the first editors printed *Ordo representacionis Ade* along with the Sibyl prophecy. This practice is no longer continued, with the text ending after the part

---

422   For arguments in favour of the text's unity as a whole (on three levels: feudal, theological and formal) see: Muir (1973). For additional testimonies (theological and exegetical) see: Hunt (1975).
423   Line numbers and all translations into English after the edition prepared by David Bevington (*Medieval Dramas*, 80–121).
424   PL 43.1123–1126. For a 12th-century version of the sermon see: Young (1933, 2.126–131).

of the Babylonian king, although certain scholars still argue that the prophecy constitutes an integral part of the work.[425]

2. The first part would begin with a Latin reading from the Bible and the singing of responsories (lines 1–2):

Tunc incipiat lectio:	Then let the lesson begin:
In principio creavit Deus celum et terram.	*In the beginning God created the heavens and the earth.*
Qua finita corus cantet:	When this is finished let the choir sing:
Formavit igitur Dominus [Deus hominem de limo terræ].	R [Responsory]: *And the Lord [God formed man].*[426]

The term *incipit* suggests a long reading from Genesis. Willem Noomen (1971) published *Ordo representacionis Ade* along with complete texts of all Latin passages, including the responsories, which makes one aware of how large a portion of the script is devoted to these parts, as well as how strong the work's ties with the liturgy must have been. Most members of the lay audience would not understand the Latin words, just like in the case of analogous lessons or chants during the Mass. Thus, they needed explanations like the ones provided in dialogues written in the French dialect and conveyed through the actions of the performers.[427]

The reading from Genesis and the responsory that follows it directly, which also quotes from Genesis, lent the spectacle a liturgical air and gravity. Parishioners who often participated in the Mass could easily discern familiar strategies.

One great example of liturgical didacticism is provided in the first lines of the dialogue between God and Adam (lines 3–5):

Quo finito dicat Figura:	When this [Responsory] is finished let the Figure [of God] say:
Adam!	*Adam!*
Qui respondeat:	Who must answer:
Sire?	*Sire?*

---

425 Accarie (1978); Accarie (2004, 28–29). Paul Aebischer (1963) is the only contemporary editor to have published *Le mysère d'Adam* alongside with *Quinze signes du Jugement*.
426 Genesis 2:7.
427 Jean-Pierre Bordier (1985) argues that *Ordo representacionis Ade* should be interpreted as an attempt to reconcile Christianity with lay culture.

FIGURA	*Fourmé te ai*	FIGURE	*I had formed you*
De limo terre.		*Of loam of the earth.*	
ADAM	*Ben le sai.*	ADAM	*I know it well.*
FIGURA		FIGURE	
Je te ai fourmé a mun semblant		*I had formed you in my likeness,*	
....		....	
A ma imagene t'ai feit de tere.		*In my image I have made you on earth.*	

In the first sentence, the Figure of God quotes in Latin a passage from the responsory everybody just heard, *De limo terre*, and translates it into French in the next line: *A ma imagene t'ai feit de tere*. This short scene expresses, in a nutshell, the chief strategy of the performance. Just like a priest during service, the Figure gains authority by using Latin, a sacred language. He orders Adam to remain obedient. When the Figure re-enters the church after the fall of Adam, it first speaks in Latin: *Adam, ubi es?* ("Adam, where are you?"; line 387). These words, sung earlier by the choir as a responsory preceding this scene, also come from Genesis. The second Latin reading from a sermon ascribed to St. Augustine opened the third part, "the procession of prophets." In order to lend themselves more credence, the prophets would also begin their speeches by quoting the Bible in Latin.

The Anglo-Norman language dominated in the dialogues, which does not allow to treat the work as a liturgical performance. Local dialects – be it French or English – did not have the authority exuded by Latin. In *Ordo representacionis Ade* the language of the people is one of error, ignorance and duplicity, used by the Devil to tempt humans. This is a language used by Adam and Eve, Cain and Abel, the prophets, as well as the public. Everyone who speaks it becomes susceptible to the workings of evil. On the stage, Adam and Eve represent the audience and play out a model scenario of the Fall, repeated by all those who sin. The devils lead everyone to hell: Adam and Eve, Cain and Abel (though the latter one is handled "more gently" [*mitius*]), as well as the prophets. They will remain there until Christ comes.

The performance would show and explain the mechanism that leads to sin, calling on the faithful to protect themselves from similar temptations and complete the story by recognizing God in Christ.

3. Adam and Eve resembled ordinary people and spoke the language of the audience. However, they were presented differently, in an intriguing manner (rubrics before line 1):

Adam indutus sit tunica rubea, Eva vero muliebri vestimento albo, peplo serico albo; et stent ambo coram Figura – Adam tamen propius, vultu composito, Eva vero parum demissiori.	Let Adam be robed in a red tunic, Eve in a woman's white garment with a wimple of white silk, and let them both stand before the Figure – Adam somewhat nearer, with peaceful countenance, Eve on the other hand not quite sufficiently humble.

Eve's attitude immediately heralded trouble. Lack of humility made the Devil's job easier and Eve was the first to succumb to temptation. Her readiness to sin is disturbing. Where does evil come from? From the Devil or from humans? Was Eve born susceptible to evil? Did this susceptibility exist before sin itself? Did Eve have any choice? Could she refuse the Devil if she was made this way? What does this intriguing asymmetry actually tell us?

Many commentators have considered the portraits of Adam and Eve to be mirroring mediaeval mentality, which was also asymmetrical. The first parents quarrelled like ordinary people. When Adam saw that Eve spoke with the Devil, he began to show symptoms of strong jealousy. Rubrics say that "Adam will come to Eve, acting annoyed" (*moleste farens*). Perhaps this is why he yielded so easily to her. Here is the entire famous dialogue (lines 277–314):

ADAM	ADAM
Di moi, muiller, que te querroit	*Tell me, wife, what was that evil Satan*
Li mal Satan? Que te voleit?	*Asking you about? What did he want from you?*
EVA	EVE
Il me parla de nostre honor.	*He talked to me about our advancement.*
ADAM	ADAM
Ne creire ja le traïtor!	*Don't believe the traitor! –*
Il est traïtre.	*Yes, he is a traitor.*
EVA	EVE
Bien le sai.	*I know it perfectly well.*
ADAM	ADAM
E tu coment?	*How do you know?*
EVA	EVE
Car l'asajai.[428]	*Because I have tried it out.*
De ço que chalt me del veer?	*What's wrong with his seeing me?*

---

428 Aebischer: "Car l'asajai"; MS: "Car io sai oi."

[ADAM]

Il te ferra changer saver.

EVA

Nel fra pas, car nel crerai
De nule rien tant que l'asai.

ADAM

Nel laisser mais venir sor toi.
Car il est mult de pute foi.
Il volst traïr ja son seignor
E so[i] poser al des halzor.
Tel paltonier qui ço ad fait
Ne voil que vers vus ait nul retrait.

Tunc serpens artificiose compositus ascendit juxta stipitem arboris vetite. Cui Eva propius adhibebit aurem, quasi ipsius auscultans consilium. Dehinc accipiet Eva pomum, porriget Ade. Ipse vero nondum eum accipiet, et Eva dicet ei:

Manjue, Adam! Ne sez que est.
Pernum ço bien que nus est prest.

ADAM

Est il tant bon?

EVA

    Tu le saveras,
Nel poez saver si'n gusteras.

ADAM

J'en duit.

EVA

    Lai le!

ADAM

Nen frai pas.

EVA

Del demorer fai tu que las.

[ADAM]

He'll make you change your mind.

EVE

No he won't, because I will believe nothing
Until I've tested him.

ADAM

Don't let him near you,
For he's a fellow of very bad faith.
He wanted to betray his Sovereign
And set himself in place of Him who is the highest.
I do not want a scoundrel who has done such things
To have access to you.

Then a serpent, artfully constructed, arises alongside the trunk of the forbidden tree. Eve will incline her ear near to it, as if hearkening to its counsel. Hereupon Eve will accept the apple, and offer it to Adam. But he will not accept it yet, and Eve will say to him:

Eat, Adam! You don't know what it is.
Let us take this good thing that is at hand for us.

ADAM

Is it so good?

EVE

    You will know soon,
But you can't know until you've tasted.

ADAM

I am fearful of it.

EVE

    Stop being afraid!

ADAM

I won't do it.

EVE

You delay out of cowardice.

ADAM

E jo le prendrai.

EVA

 Manjue. Ten!
Par ço saveras e mal e bien.
Jo en manjerai premirement.

ADAM

E jo aprés.

EVA

 Seürement?

Tunc comedet Eva[429] partem pomi, et dicet Ade:

Gusté en ai. Deus, quele savor!
Unc ne tastai d'itel dolçor.
D'itel savor est ceste pome!

ADAM

De quel?

EVA

 D'itel nen gusta home.
Or sunt mes oil tant cler veant
Jo semble Deu le tuit puissant.
Quanque fu, quanque doit estre
Sai jo trestut; bien en sui maistre.
Manjue, Adam, ne faz demore.
Tu le prendras en mult bon ore.

Tunc accipiet Adam pomum de manu Eve, dicens:

Jo t'en crerra. Tu es ma per.

EVA

Manjue. Nen poez doter.

Tunc comedat Adam partem pomi.[430]

ADAM

I'll take it.

EVE

 Eat. Take it!
By it you will know both good and evil.
I will eat some first.

ADAM

And I afterwards.

EVE

 Promise?

Then Eve will eat part of the apple, and say to Adam:

I've tasted it. My God, what a flavor!
I've never savored such sweetness.
What a taste this apple has!

ADAM

Like what?

EVE

 Like no mortal taste.
Now my eyes see so clearly
I am like the allpowerful God.
I know that has been and is to come;
I am complete master of everything.
Eat, Adam, don't hesitate.
You will take it in a lucky hour.

Then Adam will take the apple from Eve's hand, saying:

I'll trust you in this. You are my partner.

EVE

Eat. Don't be fearful.

Then let Adam eat part of the apple.

---

429 Benvington: "comedet Eva"; MS: "commedet Eve."
430 Bevington: "comedat Adam partem pomi"; MS: "commedat Adam partem pomum."

The initial asymmetry between Eve, who lacks humility, and Adam, who is submissive, develops into a fascinating dialogue. Adam, obedient to God, can stand up to the Devil, but cannot defy the woman formed from his own rib and similar to him. It is as if he could not stop himself from yielding. He does so because he is naturally submissive. Is it the case then that obedience to God has to lead to sin?

In the key moment, the action of the first part of *Ordo representacionis Ade* departs from the biblical account. After failing to tempt Adam, the Devil begins to lure Eve but departs prior to achieving his ultimate goal. Tempted by the serpent, Eve will taste the forbidden fruit in the presence of the submissive Adam and with his participation. A similar scenario appeared earlier in the Anglo-Saxon Genesis known as *Genesis B*. Both texts probably share the same source inspired by the exegetic tradition initiated by St. Augustine's work titled *De Genesi contra Manichaeos*.[431] Adam represents reason, while Eve – carnal desire. God first instructed Adam (line 21):

| Tu la governe par raison. | Govern her by reason. |

Then he taught Eve (line 35):

| A lui soies tot tens encilne. | To him be obedient all the time. |

Reason alone could reject temptation, but if desire succumbed even once, it would drag reason along. Thus, the subject of *Ordo representacionis Ade* was not the Fall of man, but rather a moral interpretation of this event.[432] The scenario of the conflict between Adam and Eve was a model one: the weak husband would sin after succumbing to the unruly and glib wife. This highly sexist scenario was repeated by the viewers every time they quarrelled at home.[433] The consequences of reiterating it were unambiguous – it led straight to loss of paradise.

---

431   Woolf (1963); Crist (1974).
432   Justice (1987, 857).
433   For a classic interpretation of the relationship between the scene of tempting and everyday life see: Auerbach (2004, 152–160).

12. *The Fall.* Cædmon Manuscript, *MS Junius 11, p. 20, The Bodleian Libraries, University of Oxford*

13. *The Fall*, St Albans Psalter, p. 17. Dombibliothek Hildesheim, Hs St God. 1 *(Property of the Basilika of St Godehard, Hildesheim)*

The Anglo-Saxon origin of the scene in which the Devil tempts Eve, absent from the Bible, seems to be suggested by iconographical sources. In Genesis, the devil tempts Eve himself (3:1-5). One of the Oxford libraries keeps a manuscript created ca. 1000: the so-called *Cædmon Manuscript*, which contains excerpts from Genesis, Exodus and Daniel in Old English, with Anglo-Saxon illustrations. In the lower part of one image showing the scene of temptation there is a scene from hell: Lucifer is sending an emissary to lure the first mother to sin (see il. 12). This tradition is also preserved in the aforementioned *St. Alban's Psalter*, created by Geoffrey de Gorham, abbot of St. Alban's monastery in the years 1119–1145, for the hermit Christina of Markyate (d. after 1155). The document was created probably several years before the composition of *Ordo representacionis Ade*. On the famous illustration, Satan appears as fallen Lucifer and spits out a serpent who hands the apple to Eve. Commentators have praised the image's composition since a long time, especially the circular shape of the tree reiterated in the "circle of sin" in which the main characters are caught.[434]

4. Latin texts in *Ordo representacionis Ade* have strong ties to the liturgy of the penultimate Sunday before Lent, the so-called Sexagesima. The reading that begins the performance – *In principio creavit Deo* – and the seven antiphons in the first two parts were all taken from *Liber responsalis* by Gregory the Great, where they are recommended for performance during the service held on Sexagesima Sunday.[435] Another element that might have been borrowed from *Liber responsalis* is the idea to combine the stories of Adam and Abel in one work. The seven responsories from Genesis constitute the framework of the story, which begins with the forming of man, and ends with the first murder. Both parts – the Fall of the first parents and the fratricide – have a similar structure: caution, offence and punishment. First, Adam and Eve were cautioned by God, while Cain – by Abel. Then, the parents would eat the forbidden fruit at the instigation of the serpent. After evil had taken root in man, no Devil was necessary to push one to murder a brother. In both cases, the punishment was announced by the Figure: Adam and Eve were expelled from paradise, while Cain was to live an eternally cursed life.

The Sexagesima Sunday marked the beginning of penance. On the next Sunday, "Halleluiah" would disappear from the liturgy, while the clergy would wear purple attire, as is appropriate for Lent.[436] Ten days after the Sexagesima Sunday, on Ash

---

434 *Cædmon's Manuscript*, Bodleian Library, Oxford, MS Junius 11, p. 20; *St. Alban's Psalter*, St. Godehard, Hildesheim, p. 17.
435 Gregory the Great, *Liber responsalis*, in: PL 78.748B-749A: *Responsoria in Sexagesimam*. Cf. Hardison (1965, 259–260).
436 Justice (1987, 853–854).

Wednesday, sinners were publicly expelled from the church during an excommunication ritual. Therefore, the subject of the original sin seems fitting for the Sexagesima: everyone should consider this sin within themselves and reject it. The Fall, however, did not end the history of humankind. The third part of *Ordo representacionis Ade* brings hope. Before being taken to hell by devils, prophets of the Old Testament predicted the coming of the Saviour, who – as was preached for example by Aaron – "will release Adam from prison" (line 782: *Cui Adam trarra de prison*). The "procession of prophets" recalled Christmas liturgy because the latter was associated with performances of *Ordo prophetarum*, which developed ideas from the sermon *Against Jews, pagans and Aryans*.

5. Stage directions contained in rubrics for the first part of *Ordo representacionis Ade* clearly refer to the tradition of the ceremony of excommunication. Could the ceremony of public banishing of sinners constitute a liturgical model on which the entire spectacle was based?

The fullest account of excommunication is contained in a collection of canon laws written in the middle of the 12th century by Gratian[437]:

Omnes penitentes, qui publicam suscipiunt aut susceperunt penitenciam, ante fores ecclesiæ se representent episcopo ciuitatis, sacco induti, nudis pedibus, uultibus in terram demissis, reos se esse ipso habitu et uultu protestantes. Ibi adesse debent decani, id est archipresbiteri parrochiarum et presbiteri penitencium, qui eorum conuersationem diligenter inspicere debent, et secundum modum culpæ penitenciam [...] iniungere. Post hec eos in ecclesiam introducat [...] cum gemitu et crebris suspiriis denunciet eis, quod sicut Adam proiectus est de paradiso, ita et ipsi pro peccatis ab ecclesia abiciuntur; postea iubeat ministris, ut eos extra ianuam ecclesiæ expellant, clerus uero prosequatur eos cum responsorio: *In sudore uultus tui uesceris pane tuo*, etc.	Let those who are assuming or who have assumed public penance present themselves to the bishop of the city before the doors of the church, clothed in sackcloth, barefoot, with faces cast down, declaring themselves guilty in dress and comportment. There the ministers – the archpriests and priests of the penitents' parishes – should be present and diligently inquire into their behaviour; they must then impose punishment according to the degree of guilt [...]. After this, let them be brought into the church [...]. Let the bishop, with groans and frequent sighs, announce to them that, as Adam was cast out of paradise, so they are cast form the church because of their sins. Then let him order the ministers to drive them from the doors of the church, and let the choir follow them, singing the responsory, *In the sweat of your brow shall you eat your bread*[438] etc.

---

437 Gratian, *Decretum*, Dist. 50, c. 64, (in: *CIC* 1.201). Trans. Justice (1987, 861). See also the above chapter on Lent.
438 Genesis 3:2.

Excommunication took the form of a horrifying spectacle in order to efficiently teach and warn all those witnessing it. John Mirk (*fl. ca.* 1382 – ca. 1414) – an Augustan canon from the tiny community of Lilleshall (Shropshire) in western England – wrote in *Instructions for Parish Priests* (lines 777–780) that upon announcing excommunication the priest should throw a candle on the floor and spit heartily. At that point the bells were supposed to start pealing.

In *Ordo representacionis Ade*, the exile of Adam is surprisingly similar to Gratian's account of the excommunication ceremony. Immediately after consuming the forbidden fruit, rubrics instructed Adam to change clothes (before line 315):

exuet sollemnes vestes et induet vestes pauperes consutas folii ficus.	he will strip off his festive garments, and will put on poor clothes sewn together with fig leaves.

The fallen Adam would not bare himself, as in the Bible, but rather don the "costume" of an excommunicated person, using it to proclaim and acknowledge his guilt.[439] The performance thus quotes the ritual of excommunication. During public penance, the penitents would appear barefoot and wearing hair shirts, with their heads obligatorily bent down. Rubrics in *Ordo representacionis Ade* instruct Adam and Eve to do the same when they stand repentant before God (after line 387):

non tamen omnino erecti, sed ob verecundiam sui peccati aliquantulum curvati et multum tristes.	yet not fully upright, but, through shame for their sins, somewhat bent forward and extremely sad.

During the excommunication ceremony, God would don a stole, the attribute of Church authority and office, as if he were a bishop.[440] By endowing God with episcopal functions, the performance recalled ideas derived from early Christians, who claimed that God operated through bishops.[441] God-as-bishop would "scrupulously" interrogate Adam, developing one question from Genesis ("Adam,

---

439 Justice (1987, 861).
440 Unwin (1939, 71).
441 This is how the bishop's office was perceived by Ignatius of Antioch, who expressed his views in letters written during the reign of Emperor Trajan. For Greek texts see: *PG* 5.649 (*Ad Ephesios* 6.2: "the bishop should be viewed as Lord himself"), 664, 668 (*Ad Magnesios* 2.1: "your godly bishop," 6.1: "the bishop who leads in place of God"), 677 (*Ad Trallianos* 3.1: "they ought to revere the bishop like they would Jesus Christ, Son of God"), 713 (*Ad Smyrnaeos* 9.1: "Who respects the bishop is respected by God"). Cf. also early Latin writers, e.g. Eligius of Noyons (d. ca. 660), *Homilia* 4 (for text see: *PL* 87.610): "Ideoque quia uices Christi agimus" ("And this is why we act as Christ's deputies"). Cf. Justice (1987, 862).

where are you?") into an entire series. This is how – according to Gratian – the penitents' behaviour was "examined" during excommunication. Sentences uttered by God were short, because they had important performative functions. They would push the action forward after Adam's fall, cornering the interrogated and heralding the inevitable sentence (lines 391–393):

Ke as tu fet? Cum as erré?	What have you done? How have you gone astray?
Qui t'a toleit de ta bonté?	Who has drawn you away from your goodness?
Que as tu fet? Por quei as honte?	What have you done? Why are you ashamed?

Two other parts of the performance lack such clear allusions to excommunication. All subsequent figures in the drama were burdened with original sin and each one had to repent. Sinners expelled from church on Ash Wednesday during public excommunication could return after Lent, on Holy Thursday. The birth of Christ signalled hope for both Adam and the prophets of the Old Testament because Jesus would release them all from hell. However, *Ordo representacionis Ade* does not end happily. All characters, except the Figure, remain in hell. Nevertheless, the truth about the prophecy that speaks of the Saviour's coming could be confirmed by the parishioners. Thus, the performance demands a supplement in the form of testimony borne by the faithful.

Despite numerous references to the liturgy and church rituals, *Ordo representacionis Ade* is a thoroughly original work. The Anglo-Norman text is not a translation of earlier Latin liturgical performances. In 1965, O.B. Hardison[442] definitively rejected the evolutionary position held by earlier scholars, who interpreted *Ordo representacionis Ade* as a drama "caught in the very act of leaving the church"[443] or as a harbinger of secularization.[444] This entirely autonomous work was developed for non-liturgical purposes, despite employing liturgical means of expression. A performance in the Anglo-Norman dialect, which quotes Latin ritual texts and reiterates official church celebrations, brought the liturgy closer to those Christians who did not know Latin. It was religious didacticism that determined this work's main performative strategies.

6. In the introduction to his edition of the text, Paul Aebischer notes that few mediaeval works are as widely discussed today as *Ordo representacionis Ade*.[445] The reconstruction of the performance remains a contentious issue, despite

---

442   Hardison (1965, 253–283).
443   Craig (1955, 64).
444   Chambers (1903, 2.89–90).
445   *Le mystère d'Adam*, ed. Aebischer, p. 7.

numerous directions contained in rubrics. The action of the performance was set in many places, referred to in rubrics with two Latin terms: *locus* and *platea*. However, these words, sometimes functioning as antonyms, are not used consistently.

In the first part, the most important *locus* is paradise, described in stage directions in an elaborate manner and with great attention to detail (rubrics before line 1):

Constituatur paradisus **loco** eminenciori; circumponantur cortine et panni serici ea altitudine ut persone, que in paradiso fuerint, possint videri sursum ad humeros; serantur odoriferi flores et frondes; sint in eo diverse arbores et fructus in eis dependents, ut amenissemus **locus** videatur.	Let paradise be constructed in a prominently high **place**; let curtains and silken hangings be placed around it at such a height that those persons who will be in paradise can be seen from the shoulders upwards; let sweet-smelling flowers and foliage be planted; within let there be various trees; and fruits hanging on them, so that the **place** may seem as delightful as possible.

Thus, paradise as *locus* was distinguished in spatial terms, and probably erected on a high scaffolding. The place called *platea* was the opposite of paradise. It was the place where devils would go about running. When Adam and Eve, instructed by the Figure, walked with admiration around paradise, rubrics instructed thus (after line 112):

Interea demones discurrant **per plateas**, gestum facientes competentem.	Meantime let devils run to and fro through the *plateae*, making appropriate gestures.

It is difficult to justify the use of the plural (*per plateas*). Soon after, when the Devil stops tempting Adam for a moment and departs from paradise in order to rest, rubrics use the singular (after line 172):

ibit ad alios demones, et faciet discursum **per plateam.**	he will go to the other demons, and make a foray through the ***platea***.

In the finale of the first part, after Adam and Eve are dragged to the gates of hell, the devils prance with joy *per plateas*.

According to Henri Rey-Flaud, the terms *platea* and *plateae* were equivalents in the Middle Ages, and thus *per plateas* ought to be read in the plural as *per plateam*.[446] However, what does this phrase mean? Years ago, Richard Southern defined the term *platea* as "public square," where the elevated stage for actors

---

446   Rey-Flaud (1973, 37). Cf. Accarie (2004, 115).

would be set up, in front of which the audience would usually stand.[447] Does *Ordo representacionis Ade* confirm Southern's definition?

After a botched attempt at tempting Adam, the instructions for the Devil were as follows (after line 204):

tristis et vultu demisso recedet ab Adam et ibi usque ad portas inferni, et colloquia habebit cum aliis demoniis. Post ea vero discursum faciet **per populum**.	sadly and with downcast countenance, he will withdraw from Adam and go to the gates of hell, and hold a conference with other demons. Thereafter he will make a foray **among the people**.

If the phrases *per plateam* and *per populum* were to be assumed to refer to the same place, *platea* could be really interpreted as "the square," where "the gates of hell" would be erected among other constructions, and as the place where the audience stood. However, these phrases are not identical.

In order to stage the first part – apart from the paradise, where Adam and Eve lived before sinning, and the gates of hell, where the devils would throw the couple in the finale – there was a need to include one more setting for action: the earth, where the first parents toiled away after being expelled from paradise. However, this place is not described in rubrics. As the opposite of paradise, earth might have been located where the devils pranced or where the audience stood. Such a solution would naturally be the most fitting one in order to convey the moral message of the performance: Adam and Eve are like every other person, while the gates to hell are present here on earth. Hell itself was not necessary for the spectacle as it would make its mark in the viewers' imagination through the smoke and noise coming from the gates. Still, rubrics do not indicate clearly that the earth and the gates are *loci* on the *platea*.

7. In the finale of the second part, the devils plunge Abel and Cain into the gates of hell. Fratricide, however, occurs on earth. Do Abel and Cain work in the same place where their parents toiled? It would seem logical from the perspective of the story, and economic from the perspective of staging. Nevertheless, rubrics do not mention this. There is only information that the brothers (before line 591):

colent terram preparatam.	will cultivate ground that has been made ready.

Adam and Eve could not make this ground "ready" because when they attempted to sow anything, the devils put thorns and thistles in their land (rubrics

---

447   Southern (1957, 235).

before line 520). Directions provided after sacrifices, on the other hand, suggest that each brother ploughed his own land (before line 668):

factis oblationibus suis ibunt ad **loca** sua.   after the oblation, they will go to their own **places**.

No additional information on these places is provided in the rubrics, which only indicate where the brothers are supposed to make their sacrifices (after line 666):

ibunt ad duos magnos lapides qui ad hoc erunt parati. Alter ab altero lapide erit remotus, ut cum ap[p]aruerit Figura, sit lapis Abel ad dexteram eius, lapis vero Chaim ad sinistram.	they will go to two great stones that have been readied for the purpose. One stone will be set at a distance from the other so that, when the Figure appears, the stone of Abel will be on his right hand, the stone of Cain on his left.

Adam's offering consisted of a lamb and thurible, while Cain's was a handful of crops. The Figure blessed Abel's gift but scorned Cain's. Then, the two brothers returned "to their own places," where Cain tried to convince Abel to go with him for a walk. Thus, these "places" could not be far away from each other. After Abel accepted the invitation, rubrics recommend moving to this part's last place of action (*locus*), where the murder occurs (after line 678):

Tunc ibunt ambo **ad locum** remotum et quasi secretum.   Then they will both go to a **place** apart and, as it were, secret.

There, Cain kills Abel, and the Figure arrives to proclaim the sentence for fratricide. This is also where the devils led the brothers to hell, but the place is not described in rubrics.

The phrase *locus secretus* appears already at the very beginning of stage directions for the performance of the third part, which begins immediately after the brothers are plunged into hell (before line 745):

Tunc erunt parati prophete **in loco** secreto singuli, sicut eis convenit.   Then the prophets will be ready, one by one, in a concealed **place**, as appropriate for them.

Rubrics provide no details regarding this special place, nor do they say where the prophets speak from. Each was introduced separately. First they spoke in Latin, quoting a sermon attributed to St. Augustine, or the Bible, and then they prophesied in a French dialect. All four – Abraham, Solomon, Daniel and Habakkuk – sat "on a bench" (*in scamno*). Where did it stand? It remains unclear, but probably somewhere in the centre.

A mysterious stage direction precedes the appearance of a Jew who initiates the dispute with Isaiah (before line 883):

Tunc exurget quidam de synagoga.	Then somebody from the synagogue will rise up.

Is "synagogue" a place this man emerges from, or is it a general description of a Jew? Was it another *locus* of the performance?

After the prophecies, the devils walked each prophet to the gates of hell, where they would wait for the coming of Christ. Salvation, however, is not addressed by the performance, which ends with prophecies.

8. The church played an intriguing role in the performance. Although it is not the place of action in any scene, rubrics refer to one direction: the Figure, or God, heads "toward the church" (*ad ecclesiam*) when His episode is finished, or arrives "from the church" (*ab ecclesiam*) in order to participate in the scene. The church is also often recalled in the "procession of prophets." Rubrics indicate that Habakkuk should make a special gesture before speaking (before line 841):

eriget manus contra ecclesiam.	He will lift up his hands toward the church.

Jeremiah's gesture is defined in even more precise terms (before line 855):

manu monstrabit portas ecclesie.	with his hand he will point to the doors of the church.

Indicating the doors, Jeremiah first spoke in Latin (rubrics before line 854):

Haec dicit Dominus Deus exercituum, Deus Israel: Bonas facite vias vestras et studia vestra, et habitabo vobiscum in **loco** isto.	Thus says the Lord of Hosts, the God of Israel: Make your ways and your doings good, and I will dwell with you in this **place**.[448]

Jeremiah refers to the church using the term *locus*, although the same rubrics never refer to the temple in this way.

The prophet continues in a French dialect (lines 859–860):

Par ceste porte volez entrer Por nostre seignor aourer.	By this door you will enter, To adore our Lord.

Church, the seat of God, was a place desired by those not allowed inside. The performance was probably meant to arouse a similar desire in the faithful. Jeremiah indicates the church's doors and turns towards the audience, inviting them inside. Would it mean that the performance was staged outside a church? This hypothesis

---

448 Jeremiah 7:3.

was formulated at the beginning of the 20th century by Gustave Cohen, and has been often repeated since then.[449]

In a brilliant 1968 article, Willem Noomen notes that Latin directions contained in rubrics are rather ambiguous. The phrase *vadare ad ecclesiam*, which describes the movement of the Figure of God, does not mean "enter the church," but rather "go to the church." Thus, the text does not make it clear whether the performance used a real building or a mansion. Moreover, Noomen observes that certain staging problems can be simplified if we assume that the performance was staged not on a square in front of the church but inside it. This idea was developed by a scholar from Nice, Maurice Accarie.[450] In the book *Théâtre, littérature et société au Moyen Age*, he devotes an entire chapter to a meticulous reconstruction of the performance inside the church. He reiterates arguments developed by Noomen, adding that the key to the staging ought to be sought in the final part of *Ordo representacionis Ade*, i.e. the "procession of prophets."[451] According to the French scholar, this scene alludes to the popular mediaeval dispute between the church and the synagogue. Accarie interprets the stage direction *exurget quidam de synagoga* (rubrics before line 883) as proof that a synagogue-mansion was used in the performance. He assumes, therefore, that the space of the performance is subordinated to two perpendicular axes expressing opposites fundamental for the contents of all three parts:

	PARADISE	
SYNAGOGUE	*platea*	CHURCH
	HELL	

Accarie locates the *platea* right in the middle, at the place where the axes intersect. He proposes to consider this term as "stage space." Its meaning can vary, depending on the play of the performers. This would be the place where all earth scenes were staged. The audience would stand on both sides of the *platea*. Accarie also notes that the rubrics before the onset of the third part instruct that the beginning of chapter IX of the sermon *Against Jews, pagans and Aryans* be read "in the choir" (*in choro*), which he claims to confirm that the performance was staged inside the

---

449 Cohen (1926); the argument is reiterated by Konigson (1975, 92).
450 Accarie (1979); (2004, 109–123; chapter "La Mise en Scène du *Jeu d'Adam*").
451 Jean-Charles Payen (1972) argued earlier that *Ordo representacionis Ade* is an extended version of *Ordo prophetarum*, with the former's first parts constituting a development of Adam's and Abel's prophecies, as a result of which they became autonomous plays.

church. In the part called choir, the cantor would stand reciting subsequent readings, with singers chanting responsories. Thus, the French medievalist concluded that the final spatial outline of the performance would look as follows:

	CHOIR	
SYNAGOGUE	PARADISE	CHURCH
audience	*platea*	audience
	HELL	

Accarie locates the mansion with hell at the church doors. The gates of hell would thus also be the door leading outside: whoever was plunged in there, had to leave the church. Although Accarie does not note this himself, his model also reiterates the ceremony of excommunication, to which the text alludes in many places.

Accarie emphasizes that the spatial model he proposed is reminiscent of solutions adopted in famous religious performances of late Middle Ages: it allows for the performance of *Ordo representacionis Ade* to take place anywhere, also outside the church, on any square, without the need to use the real church building.

9. The argumentation proposed by the French scholar proceeds, as it were, backwards. The "procession of prophets," the last part of *Ordo representacionis Ade*, was supposed to establish the main spatial layout used in previous parts, while later artistic practices – spectacles like *The Castle of Perseverance* – were to justify the form of the performance in the 12th century. Was the church, so often recalled in the performance and in such special way, to be merely a theatrical dummy? A mansion? It seems that the performance realized a clear-cut programme of a propagandist and moralizing character: it showed the church to the faithful as a very special place, one to be longed for and desired! The viewers were treated as performers from the very beginning.

At first, the audience would be assigned the role of penitents who were not allowed to enter the church. Only one character would be granted passage inside – the Figure. Thus, the church functioned as the inaccessible seat of God. Consequently, the audience would be treated as the Devil's ally. Fratricide would occur on the earth, almost among the audience. Everyone would stand witness murder. People would be lured into the plot, suggesting that they might have prevented the crime. Similar strategies were already used for a long time in liturgical performances in order to provoke a sense of co-responsibility in the participants, and deepen the reality of this experience.

The main message of the performance – loss of paradise – would acquire particularly convincing power if the performance were to be played on a square in front of the church's western gates. Paradise could be then located on a scaffolding at the top of the stairs, next to the door. After being expelled from paradise, Adam and Eve would have to descend down the stairs leading to the church. The meaning of this performance would be obvious for everyone: returning to paradise means returning to church. Like a modern advertising campaign, the performance conveyed a clear message, positing the temple as "paradise" – a place where saving powers operate. The first rubric closes with a remarkable stage direction:

| Quicunque nominaverit paradisum, | Whoever will mention the name of paradise, let him |
| respiciat eum et manu demonstret. | look in its direction and point it out with his hand. |

Extending their hands upwards, towards paradise, the performers would each time naturally indicate the church.

The longing for paradise expressed by the exiled Adam would stimulate yearning for the church among the viewers. Pointing to the paradise/church, Adam laments (lines 523–524):

| Oi, paradis, tant bel maner! | O paradise, how sweet to dwell there! |
| Vergier de glorie, tant vus fet veer! | Garden of glory, what a beautiful sight you make! |

A similarly unfulfilled longing was expressed by Abel when he was dying on his knees, facing east (*ad orientem*). If, as most commentators suppose today, the performance was staged at the western portal, Abel would kneel with his back to the public and turn towards the lost paradise – the church. This was also the object of longing for the prophets, who would in turn force the audience into the role of Jews doubting Christ. If the viewers watched the show while standing in front of the building where all characters in the drama were so eager to enter, perhaps this feeling would grow and intensify among the public. Church doors at the top of the stairs symbolized the gate to heaven. Entering the temple would be thus equivalent to Adam and Eve "returning" to paradise, and the "returning" of the excommunicated to the church. The show would therefore practically become the clergy's ideological manifesto. In his first monologue, Abel even called on his brother, and on the audience, to pay the tithe!

Performing *Ordo representacionis Ade* on a square in front of the church would also be captivating because it recalled the practices of ancient theatre. Anonymous Christian artists could not be aware of having actually deployed strategies similar to those adopted by Aeschylus in *Oresteia*. In the Athenian Theatre of Dionysus, the *skene* building, behind the orchestra, as well as the gate leading to it, also played a key role in the performance. A mediaeval cleric, free from the limitations of the liturgy, indicated a surprisingly mature understanding of the "theatricality." Performing *Ordo representacionis Ade* inside the church – as Maurice Accarie and others claim – would dissolve the crucial components of its message and weaken its pedagogical impact. Similarly, performing *Oresteia* inside the *skene* would annihilate the entire dramatic trilogy. For the duration of the performance, the inside of the church should remain inaccessible both in the plot and in reality.

On the assumption that *Ordo representacionis Ade* was played on a square in front of a real church, the structure of the performance's cosmos would be clear:

- at the bottom: earth, populated by people and devils; a place where hard work is obligatory and offerings need to be made; the gates of hell are located there;
- at the top: paradise, where the first people used to live; now, only the lonely Figure sometimes wanders there; also: the church, seat of God.

The spatial schema of the performance could be as follows:

	audience		
GATE TO HELL	*platea*	PARADISE	church building
	audience	CHOIR	

Performative analyses confirm that the traditional reconstructions were right: the performance would affect the public to the greatest degree if staged at a square in front of the church. Perhaps it was the specificity of the lay of the land in the place for which the text was originally prepared that made the author use the plural in the phrase *per plateas* when instructing that the devils run around on different "squares." A synagogue might have also stood in the vicinity, because the Jewish community was ultimately expelled from England in 1290.[452] However, it seems unlikely; the phrase *quidam de synagoga* ("someone from the synagogue") should be rather understood as a general description of a Jew. The performance would require only two mansions described in rubrics: paradise and the gates of hell. Staging the show "at the threshold" of a real church would also reinforce references to the excommunication ritual. According to Gratian, who is quoted above, the expelled sinners would wait outside the church and make their public confession there.

10. Borrowings from church rituals could not be a matter of coincidence. This performance, one of the earliest ones, clearly employs the language of liturgy. References to the excommunication ritual deepened the meanings of the spectacle and augmented its pedagogical message. The ending of *Ordo representacionis Ade* is lost. Nevertheless, it does not seem probable that the performance's finale

---

452   Mundill (1998); Nirenberg (1996).

could feature a symbolic return of the excommunicated sinners to the bosom of the Church, just like on Holy Thursday. This act ought to be completed by parishioners themselves, who would first learn the shocking lesson about the first parents, their sons and the prophets of the Old Testament, and then would "return" to the Church, going inside the building and participating in the Mass with a heightened religious awareness.

As Steven Justice observed, the performance *Ordo representacionis Ade* would work most efficiently if staged shortly after Ash Wednesday when sinners were publically expelled from Church, because the excommunication ritual would be still vividly remembered by everyone. Despite using the language of liturgy and ritual, *Ordo representacionis Ade* was not a script of a liturgical performance. Freed from the domination of Latin, the work brought biblical stories closer to the parishioners, explicating the meaning of Christian rituals. Thus, it was a largely autonomous piece, which could be staged independently of Church practices, although its deepest meaning would be revealed when staged at the beginning of Lent.

11. One of the first dramatic pieces created in a vernacular language, *Ordo representacionis Ade* surprises with the richness of staging and artistic maturity. It features eighteen speaking roles, most probably played by eighteen different performers. Additionally, the production needed "three or four devils," a choir singing responsories, a mute angel and some animals: Abel sacrifices a sheep on a rock, prophet Balaam rides a donkey and the temptation scene required "a serpent, artfully constructed" (*serpens artificiose compositus*). Every performer would wear a characteristic costume, often holding appropriate props. Paradise had to be constructed on a scaffolding. Smoke and the sound of breaking dishes would come from the gates of hell, which had to be large enough to hold the numerous devils, Adam, Eve, Cain and Abel, as well as at least eleven prophets. The angel who expelled the first parents would wield a "flaming sword" (*radientem gladium*) (see il. 11). Abel and Cain would make offerings on two separate stones, while Abraham, Solomon, Daniel and Habakkuk would sit on a bench.

Rubrics also abound in stage directions meant for performers. Instructions provided before the first part end with some notable remarks (rubrics before line 1):

Et sit ipse Adam bene instructus quando respondere debeat, ne ad respondenum nimis sit velox aut nimis tardus. Nec solum ipse, sed omnes persone sic instruantur ut composite loquantur et gestum faciant convenientem rei de qua loquuntur ; et in rhithmis nec syllabam addant nec demant, sed omnes firmiter pronuncient, et dicantur seriatim que dicenda sunt.	And let this Adam be well coached when he must give answers, lest in answering he should be either too hasty or too slow. Nor him alone, but let all persons be coached thus, so that they may speak in an orderly manner and make gestures appropriate to the things of which they speak; and, in their verses, let them neither add nor subtract a syllable, but pronounce them all steadily, and speak those things that are to be spoken in their due order.

The primary task of the performers was to communicate meanings lucidly. Clarity was especially important with regard to the prophecies. Rubrics before the third part instruct the performers in the following way (before line 745):

et cum processeri[n]t, honeste veniant et prophetias suas aperte et distincte pronuntient.	and, when they come forward, let them proceed with dignity and announce their prophecies clearly and distinctly.

As in the case of liturgical performances, the reality of the events was guaranteed by the clarity of the message, not the credibility of acting. When Cain kills Abel, stage directions are quite unambiguous (rubrics after line 722):

Tunc Abel flectet genua ad orientem. Et habebit ollam coopertam pannis suis, quam percutiet Chaim, quasi ipsum Abel occideret. Abel autem jacebit prostratus, quasi mortuus.	Then Abel will kneel to the east. And he will have a pot concealed in his garments, which Cain will strike violently, as though killing Abel. Abel will lie prostrate as though dead.

Hitting the pot was meant to draw the public's attention to the scene's key moment. The sound signal focused the attention of audience members, but was not realistic. Directions do not recommend using blood or simulating a real murder. Just like in liturgical performances, the way in which actors were supposed to play was not mimetic but representative.

Rubrics also demand that performers use a whole range of meaningful gestures and facial expressions. Whenever it was possible, the performers would point their hands in the direction of objects and people they currently referred to or turned towards. Moreover, they would assume meaningful body positions. After committing sin, Adam and Eve would stand before the Figure with their heads bent, while after being expelled from paradise they would express their grief by falling on the ground, as well as beating their breasts and thighs (before line 519). The devils would run around among the audience, making "appropriate" gestures, which probably means they were vulgar, and then would dance with joy after successfully plunging the first parents into hell.

Instructions for performers in the second part are particularly intriguing. When advised by Abel, Cain was to look at his brother "as if mocking him" (before line 611: *quasi sub-san[nan]s*). Then, he would respond "as if Abel's counsel has pleased him" (before line 639: *quasi placuerit ei consilium Abel*). He also had to make a "savage face" (before line 667: *torvum vultum*). Before the murder, he was to start towards Abel "like a madman" (before line 678: *quasi furibundus*). After the fratricide, Abel was to fall on the ground "as though dead" (before line 722: *quasi mortuus*), while God addressed Cain "as though very angry" (before line 723: *quasi iratus*). All these "quasi" elements, the "as ifs," inclined the performers to behave in an even more everyday-like way than during the argument between Adam and Eve. Performers were forced to visibly express their emotional attitude to the character they played and to other characters on the stage. The main means of expressing these emotions was the body, primarily the bare face. Liturgical gestures were supplemented with exemplary ones, and with facial expressions, both representing the reactions of real people.

The performance would call on the audience to act. Its members were supposed to enter the church, albeit advised and transformed, like sinners after a long penance. Participation in the spectacle would thus be meant to transform everybody – both the performers and the witnesses. Everyone would receive a specific task. The 12th-century author displays an astonishing awareness of performance art, focusing attention on the performers' corporeality. This could not have been accidental. The body played a central role already in performances of Anglo-Saxon monks as the vehicle of transformation. By stimulating the performers to gesticulate and make facial expressions, the mediaeval "as if" initiated internal transformations from the outside.

RECAPITULATION

A performative perspective allows to reveal the continuity of artistic practices adopted by Anglo-Saxon monks and 12th-century clerics. The first spectacle in a vernacular, non-Latin language was constructed using the means of artistic expression developed by monks. The author of *Ordo representacionis Ade*, who hailed from the clergy, resembles Cædmon insofar as he has initiated the history of religious theatre by creating a work characterized by an exceptionally rich and mature structure. Its performativity alludes to the practices of Anglo-Saxon monks and parish services:

- the terms *platea* and *loci*, present in the text, defined the spatial strategies of the performance as mnemotechnics;
- quoting Latin liturgical texts and excerpts from official rituals gave the performance the status of truth;
- the performers staged the spectacle in the world of the viewers;
- space had a performative character, while key roles in the spectacle were played by real buildings;
- performative strategies allowed every performer and viewer to experience the spectacle as a real event;
- performers played without masks: bare faces turned them into witnesses of the characters they played, and allowed something like "transubstantiation" in key moments;
- all participants and witnesses were treated as performers;
- viewers were encouraged to "complete" the spectacle by "returning" to the church in the finale;
- realism was achieved by adopting liturgical strategies;
- members of the clergy would perform the text and deliver their performances by addressing the lay audience directly; in this way, they promoted the clergy and the Church as an institution;
- images, supplemented with passages in the vernacular, and sound effects, were the main vehicle of conveying the emotional message of the performance;
- performers used two kinds of gestures: liturgical and representative[453];
- making certain figures "present" by way of utilizing the corporeality of the performers intensified the presence of the latter and stimulated their transformation;
- internal transformation of every participant was the main goal of the performance.

---

453   Ogden (2001, 33–34).

Towards Christian Performativity

1. Although Anglo-Saxon monks invented theatre, they did not practice it themselves. However, they did formulate a revolutionary artistic programme. Monastic performative practices had little in common with the ancient tradition, although the Romans began constructing theatres in Britain almost immediately after invading the island. In the first capital of this Roman province, Camulodunum (today's Colchester in Essex), one such building must have been erected shortly after establishing a military outpost in AD 49. In his account of the bloody suppression of Queen Boudicca's rebellion in 61, Tacitus wrote that "the theatre had rung with shrieks" (*consonuisse ululatibus theatrum*).[454] After the destruction of Camulodunum, the capital was moved to Londinium (today's London). Presumably a theatre was soon built there too, although no traces of it have been found yet. Archaeologists have identified only seven Roman theatrical buildings in Great Britain. The best preserved one is located in Verulamium (today's St. Albans in Hertfordshire). It was erected in the middle of the 2nd century and then twice rebuilt. Remains of two other theatres were unearthed in Canterbury. They were probably linked to an old sanctuary from before the Roman invasion. Their huge auditoriums could hold seven thousand people.[455] Elements of amphitheatres have also survived in fifteen places.[456]

There is no information on who performed in these theatres, what was being staged there, or how the auditoriums were filled. Frequent rebuilding suggests intense use, but after the departure of Romans in the year 400 theatres turned into ruin almost overnight. They were then mainly used as quarries providing construction materials for the local populations. The history of Verulamium becomes emblematic in this context. St. Alban, the first Christian martyr, died near the theatre. The monument and abbey erected many years later in his name attracted crowds of Christian pilgrims. They would piously pay their respects to the saint near an old pagan temple and theatre, where several centuries earlier a different kind of audience practiced its own rituals.[457]

---

454 Tacitus, *Annales* 14.32. Trans. J. Jackson (Loeb).
455 Sear (2006, 97–98 [commentary]; 196–198 [catalogue of theatres]). Theatres have been identified in St. Albans, Brough-on-Hunter, Canterbury (two), Catterick, Cirencester and Colchester.
456 St. Albans, Caerwent, Caister-by-Norwich, Carmarthen, Chichester, Colchester, Dorchester, Leicester, Londyn, Sarmizagethusa, Silchester, Trier, Wroxeter and York.
457 Coldewey (2004, 19).

2. The essentials of Christian performativity have been formulated by monks during the Anglo-Saxon period. Closed, self-sufficient monasteries were perfect laboratories of religious practices. In the Norman period, the clergy developed further the monastic strategies and adopted them for non-liturgical performances. Later on, the Christian art of performance was enriched by parishioners and professional artists. The creative explosion of Anglo-Saxon monks fundamentally shaped the form of modern theatre. The heritage of ancient drama was expanded with a new, deepened understanding of theatrical practices. A comparison of crucial categories in ancient and monastic performativity may fully reveal the extent of the revolutionary nature and originality of the monks' invention:

ANCIENT PERFORMATIVITY	MONASTIC PERFORMATIVITY
MASK covering the face	FACE is bare
BODY perfect and protected, altered by costume	BODY frail and susceptible to wounding, bare
PERFORMATIVE SPACE	PERFORMATIVE SPACE
theatre	church, monastery, square
orchestra, *skene*	*platea*, *locus*
costume and mask	liturgical attire
prop	liturgical instrument
CHOREA	LITURGY
(dancing, singing, music and poetry)	(cult, meditation and imitation of Christ)
DRAMA	CULT
comedy	Immaculate Conception
tragedy	Passion
satyr play	Resurrection
Homer	Bible
Dionysius	Jesus
PERFORMATIVE TECHNIQUES	PERFORMATIVE TECHNIQUES
choreographic gesture	liturgical gesture
singing to the *aulos*	singing without accompaniment
spoken dialogue	sung dialogue (antiphon)

THE ART OF PERFORMANCE	THE ART OF PERFORMANCE
mimesis	representacio[458]
craft (téchnē in Greek)	confession (confessio in Latin)
deception (apátē in Greek)	testimony (martýrion in Greek [459])
illusion	truth
THE ART OF THE PERFORMER	THE ART OF THE PERFORMER
manipulation	transubstantiation
play	transformation
originality	memory
PERFORMANCES OF THE VIEWERS	PERFORMANCES OF THE VIEWERS
interpretation	strengthening in faith
transfer into the world of the play	experiencing the performance here and now

The monastic performativity outlined in this study suggests a possible direction in research leading towards a fuller account of Christian performativity. However, this is not an easy task. Lack of Catholic documents, which were destroyed on a mass scale during the turmoil of the Reformation, makes the reconstruction of early English theatre significantly more difficult. For example, little is known about the actual impact of continental practices on Anglo-Saxon liturgy. Although they are later documents than *Regularis concordia*, scripts for *Visitatio Sepulchri* and other liturgical performances have been preserved mostly on the territories of today's France and Germany. The earliest drama to be staged in England – *Ordo representacionis Ade* – was written in Old French. It remains unknown whether English monks would adapt ancient dramas into Christian ones as a form of exercise, which was done for example by Hrotswith (ca. 935 – ca. 1002) in the Benedictine Gandersheim monastery in Lower Saxony. Many monks learned Latin from comedies by Terence. Christian theatre contained elements of ancient practices. Were they really invented anew? Does this prove the universal character of performance art? After all, mediaeval clerics had little understanding of ancient theatre, and rejected it thoroughly. Another tradition, much more difficult to capture, is folk culture, transmitted orally for a long time. Performances of travelling preachers, musicians, clowns, ventriloquists, surgeons, jugglers etc. also impacted the art of mediaeval shows. All of these issues demand further,

---

458 The mediaeval form of the Latin word *repraesentatio* meaning "to make present again."
459 Hence *martýr* in Greek, meaning "martyr" or "sufferer."

deepened research. In the light of what is certain today, it remains possible to formulate only a handful of hypotheses.

CHRISTIAN PERFORMATIVITY – FIRST HYPOTHESES
bare face
body – frail and susceptible to wounding

platea, locus
liturgical attire + costume

representacio
testimony

dialogue
singing
liturgical + representative gestures

memory
staging in the world of the audience

A personal epilogue: Performer as Monk

In the late 1980s, Jerzy Grotowski wrote in Tuscany a short "travel report," attempting to define the chief task of an artist called the Performer (with a capital letter). The document remains a unique testimony left by one of the greatest cultural innovators of the 20th century and one of the most insightful scholars in the art of acting to emerge in the history of theatre. The crucial element of Grotowski's cultural revolution was the enlivening of "bodily memory." "I don't look to discover something new," he writes in *Performer*, "but something forgotten." Grotowski reformed theatre by returning to the sources of performance art. The path of his career, marked by a series of transformations, was truly incredible: from actor and director, through politician, scholar and dissenter, to guru and hermit. *Performer* was written during the last period, and formulates the vision of a total artist, which has been also expressed – to my mind – in liturgical practices of early Christian monks.

Grotowski's text can be thus employed here to recapitulate once more the achievements of Anglo-Saxon monks, albeit using a modern language we all understand, and without attempting to assume a falsely objective perspective lined with common condescension, or trying to fruitlessly describe the 10th century with terms derived from that period. In this elaboration on the monastic performativity no attempt is made to define the term "performer" in strictly "scientific" categories. Instead, the following meditation follows hints offered by a practitioner and hermit who called himself "the Performer's teacher." Hopefully, the gravity of Grotowski's musings can help us grasp the artistic message conveyed by the performative practices of mediaeval monks, at the same time avoiding banalization or vulgarization of the liturgical dimension.

Quotations from Grotowski are marked in italics.

Performer is a state of being
When a monk crossed the threshold of the monastery – having decided to effect a radical change in the way he looked and lived, and alter the rhythm of life and eating habits – he would in fact transform both his self-understanding and his notion of the world. "This message of mine is for you," wrote Benedict in the prologue to the Rule, "armed with the strong and noble weapons of obedience." New patterns of behaviour, practiced incessantly and with absolute humility, day and night, would transform the neophyte into a new person. Being a monk is, in this model, a way of being in striving towards God, which constitutes a path to be followed by every Christian.
Personal transmutation is in some way the task of everyone

Performer – with a capital letter – is a man of action
Life in the monastery, regulated in great detail, in fact boiled down to the diligent realization of performances, which repeated in daily, weekly and annual cycles. Every activity would have to contribute to the superior goal of holy service. Every performance, be it psalmody, meditation, reading, vigil, prayer, procession or liturgy, would have to testify to the truth. Monks would put things into practice. Their aim was to achieve the total act, i.e. complete transformation, which entailed the forging of a new identity.
With age, it's possible to pass from the body-and-essence to the body of essence

A man of knowledge – a rebel face to whom knowledge stands as duty
In order to submit themselves to total, regulated discipline, monks would have to renounce everything that made their lives meaningful outside the monastery, rejecting the world in order to become immersed in transcendence. Monks are rebels, for whom learning the truth is a duty. All their actions and gestures have the rank of confession.
The key question is: What is your process?

A man of knowledge has at his disposal **the doing**
Fulfilling the duties specified by the rule required ceaseless activity, especially in terms of patience. The many-hour-long psalmodies must have been the most burdensome element of monastic life. Every week, Anglo-Saxon monks would sing the entire psalter. During Lent, monks in Cluny would perform 150 psalms every day. Studying transcendence did not involve reading, but action. The content of songs was fathomed through meditation while singing the never-ending melismatic cascades of sounds. Active cognition transformed and purified the Performer. Monks dealt in actions.
Knowledge is a matter of doing

Performer knows to link body impulses to the song
Singing and reciting filled most days in Anglo-Saxon monasteries. *Regularis concordia* (8) instructed that prayers be sung at a modest pace so as not to anger God. The body, subjected to strict discipline from the outside, and vibrating with voice on the inside, would learn how to live again. Monks would not reject the body, because it was the vehicle of transformation. Rather, they would link its impulses to the song, like warriors.
For the warrior with organicity in full, the body and essence can enter into osmosis: it seems impossible to dissociate them

Ritual is a time of great intensity
Psalmodies could last hours, just like liturgical performances. However, the structure of these compositions intensified the experience. Monotonous singing would

induce an altered state of consciousness in the performer, inciting permanent rapture. Liturgy made Christ present on the Cross, which in turn could provoke particularly strong feelings and emotional outbursts.

Performer must develop not an organism of muscles, but an organism-channel through which the energies circulate, the energies transform

The things to be done must be precise

Psalmodic singing was difficult. "Let all these prayers be chanted distinctly," *Regularis concordia* instructs (8), following Benedict's Rule (19.7), "so that mind and voice agree" (*ut mens nostra concordet voci nostrae*). Appropriate performance of elaborate *responsoria* demanded laborious training. Every song had to be performed in the right way. Monks would repeat words and melodies for hours before fully mastering the technique of singing. Detailed rules also regulated the course of liturgical performances.

Performer should ground his work in a precise structure

The stream of life should be articulated in forms

Strict discipline was imposed on the bodies of monks. Their attire, step, posture, gestures and sounds were all directed and brought under control. In the monastery, a single proper pattern of behaviour was defined for each performance. Monks would begin their training from imitating forms, i.e. learning how to kneel, lie prostrate, sing and meditate. In this way, they would acquaint themselves with the detailed scenarios of liturgical performances. It was only then – when the form imposed from outside ceased to be hindering and became a new way of being in the world – that the monk would transform into someone who testifies to the truth. His life would thus acquire meaning due to the ability to achieve, as the Rule has it, "the loftier summits of the teaching and virtues" (73.9). In the monastery, the stream of life would be articulated in forms, vehicles for inner transformation.

Adjusted to process, the body becomes non-resistant, nearly transparent

The witnesses enter into state of intensity because, so to say, they feel presence

Liturgical performances intensified and concentrated the experiences of their participants, because – following the model of Eucharistic liturgy – they stimulated the experience of transcendence's real presence. The Cross would become the Crucified. Three brothers wielding thuribles and demonstrating the empty shroud would transform those who participated in the celebrations into witnesses of Resurrection. During *Tenebrae*, on the other hand, the growing darkness and fading chants of boys evoked the shocking experience of God's death, absolute emptiness and lack of presence. *Regularis concordia* instructed monks to receive

the Eucharist every day. As a result, monks are the ones who offer testimony to real presence in the liturgy and in the Sacrament, including their own presence.
Active: to be present

What is the quality of submission to your own destiny?
In the monastery, Christ became the destiny of every member of the community. "First of all," Benedict teaches in the prologue to the Rule (4), "every time you begin a good work, you must pray to him most earnestly to bring it to perfection." The discovery of one's destiny thus involved a very painful process of renouncing everything one had: objects, ideas, desires, dreams and illusions. Subjecting the monk to his destiny – i.e. Christ – had to be absolute.
One can catch the process if what one does is in keeping with himself

The question is to be passive in action and active in seeing
Ceaseless testifying to the truth is an immensely challenging task. Monks who spent most of their time singing psalmodies usually displayed very limited outside activity, which consisted mainly in standing, kneeling or lying prostrate. They had to be passive in order to experience the effect of the overwhelming transformative power of monotonous singing. When meeting God, the initiative is not on the side of human beings. Striving towards unity with transcendence, monks would have to be passive in order to allow God to operate. Conversely, they would have to be active in perceiving in order to respond to God's calling.
Passive: to be receptive

One access to the creative way consists of discovering in yourself an ancient corporeality to which you are bound by a strong ancestral relation
In the monastery, everyone would imitate Christ, but only performances of radical humility allowed monks to find a trace of God within themselves; it was only through humiliation that elevation was made possible. Washing the feet of the poor, performing all offices, kneeling and standing for many hours, keeping vigils, representing women in liturgical performances, and fasting – all of these contributed to discovering within oneself a source corporeality, God incarnate.
Starting from details you can discover in yourself somebody other

Discoveries are behind us and we must journey back to reach them
Liturgical performances brought sacred time into existence. The experience of its reality escapes human reason. Within sacred time, the here and now, it is not only the present that reveals itself, but also the past (Incarnation, Crucifixion and Resurrection). The entire truth has already been revealed – in order to reach it, one must travel backwards.
Performer is pontifex, maker of bridges

Bibliography

Primary Sources
- *Acta Johannis* (CCSA 1-2), eds. E. Junod and J.-D. Kaestli (Turnhout, 1983).
- *Ælfric's Catholic Homilies. The First Series: Text* (EETS SS 17), ed. P. Clemoes (Oxford, 1997).
- *Alcvini sive Albini epistolae*, ed. E. Dümmler, in MGH, *Epistolae* 1, vol. 4 (Berlin, 1845), pp. 1–493.
- *Amalarii episcopi Opera liturgica omnia*, vol. 3 (Studi e testi 140), ed. J.M. Hanssens (Vatican City, 1950).
- *The Anonymous Sayings of the Desert Fathers: A Selected Edition and Complete English Translation*, trans. J. Wortley (Cambrigde, 2013).
- *S. Aureli Augustini Hipponensis Episcopi Epistulae*, Pars 3: *Ep. CXXIV-CLXXXIV* (CSEL 44, S. Aureli Augustini opera; Sectio 2: *Epistulae*), eds. A. Goldbacher and F. Trempsky (Vienna, 1904).
- BASILE SAINT, *Lettres*, ed. Y. Courtonne, 3 vols. (Paris, 1957–66).
- BEDE, *Epistola ad Ecgbertum Episcopum*, ed. C. Plummer, in Bede, *HE* 1, pp. 405–423.
- BEDE, *Historia abbatum*, ed. C. Plummer, in Bede, *HE* 1, pp. 364–387.
- BEDE, *De temporum ratione*, in *Bedae opera didascalica* (CCSL 123B), ed. C.W. Jones (Turnhout, 1977), pp. 241–544.
- *The Benedictional of St Aethelwold: A Masterpiece of Anglo-Saxon Art* (The British Library, Facsimile edition), ed. A. Prescott (London, 2002).
- *Die Briefe des Heiligen Bonifatius und Lullus*, MGH 1, *Epistolae selectae* I, ed. M. Tangl (Berlin, 1916).
- BUBER M., *Elija. Ein Mysterienspiel* (Heidelberg, 1963).
- *A Descritption or Briefe Declaration of All the Ancient Monuments, Rites, and Customes Belonginge, or Beinge within, the Monastical Church of Durham before the Suppresion, written 1593*, ed. J. Raine (London, 1842; repr. 2009).
- *The Etymologies of Isidore of Seville*, trans. S.A. Barney, W.J. Lewis, J.A. Beach and O. Berghof (Cambridge, 2006).
- *Giraldi Cambrensis opera* (Rolls Series 21), eds. J.S. Brewer, J.F. Domock and G.F. Warner, 8 vols. (London, 1861–1891).
- HESIOD, *Theogony*, ed. M.L. West (Oxford, 1966).

- *Historia monachorum in Aegypto: édition critique du texte grec*, ed. A.-J. Festugière (Brussels, 1961).
- *The Homilies of Wulfstan*, ed. D. Bethurum (Oxford, 1957, 1971²).
- *Die Hirtenbriefe Ælfric's in altenglischer und lateinischer Fassung* (Bibliothek der angelsächsischen prosa 9), ed. B. Fehr (Hamburg, 1914).
- LAMBARDE WILLIAM (1536–1601), *Dictionarium Angliæ Topographicum et Historicum: An alphabetical description of the chief places in England and Wales* (London, 1730).
- *The Late Medieval Religious Plays of Bodleian Mss. Digby 133 and E Museo 160* (EETS ES 238), eds. D.C. Baker, J.L. Murphy and L.B. Hall (London, 1982).
- *The Leofric Collectar* (HBS 45, 46), eds. E.S. Dewick and W.H. Frere, vols. 2.1–2 (London, 1914–1921).
- *Liber sacramentorum Romanae Aeclesiae ordinis anni circuli: Cod. Vat. Reg. lat. 316, Paris Bibl. Nat. 7193, 41/56 (Sacramentarium Gelasianum)*, Rerum ecclesiastiorum documenta 4, Series maior, Fontes, ed. M. Letts *et al.* (Roma 1981³).
- *The Lives of the Desert Father*, intr. by B. Ward, trans. by N. Russell (London, 1980).
- *The Lives of Symeon Stylites* (CS 112), ed. R. Doran (Kalamazoo, 1992).
- *Medieval Drama*, ed. D. Bevington (Boston, 1975).
- *Memorials of St Dunstan, archbishop of Canterbury*, ed. W. Stubbs (London, 1874).
- *The Middle-English Harrowing of Hell and Gospel of Nicodemus* (EETS ES 100), ed. W.H. Hulme (London, 1908, repr. 1976).
- *Le mystère d'Adam (Ordo representacionis Ade)*, texte complet du manuscrit de Tours; publié avec une introduction, des notes et un glossaire, ed. P. Aebischer (Genève-Paris, 1963).
- *Nine Medieval Latin Plays* (Cambridge Medieval Classics 1), ed. P. Dronke (Cambridge, 1994).
- *Old and Middle English c. 890-c.1450: An Anthology*, ed. and trans. E. Treharne (Chichester, West Sussex, 2010³).
- *The Old English Life of St. Machutus* (Toronto Old English series 9), ed. D. Yerkes (Toronto, 1984).
- *The Ordinale and Customary of the Benedictine Nuns of Barking Abbey: University College, Oxford, MS 169* (HBS), ed. J.B.L. Tolhurst, 2 vols. (London 1927–8).

- *Pachomian Koinonia: The Lives, Rules and Other Writings of Saint Pachomius and His Disciples* (CS 46), ed. and trans. A. Veilleux, 3 vols. (Kalamazoo, 1981).
- *Paenitentiale Merseburgense A*, ed. R. Kottje, in *Paenitentalia minora Franciae et Italiae saeculi VIII–IX* (CCSL 156.1), vol. 1, eds. R. Kottje, L. Körntgen and U. Spengler-Reffgen (Turnhout 1994).
- PASCHASIUS RADBERTUS, *De corpore et sanguine domini* (CCCM 16), ed. B. Paulus (Turnhout, 1969).
- *La „prière universelle" dans les liturgies anciennes: Témoignages patristiques et textes liturgiques* (LQF 62), ed. P. De Clerck (Münster, 1977).
- RATRAMNUS, *De corpore et sanguine domini* (Verhandelingen der Koninklijke Nederlandse Akademie van Wetenschappen. Afd. Letterkunde. Nieuwe reeks 61.1), ed. J.N. Bakhuizen van der Brink (Amsterdam, 1974²).
- *Regularis concordia anglicae nationis monachorum santcimonialiumque / The Monastic Agreement of the Monks and Nuns of the English Nation* (Nelson's Medieval Classics), ed. T. Symons OSB (London, 1953).
- *Die „Regularis Concordia" und ihre altenglische Interlinearversion. Mit Einleitung und Kommentar* (Müncher Universitäts-Schriften: Texte und Untersuchungen zur Englischen Philologie 17), ed. L. Kornexl (München, 1993).
- *The Revelation of the Monk of Eynsham* (EETS OS 318), ed. R. Easting (Oxford, 2002).
- RUFINUS, *Historia ecclesiastica*, in *Kirchengeschichte*, ed. T. Mommsen, GCS 9.1 (Berlin, 1908).
- THEODORET OF CYRRHUS, *A History of the Monks of Syria* (CS 88), trans. R.M. Price (Kalamazoo, 1985).
- *The Travels of Leo of Rosmital trough Germany, Flanders, England, France, Spain, Portugal and Italy, 1465–1467*, ed. M. Letts (Cambridge, 1957).
- *The Vercelli Book*, ed. G.P. Krapp (New York, 1932).
- WULFSTAN, *Vita S. Æthelwoldi*, in Wulstan of Winchester, *The Life of Saint Æthelwold*, eds. M. Lapidge and M. Winterbotton (Oxford, 1991).

Secondary Sources

- ACCARIE, M. (1978) 'Théologie et morale dans le Jeu d'Adam', *Revue des langues romanes* 83, pp. 123–147.
- ACCARIE, M. (1979) 'La mise en scène du *Jue d'Adam*', in *Mélanges de langue et littérature françaises du Moyen-Âge offerts à Pierre Jonin* (Sénéfiance 7), CUER MA (Aux-en-Provience), pp. 3–16.

- ACCARIE, M. (2004) *Théâtre, littérature et société au Moyen Age* (Nice).
- ANGENENDT, A. (2004) '"Mit reinen Händen": das Motiv der kultischen Reinheit in der abendländischen Askese', in A. Angenendt, Th. Flammer and D. Meyer (eds.) *Liturgie im Mittelalter: Ausgewählte Aufsätze zum 70. Geburtstag* (Ästhetik-Theologie-Liturgik 35) (Münster), pp. 245–267.
- ANGENENDT, A. (2008) 'Sacrifice, gifts, and prayers in Latin Christianity', in *CHC* 3, pp. 453–471.
- ANGENENDT, A., TH. FLAMMER and D. MEYER (eds.) (2004) *Liturgie im Mittelalter: Ausgewählte Aufsätze zum 70. Geburtstag* (Ästhetik-Theologie-Liturgik 35) (Münster).
- APEL, W. (1958) *Gregorian chant*, Bloomington.
- ARBIB, M.A. (2012) *How the Brain Got the Language: The Mirror System Hypothesis* (New York).
- ARMSTRONG, D.F., and S.E. WILCOX (2007) *The Gestural Origin of Language* (Oxford).
- ASAD, T. (1993) *Genealogies of Religion. Discipline and Reason of Power in Christianity and Islam* (Baltimore-London).
- ASTON, M. (1993) *Faith and Fire. Popular and unpopular religion, 1350–1600* (London).
- AUERBACH, E. (2003) *Mimesis: The Representation of Reality in Western Culture*, trans. W.R. Trask (Princeton, New Jersey).
- BALDWIN, J.W. (1997) 'The Image of the jongleur in Northern France around 1200', *Speculum* 72.3, pp. 635–663.
- BANHAM, D. (1991) *Monasteriales Indicia: The Anglo-Saxon Monastic Sign Language* (Pinner).
- BARROW, J. (1996) 'The community of Worcester, 961-c.1100', in N. Brooks and C. Cubitt (eds.) *St. Oswald of Worcester: Life and Influence* (London), pp. 84–99.
- BARTLETT, R. (1982) *Gerald of Wales 1146–1223* (Oxford).
- BEADLE, R. (ed.) (1994) *The Cambridge Companion to Medieval English Theatre* (Cambridge).
- BECKWITH, S. (2001) *Signifying God: Social Relation and Symbolic Act in the York Corpus Christi Plays* (Chicago).
- BEDINGFIELD, M.B. (2002) *The Dramatic Liturgy of Anglo-Saxon England* (Anglo-Saxon Studies 1) (Woodbridge).
- BIGONGIARI, D. (1946) 'Were there theatres in the twelfth and thirteenth centuries?', *Romanic Review* 37, pp. 201–224.

- BLAIR, J. (2005) *The Church in Anglo-Saxon Society* (Oxford).
- BLAIR, J., and G. SHARPE (eds.) (1992) *Pastoral Care before the Parish* (Leicester).
- BLAKESLEE, S. (2006) 'Cells that read minds', *New York Times* (Science section) January 10.
- BONNER, G. (ed.) (1976) *Famulus Christi: Essays in Commemoration of the Thirteenth Centenary of the Birth of the Venerable Bede* (SPCK) (London).
- BOOR, H. DE (1967) *Die Textgeschichte der lateinischen Osterfeiern* (Hermaea: germanistische Forschungen, neue Folge 22) (Tübingen).
- BORDIER, J.-P. (1985) 'Le Fils et le fruit: *Le Jeu d'Adam* entre la théologie et la myth', in H. Braet, J. Nowé and G. Tournoy (eds.) *The theatre in the Middle Ages* (Maediaevalia Lovaniensia 13.1) (Leuven), pp. 84–102.
- BOUREAU, A. (2008) *Visions of God*, in *CHC* 3, pp. 491–509.
- BOYLE, L.E. (1955) 'The *Oculus Sacerdotis* and some other works of William of Pagula', *Transactions of the Royal Historical Society*, vol. 5, pp. 81–110.
- BRADSHAW, P. (2004) *Eucharistic Origins* (London).
- BRAET, H., J. NOWÉ and G. TOURNOY (eds.) (1985) *The theatre in the Middle Ages* (Maediaevalia Lovaniensia 13.1) (Leuven).
- BRESSLOFF, P.C., J.D. COWAN, M. GOLUBITSKY, P.J. THOMAS and M.C. WIENER (2000) 'Geometric visual hallucinations, Euclidean symmetry and the functional architecture of the striate cortex', *Philosophical transactions of the Royal Society*, Series B, vol. 356, pp. 299–330.
- BROOKS, N., and C. CUBITT (eds.) (1996) *St. Oswald of Worcester: Life and Influence* (London).
- BROWN, M.P. (1996) *The Book of Cerne: Patronage and Power in Ninth-Century England (Cambridge University Library Manuscript L1.1.10)*, British Library studies in medieval culture (London-Toronto).
- BROWN, P. (1989²) *The World of Late Antiquity: AD 150–750* (New York).
- BROWN, P. (2003²) *The Rise of Western Christendom: Triumph and Diversity, AD 200–1000* (Oxford).
- BROWN, P. (1988) *The Body and Society: Men, Women, and Sexual Renunciation in Early Christianity* (New York).
- BRUCE, S.G. (2007) *Silence and Sign Language in Medieval Monasticism: The Cluniac Tradition c. 900–1200* (Cambridge Studies in Medieval Life and Thought, Fourth Series) (Cambridge).
- BUTTERWORTH, P. (2005) *Magic on the Early English Stage* (Cambridge).

- CAMPBELL, T.P. (2001) 'Liturgical drama and community discourse', in T.J. Heffernan and E.A. Matter (eds.) *The Liturgy of the Medieval Church* (Kalamazoo), pp. 619–644.
- CAMPBELL, T.P. and C. DAVIDSON (eds.) (1985) *The Fleury Playbook: Essays and Studies* (EDAM Monograph Series, 7) (Kalamazoo).
- CARRUTHERS, M. (2008) *The Book of Memory: A Study of Memory in Medieval Culture* (Cambridge, 1990[1]).
- CASSIDY, B. (ed.) (1992) *The Ruthwell Cross: Papers from the Colloquium Sponsored by the Index of Christian Art, Princeton University, 8 December 1989* (Princeton).
- CHADWICK, H. (1989) 'Ego Berengarius', *Journal of Theological Studies* 40.2 (October), pp. 414–448.
- CHAMBERS, E.K. (1903) *The Medieval Stage*, 2 vols. (Oxford).
- CHOAT, M. (2002) 'The development and the usage of terms for "monks" in late antique Egypt', *JAC* 45, pp. 5–23.
- CHRISTIANSEN, M.H., and S. KIRBY (eds.) (2003) *Language Evolution* (Oxford).
- CLAYTON, M. (1990) *The Cult of the Virgin Mary in Anglo-Saxon England* (CSASE 2) (Cambridge).
- COHEN, G. (1926[2]) *Histoire de la mise en scène dans le théâtre religieux français du Moyen Âge* (Paris).
- COLDEWEY, J.C. (1975) 'The Digby Plays and the Chelmsford Records', *Research Opportunities in Renaissance Drama* 18, pp. 103–121.
- COLDEWEY, J.C. (2004) 'From Roman to Renaissance in drama and theatre', in *CHBT* 1, pp. 3–69.
- COLGRAVE, B., and R.A.B. MYRONS (eds. and trans.) (1969) *Bede's Ecclesiastical History of the English People* (Oxford Medieval Texts) (Oxford).
- COTTON, N. (1978) 'Katherine of Sutton: the first English woman playwright', *ETJ* 30, pp. 475–481.
- COUNSELL, C. (1996) *Signs of Performance: An Introduction to Twentieth-Century Theatre* (London).
- COWDREY, H.E.J. (2003) *Lanfranc: Scholar, Monk, and Archbishop* (Oxford).
- CRAIG, H. (1955) *English Religious Drama in the Middle Ages* (Oxford).
- CRÉPIN, A. (1976) 'Bede and the vernacular', in G. Bonner (ed.) *Famulus Christi: Essays in Commemoration of the Thirteenth Centenary of the Birth of the Venerable Bede* (SPCK) (London), pp. 170–192.

- CRIST, L.S. (1974) 'Le Jeu d'Adam et l'exégèse de la chute', in *Études de civilisation medieval (IXe-XIIe siècle)*: mélanges offerts à Edmond-René Labande à l'occasion de son départ à la retraite et du XXe anniversaire du C.É.S.C.M., par ses amis, ses collegues, ses eleves (Poitiers).
- CSAPO, E. and M.C. MILLER (eds.) (2007) *The Origins of Theater in Ancient Greece and Beyond: From Ritual to Drama* (Cambridge).
- DAVIDSON, C. (1991) *Illustrations of the Stage and Acting in England to 1580* (EDAM Monograph Series 17) (Kalamazoo).
- DAVIDSON, C. (ed.) (2001) *Gesture in Medieval Drama and Art* (EDAM Monograph Series 28) (Kalamazoo).
- DAVIDSON, C. (ed.) (2005) *The Dramatic Tradition of the Middle Ages* (Brooklyn).
- DAVIDSON, C. (2007) *Festivals and Plays in Late Medieval Britain* (Aldershot).
- DAVIDSON, C., and A.E. NICHOLS (eds.) (1989) *Iconoclasm vs. Art and Drama* (EDAM Monograph Series 11) (Kalamazoo).
- DAVIDSON, C., and T.H. SEILER (eds.) (1992) *The Iconography of Hell* (EDAM Monograph Series 17) (Kalamazoo).
- DAVIDSON, C., and J.H. STROUPE (eds.) (1990) *Drama in the Middle Ages: Comparative and Critical Essays. Second Series* (AMS Studies in the Middle Ages 18) (New York).
- DAVIES, N. (ed.) (1970) *Non-Cycle Plays and Fragments* (EETS SS1) (Oxford).
- DESHMAN, R. (1995) *The Benedictional of Æthelwold* (Studies in Manuscript Illumination 9) (Princeton).
- DILLER, H.-J. (1973) *Redeformen des englischen Misterienspiels* (München).
- DILLON, J. (2006) *The Cambridge Introduction to Early English Theatre* (Cambridge).
- DOBBIE, E. VAN K. (1937) *The Manuscripts of Caedmon's Hymn and Bede's Death Song* (New York).
- DODWELL, C.R. (2000) *Anglo-Saxon Gestures and the Roman Stage* (CSASE 28) (Cambridge).
- DOHRN-VAN ROSSUM G. (1996) *History of the Hour: Clocks and Modern Temporal Orders*, trans. T. Dunlap, Chicago (*Die Geschichte der Stunde: Uhren und moderne Zeitordnung*, München 1992).
- DOLAN, D. (1975) *Le drame liturgique du Pâques en Normandie et Angleterre au Moyen-âge* (Université de Poitiers 16) (Paris).
- DORIVAL, G. (1999) 'Les débuts du christianisme à Alexandrie', in *Alexandrie: Une mégapole cosmopolite* (Actes du 9ème colloque de la Villa Kérylos à Beaulieu-sur-Mer les 2&3 octobre 1998) (Paris), pp. 1–10.

- Dox, D. (2004) *The Idea of the Theater in Latin Christian Thought: Augustinus to the Fourteenth Century* (Ann Arbor).
- Duffy, E. (1992) *The Stripping of the Altars: Traditional Religion in England 1400–1580* (New Haven-London).
- Duggan, J.J. (ed.) (1975) *Oral Literature: Seven Essays* (Edinburgh).
- Dumville, D.N. (1972) 'Liturgical drama and panegyric responsory from the eight century? A re-examination of the origin and contexts of the ninth-century section of the Book of Cerne', *JTS* 23, pp. 375–406.
- Dunn, M. (2000) *The Emergence of Monasticism: From the Desert Fathers to the Early Middle Ages* (Oxford).
- Dunn, M. (2007) 'Asceticism and monasticism, II: Western', in *CHC* 2, pp. 669–690.
- Dyer, J. (1989) 'The singing of psalms in the early-medieval Office', *Speculum* 64.3, pp. 535–578.
- Edwards, O.T. (1996) 'Dynamic qualities in the medieval Office', in E.L. Lillie and N.H. Petersen (eds.) *Liturgy and the Arts in the Middle Ages: Studies in Honour of C. Clifford Flanigan* (Copenhagen), pp. 36–63.
- Ender, J. (1992) *Rhetoric and the Origins of Medieval Drama* (Rhetoric and Society) (Ithaca-London).
- Faulkner, A. (1992) 'The Harrowing of Hell at Barking Abbey and in modern production', in C. Davidson and T.H. Seiler (eds.) *The Iconography of Hell* (EDAM Monograph Series 17) (Kalamazoo), pp. 141–157.
- Ferrari, G. (1957) *Early Roman monasteries: Notes for the history of the monasteries and convents at Rome from the V through the X century* (Studi di Antichità Cristiana pubblicati per cura del Pontificio Istituto di Archeologia Cristiana 23) (Citta del Vaticano).
- Ferrari, P.F., P. Gallese, P. Rizzolatti and L. Fogassi (2003) 'Mirror neurons responding to the observation of ingestive and communicative mouth movements in the monkey ventral premotor cortex', *European Journal of Neuroscience* 17, pp. 1703–1714.
- Flanigan, C.C. (1974) 'The Roman rite and the origins of the liturgical drama', *University of Toronto Quarterly* 43, pp. 263–284.
- Flanigan, C.C. (1985) 'The traditions of medieval Latin drama and modern scholarship', in T.P. Campbell and C. Davidson (eds.) *The Fleury Playbook: Essays and Studies* (EDAM Monograph Series, 7) (Kalamazoo), pp. 1–25.
- Flanigan, C.C. (1996) 'Medieval liturgy and the arts: Visitatio Sepulchri as paradigm' in E.L. Lillie and N.H. Petersen (eds.) *Liturgy and the Arts in*

the Middle Ages: Studies in Honour of C. Clifford Flanigan (Copenhagen), pp. 9-35.
- FLANIGAN, C.C., ASHLEY, K., and P. SHEINGORN (2001) 'Liturgy as social performance: expanding the definitions', in T.J. Heffernan and E.A. Matter (eds.) *The Liturgy of the Medieval Church* (Kalamazoo), pp. 695-714.
- FLETCHER, A.J., and M. EGAN-BUFFET (1990) 'The Dublin Visitatio Sepulcri play', *PRIA Section C* 90.7, pp. 159-241.
- FLETCHER, A.J., and W. HÜSKEN (eds.) (1997) *Between Folk and Liturgy* (Amsterdam).
- FLINT, V.I.J. (2000) 'Space and discipline in early medieval Europe', in B.A. Hanawalt and M. Kobialka (eds.) *Medieval Practices of Space* (Minneapolis-London), pp. 149-166.
- FOOT, S. (1992) 'Anglo-Saxon minster: a review of terminology', in J. Blair and G. Sharpe (eds.) *Pastoral Care before the Parish* (Leicester), pp. 212-225.
- FOOT, S. (2006) *Monastic Life in Anglo-Saxon England, c. 600-900* (Cambridge).
- FRANK, S. (1964) Ἀγγελικὸς Βίος: *Begriffsanalytische und begriffsgeschichtliche Untersuchung zum „engelgleichen Leben" im frühen Mönchtum* (Beiträge zur Geschichte des alten Mönchtums und des Benediktinerordens 26) (Münster).
- FRANTZEN, A.J. (1990) *Desire for Origins: New language, Old English, and Teaching the Tradition* (New Brunswick, New Jersey).
- FRANTZEN, A.J., and J. HINES (eds.) (2007) *Cædmon's Hymn and Material Culture in the World of Bede* (Medieval European Studies 7) (Morgantown).
- FRENCH, K.L. (2001) *The People of the Parish: Community Life in a Late Medieval English Diocese* (Philadelphia).
- FRIEDMAN, M. (ed.) (1970) *Martin Buber and the Theater* (New York).
- FRY, D.K. (1974) 'Cædmon as a formulaic poet', *Forum for Modern Language Studies* 10.3, pp. 227-247.
- FULTON, R. (2002) *From Judgment to Passion: Devotion to Christ and the Virgin Mary, 800-1200* (New York).
- GALLESE, V. (2003) 'The roots of empathy: the shared manifold hypothesis and the neural basis of intersubjectivity', *Psychopathology* 36.4, pp. 171-180.
- GALLESE, V. (2008) 'Empathy, embodied Ssimulation, and the brain: commentary on Aragno and Zepf/Hartmann', *Journal of American Psychoanalytic Association* 56.3, pp. 769-781.
- GALLESE, V. (2008a) 'Il corpo teatrale: mimetismo, neuroni specchio, simulazione incarnata', *Culture Teatrali* 16, pp. 13-38.

- GALLESE, V., L. FADIGA, L. FOGASSI and G. RIZZOLATTI (1996) 'Action recognition in the premotor cortex', *Brain* 119, pp. 593–609.
- GIBSON, M. (1978) *Lanfranc of Bec* (Oxford).
- GNUESS, H. (1997) 'Origin and provenance of Anglo-Saxon manuscripts – the case of Cotton Tiberius A.III', in P.R. Ribinson and R. Zim (eds.) *Of the Making of Books: Medieval Manuscripts, their Scribes and Readers. Essays Presented to M.B. Parkes* (Aldershot), pp. 13–48.
- GOEHRING, J.E. (1999) *Ascetics, Society and the Desert: Studies in Early Egyptian Monasticism* (Harrisburg).
- GOLDSTEIN, L. (2004) *The Origin of Medieval Drama* (Madison).
- GREENFIELD, S.B., and D.G. CALDER (1986) *A New Critical History of Old English Literature* (New York).
- GRETSCH, M. (1999) *The Intellectual Foundations of the English Benedictine Reform* (Cambridge Studies in Anglo-Saxon England 25) (Cambridge).
- GROVES, B. (2007) *Texts and Traditions. Religion in Shakespeare 1592–1604* (Oxford English Monographies) (Oxford).
- HANAWALT, B.A., and M. KOBIALKA (eds.) (2000) *Medieval Practices of Space* (Minneapolis-London).
- HARDISON JR., O.B. (1965) *Christian Rite and Christian Drama in the Middle Ages: Essays on the Origin and Early History of Modern Drama* (Baltimore-London).
- HARMLESS, W. SJ (2009), *Desert Christians: An Introduction to the Literature of Early Monasticism* (Oxford).
- HEFFERNAN, T.J., and E.A. MATTER (eds.) (2001) *The Liturgy of the Medieval Church* (Kalamazoo).
- HEIDEGGER, M. (1962), *Being and Time*, trans. J. Macquarrie and E. Robinson (San Francisco).
- HEITZ, C. (1963) *Recherches sur les rapports entre architecture et liturgie à l'époque carolingienne* (Paris).
- HICKOK, G. (2014), *The Myth of Mirror Neurons: The Real Neuroscience of Communication and Cognition* (New York).
- HILL-VÁSQUEZ, H. (2007) *Sacred Players: The Politics of Response in the Middle English Religious Drama* (Washington DC).
- HINES, J. (2007) 'Changes and exchanges in Bede's and Cædmon's work', in A.J. Frantzen and J. Hines (eds.) *Cædmon's Hymn and Material Culture in the World of Bede* (Medieval European Studies 7) (Morgantown), pp. 191–220.

- HISCOCK, N. (ed.) (2003) *The White Mantle of Churches: Architecture, Liturgy, and Art Around the Millennium* (International Medieval Research, 10) (Turnhout).
- HOLLOWAY, J.B. (1990) 'The *Dream of the Rood* and the liturgical drama', in C. Davidson and J.H. Stroupe (eds.) *Drama in the Middle Ages: Comparative and Critical Essays. Second Series* (AMS Studies in the Middle Ages 18) (New York), pp. 24–42.
- HOLSCHNEIDER, A. (1968) *Die Organa von Winchester: Studien zur ältesten Repertoire polyphoner Musik* (Hildesheim).
- HUGHES, A. (1991) 'Liturgical drama: falling between the disciplines', in E. Simon (ed.) *The Theatre of Medieval Europe: New Research in Early Drama* (Cambridge), pp. 42–62.
- HUGHES, J. (1988) *Pastors and Visionaries: Religion and Secular Life in Late Mediaeval Yorkshire* (Woodbridge).
- HUNT, T. (1975) 'The unity of the *Play of Adam* (*Ordo representacionis Ade*)', *Romania* 96, pp. 368–388, 497–527.
- HUPPÉ, B.F. (1968) *Cædmon's Hymn*, in M. Stevens and J. Mandel (eds.) *Old English Literature: Twenty-two analytical essays* (Lincoln, Nebrasca), pp. 117–138.
- ILNITCHI, G. (2001) 'Music in the liturgy', in T.J. Heffernanand and E.A. Matter (eds.) *The Liturgy of the Medieval Church* (Kalamazoo), pp. 645–671.
- IZYDORCZYK, Z. (ed.) (1997) *The Medieval Gospel of Nicodemus: Texts, Intertexts, and Contexts in Western Europe* (Medieval and Renaissance Texts and Studies 158) (Tempe).
- JANSEN, K. (2009) 'The word and its diffusion', in *CHC* 4, pp. 114–132,
- JARECKI, W. (1981) *Signa Loquendi: Die cluniacensischen Signa-Listen eingeleitet und herausgegeben* (Saecula spiritalia 4) (Baden-Baden).
- JENSEN, R.M. (2006) 'Towards a Christian material culture', in *CHC* 1, pp. 568–585.
- JOHNSTON, A.F. (1996) '*What revels are in hand?* Dramatic activities sponsored by the parishes of the Thames Valley', in A.F. Johnston and W. Hüsken (eds.) *English Parish Drama* (Ludus MERTD 1) (Amsterdam), pp. 95–104.
- JONES, L.W., and C.R. MOREY (1930-1931) *The Miniatures of the Manuscripts of Terence Prior to the Thirteenth Century* (Department of Art and Archeology of Princeton University. Illuminated manuscripts of the middle ages), vol. 1: Text, vol. 2: Plates (Princeton).
- JONES, P.F. (1929) *A Concordance to the Historia Ecclesiastica of Bede* (Cambridge, Mass.).

- JONSSON, R. (1975) 'Avant-propos', in R. Jonsson (ed.), *Corpus Troporum 1: Tropes du propre de la messe Cycle de Noël* (Stockholm).
- JUDGE, E.A. (1977) 'The earliest use of monachos for „Monk" (P.Coll. Youtie 77) and the origins of monasticism', *JAC* 20, pp. 72–89.
- JUNGMANN, J.A. (1992) *The Mass of the Roman Rite: Its Origins and Development (Missarum Sollemnia)*, trans. F.A. Brunner, 2 vols. (Westminster, Maryland).
- JUSTICE, S. (1987) 'The authority of ritual in the *Jeu d'Adam*', *Speculum* 62.4, pp. 851–864.
- KELLY, H.A. (2000) *Chaucerian Tragedy* (Cambridge).
- KENDON, A. (1988) *Sign Languages of Aboriginal Australia* (Cambridge).
- KER, N.R. (1957) *Catalogue of Manuscripts Containing Anglo-Saxon* (Oxford).
- KIENZLE, B.M. (2002) 'Medieval sermons and their performance: theory and record', in C.A. Muessig (ed.) *The Sermon in the Middle Ages* (Leiden), pp. 89–124.
- KIENZLE, B.M. (2009) 'Religious poverty and the search for perfection', in *CHC* 4, pp. 39–53.
- KING, P. (2006) *The York Mystery Cycle and the Worship of the City* (Westfield Medieval Studies 1) (Cambridge).
- KNOWLES, D. (1963²) *The Monastic Order in England: A History of its Development from the Times of St Dunstan to the Fourth Lateran Council, 940–1216* (Cambridge).
- KOBIALKA, M. (1999) *This Is My Body: Representational Practices in the Early Middle Ages* (Ann Arbor).
- KOCUR, M. (2005) *We władzy teatru: Aktorzy i widzowie w antycznym Rzymie* (Wrocław).
- KOCUR, M. (2007) 'Ciało w teatrze chrześcijańskim', in A. Wieczorkiewicz and J. Bator (eds.) *Ucieleśnienia: Ciało w zwierciadle współczesnej humanistyki. Myśl. Praktyka. Reprezentacja* (Warszawa), pp. 199–217.
- KOCUR, M. (2007a) 'Tragedia jako objawienie: Geneza tragiczności chrześcijańskiej', in K. Łukaszewicz and D. Wolska (eds.), *Kultura i tragiczność* (Acta Universitatis Wratislaviensis 3038, Prace Kulturoznawcze X) (Wrocław), pp. 128–148.
- KOCUR, M. (2008) 'Papirus z *Alkestis*', *Dialog* 12, pp. 57–61.
- KOCUR, M. (2009) 'Sztuka performansu średniowiecznych parafian: Zwrot performatywny w naukach historycznych', in S. Bednarek and K. Łukasiewicz (eds.) *O kulturze i jej poznawaniu: Prace ofiarowane Profesorowi Stanisławowi Pietraszce* (Wrocław), pp. 142–152.

- KOCUR, M. (2012) *Teatr bez teatru: Performanse w Anglii Wschodniej u schyłku średniowiecza* (Wrocław).
- KOCUR, M. (2013) *Źródła teatru* (Złota Seria Uniwersytetu Wrocławskiego) (Wrocław).
- KOCUR, M. (2016) *On the Origins of Theater* (Interdisciplinary Studies in Performance 4) (Frankfurt am Main).
- KONIGSON, E. (1975) *L'Espace théâtral médiéval* (Paris).
- LANCASHIRE, I. (1979) 'Ioly Wat and Malkyng: a Grimsby Puppet Play in 1431', *REEDN* 2, pp. 6–8.
- LAPIDGE, M. (1975) 'The hermeneutic style in tenth-century Anglo-Latin literature', *Anglo-Saxon England* 4, pp. 67–111.
- LAPIDGE, M. (ed.) (1999) *The Blackwell Encyclopaedia of Anglo-Saxon England* (Oxford).
- LAWLESS, G. (1987) *Augustine of Hippo and His Monastic Rule* (Oxford).
- LECLERCQ, J. (1961) *The Life of Perfection: Points of View on the Essence of the Religious State*, trans. L.J. Doyle (Collegeville).
- LERUD, T.K. (2008) *Memory, Images, and the English Corpus Christi Drama* (New York).
- LICHTHEIM, M. (1983) *Late Egyptian Wisdom in the International Context: A Study of Demotic Instructions* (Orbis biblicus et orientalis 52) (Göttingen).
- LIETZMANN, H. (1908) *Das Leben des heiligen Symeon Styliste* (TU 32.4) (Leipzig).
- LILLIE, E.L., and N.H. PETERSEN (eds.) (1996) *Liturgy and the Arts in the Middle Ages: Studies in Honour of C. Clifford Flanigan* (Copenhagen).
- LINDENBAUM, S. (2007) 'Drama as textual practice', in P. Strohm P. (ed.) *Middle English* (Oxford), pp. 386–400.
- Lipton S., 2005, '"The Sweet Lean of His Head": Writing about Looking at the Crucifix in the High Middle Ages', *Speculum* 80, pp. 1172–1208.
- LIPTON, S. (2009) 'Images and their uses', in *CHC* 4, pp. 254–282.
- LUNDBERG, M. (2011), Tonus Peregrinus: *The History of a Psalm-tone and its use in Polyphonic Music* (Farnham, 2011).
- LUTTERBACH, H. (1999) *Sexualität im Mittelalter: Eine Kulturstudie anhand von Bußbüchern des 6. bis 12. Jahrhunderts* (Beihefte zum Archiv zur Kulturgeschichte 43) (Köln-Weimar-Wien).
- MACCOBY, H. (1991) *Paul and Hellenism* (London).
- MCGEE, T. (1976) 'Liturgical placements of the "Quem quaeritis" dialogue', *Journal of the American Musicological Society* 29.1 (Spring), pp. 1–29.

- McGowan, A.B. (1997) 'Naming the feast: the 'agape' and the diversity of early Christian ritual meals', *Studia Patristica* 30, pp. 314–318.
- McKinnon, J. (ed.) (1987) *Music in Early Christian Literature* (Cambridge).
- Meredith, P. (1997) 'The Bodley Burial and Resurrection: late English liturgical drama?', in A.J. Fletcher and W. Hüsken (eds.) *Between Folk and Liturgy* (Amsterdam), pp. 133–155.
- Miyashita, Y. (1995) 'How the brain creates imagery: projection to primary visual cortex', *Science* 268, pp. 1719–1720.
- Montclos, J. de (1971) *Lanfranc et Bérengar: La controverse eucharistique du XIe Siècle* (Spicilegium sacrum Lovaniense, études et documents; fasc. 37) (Louvain).
- Muessig, C.A. (ed.) (2002) *The Sermon in the Middle Ages* (Leiden).
- Muir, L.R. (1973) *Liturgy and Drama in the Anglo-Norman Adam* (Medium Aevum monographs, new series 3) (Oxford).
- Muir, L.R. (1995) *The Biblical Drama of Medieval Europe* (Cambridge).
- Mundill, R.R. (1998) *England's Jewish Solution: Experiment and Expulsion, 1269–1290* (Cambridge).
- Newbigin, N. (1990) 'The world made flesh: the rappresentazione of mysteries and miracles in fifteenth-century Florence', in T. Verdon and J. Henderson (eds.) *Christianity and Renaissance: Image and Religious Imagination in the Quattrocento* (Syracuse), pp. 361–376.
- Niblett, R. (1995) *Roman Hertfordshire* (Stanbridge, Dorset).
- Nirenberg, D. (1996) *Communities of Violence* (Princeton).
- O'Donell, D.P. (2005) *Cædmon's Hymn: A Multimedia Study, Edition and Archive* (SEENET A.8), with the assistance of D. Collins *et al.* (Cambridge).
- O'Donell, D.P. (2007) 'Material differences: the place of Cædmon's Hymn in the history of Anglo-Saxon vernacular poetry', in A.J. Frantzen and J. Hines (eds.) *Cædmon's Hymn and Material Culture in the World of Bede* (Medieval European Studies 7) (Morgantown), pp. 15–50.
- Ogden, D.H. (2001) 'Gesture and characterization in the liturgical drama', in C. Davidson (ed.) *Gesture in Medieval Drama and Art* (EDAM Monograph Series 28) (Kalamazoo), pp. 26–47.
- Ogilvy J.D.A. (1963) 'Mimi, scurrae, histriones: entertainers of the early Middle Ages', *Speculum* 38.4, pp. 603–619.
- O'Keeffe, K.O'B. (1987) 'Orality and the developing text of Caedmon's Hymn', *Speculum* 62.1, pp. 1–20.
- O'Keeffe, K.O'B. (1990) *Visible Song: Transitional Literacy in Old English Song* (Cambridge Studies in Anglo-Saxon England 4) (Cambridge).

- OTTOSEN, K. (1996) 'Liturgy as a theological place: possibilities and limitations in interpreting liturgical texts as seen for instance in the Office of the Dead', in E.L. Lillie and N.H. Petersen (eds.) *Liturgy and the Arts in the Middle Ages: Studies in Honour of C. Clifford Flanigan* (Copenhagen), pp. 168–180.
- PAGE, C. (2010) *The Christian West and Its Singers: The First Thousand Years* (New Haven-London).
- PALAZZO, É. (2008) 'Performing the liturgy', in *CHC* 3, pp. 472–488.
- PALFREY, S., and T. STERN (2007) *Shakespeare in Parts* (Oxford).
- PAYEN, J.-CH. (1972) 'Idéologie et théâtralité dans *l'Ordo Representacionis Ade*', *Études Anglaises* 25, pp. 19–29.
- PEARSON, B.A. (2006) 'Egypt', in *CHC* 1, pp. 331–350.
- PERRON, A. (2009) 'The bishops of Rome, 1100–1300', in *CHC* 4, pp. 22–38.
- PETERSEN, N.H. (2000) 'Les textes polyvalents du Quem quaeritis à Winchester au Xe siècle', *Revue de Musicologie* 86.1, pp. 105–118.
- PETERSEN, N.H. (2003) 'The representational liturgy of the *Regularis Concordia*', in N. Hiscock (ed.) *The White Mantle of Churches: Architecture, Liturgy, and Art Around the Millennium* (International Medieval Research, 10) (Turnhout), pp. 107–117.
- PETERSEN N.H. (2007) 'Representation in European devotional rituals: the question of the origin of medieval drama in medieval liturgy', in E. Csapo and M.C. Miller (eds.) *The Origins of Theater in Ancient Greece and Beyond: From Ritual to Drama* (Cambridge), pp. 329–360.
- PLANCHART, A.E. (1977) *The Repertory of Tropes at Winchester*, 2 vols. (Princeton).
- RAASTED, J. (1996) 'Length and festivity: on some prolongation techniques in Byzantine chant', in E.L. Lillie and N.H. Petersen (eds.) *Liturgy and the Arts in the Middle Ages: Studies in Honour of C. Clifford Flanigan* (Copenhagen), pp. 75–84.
- RANKIN, K.S. (1981) 'A new English source of the *Visitatio Sepulchri*', *Journal of the Plainsong and Mediaeval Music Society* 4, pp. 1–11.
- RANKIN, K.S. (1985) 'Musical and ritual aspects of *Quem quaeritis*', *Münchener Beiträge zur Mediävistik und Renaissanceforschung* 36, pp. 181–192.
- RANKIN, K.S. (1989) *The Music of the Medieval Liturgical Drama in France and England* (Outstanding dissertations in music from British universities), 2 vols. (New York-London).
- RANKIN, K.S. (1990) 'Liturgical drama', in *The New Oxford History of Music*, vol. 2: *The Early Middle Ages to 1300* (Oxford), pp. 310–356.

- Rastall, R. (1996) *The Heaven Singing: Music in Early English Religious Drama* (Woodbridge).
- Rey-Flaud, H. (1973) *Le cercle magique: Essai sur le théâtre en rond à la fin du Moyen Age* (Bibliothèque des idées) (Paris).
- Rey-Flaud, H. (1980) *Pour une dramaturgie du Moyen age* (Litteratures modernes 22) (Paris).
- Rizzolatti, G., and C. Sinigaglia (2008) *Mirrors in the Brain: How Our Minds Share Actions and Emotions*, trans. F. Anderson (Oxford).
- Robinson, P.R., and R. Zim (eds.) (1997) *Of the Making of Books: Medieval Manuscripts, their Scribes and Readers. Essays Presented to M.B. Parkes* (Aldershot).
- Rogers, N.J. (2005) 'Mechanical images at Salisbury', in C. Davidson (ed.) *The Dramatic Tradition of the Middle Ages* (Brooklyn), pp. 46–47.
- Rowntree, C.B. (1990) 'A Carthusian world view: Bodleian Manuscript E Museo 160', *Analecta Cartusiana* 35.9, pp. 5–72.
- Rubenson, S. (2007) 'Ascetism and monasticism, 1: Egypt', in *CAC* 2, pp. 637–638.
- Rubin, M. (1991) *Corpus Christi: The Eucharist in Late Medieval Culture* (Cambridge).
- Schiller, G. (1971) *Ikonographie der christlichen Kunst*, vol. 3: *Die Auferstehung und Erhöhung Christi* (Gütersloh).
- Semmler, J. (1980) 'Mönche und Kanoniker im Frankenreich Pippins III. und Karls des Großen', in Max-Planck-Institut für Geschichte (ed.), *Untersuchungen zu Kloster und Stift* (Veröffentlichungen des Max-Planck-Instituts für Geschichte 68, Studien zur Germania sacra 14) (Göttingen), pp. 78–111.
- Sharpe, K. (1979) *Sir Robert Cotton, 1586–1631: History and Politics in Early Modern England* (Oxford).
- Sheingorn, P. (1987) *The Easter Sepulchre in England* (EDAM Reference Series, 5) (Kalamazoo).
- Sheingorn, P. (1989) '"No Sepulchre on Good Friday": the impact of the Reformation on the Easter rites in England', in C. Davidson and A.E. Nichols (eds.) *Iconoclasm vs. Art and Drama* (EDAM Monograph Series 11) (Kalamazoo), pp. 145–163.
- Simon, E. (ed.) (1991) *The Theatre of Medieval Europe: New Research in Early Drama* (Cambridge).
- Smith, A.H. (ed.) (1969) *Three Northumbrian Poems: Caedmon's Hymn, Bede's Death Song and The Leiden Riddle*, revised ed. (London).

- SMOLDON, W.L. (1980) *The Music of the Medieval Church Dramas*, ed. C. Bourgeault (London).
- SOUTHERN, R. (1957) *The Medieval Theatre in the Round: A Study of the Staging of* The Castle of Perseverance *and Related Matters* (London, 1975²).
- SPURELL, M. (1992) 'The architectural interest of the *Regularis concordia*', *ASE* 21, pp. 161–176.
- STEMMLER, T. (1970) *Liturgische Feiern und geistliche Spiele: Studien zu Erscheinungsformen des Dramatischen im Mittelalter* (Habilitationsschrift) (Tübingen).
- STEVENS, M, and J. MANDEL (eds.) (1968) *Old English Literature: Twenty-two Analytical Essays* (Lincoln, Nebrasca).
- STOCK, B. (1983) *Implication of Literacy: Written Language and Models of Interpretation in the Eleventh and Twelfth centuries* (Princeton).
- STOKOE, W.C. (1960) *Sign Language Structure: An Outline of the Visual Communication Systems of the American Deaf* (Studies in Linguistics, Occasional papers 8) (Buffalo).
- STROHM, P. (ed.) (2007) *Middle English* (Oxford).
- TAMBURR, K. (2007) *The Harrowing of Hell in Medieval England* (Cambridge).
- TARUSKIN, R. (2005) *The Oxford History of Western Music*, vol. 1: *The Earliest Notations to the Sixteenth Century* (Oxford).
- TATARKIEWICZ, W. (1965) 'Theatrica, the science of entertainment from the XIIth to th XVIIth century, *Journal of the History of Ideas* 26, pp. 263–272.
- TEMPLE, E. (1976) *Anglo-Saxon Manuscripts 900–1066* (London).
- THUNDY, Z. P. (1989) 'The Qur'ān: source or analogue of Bede's Cædmon story?', *Islamic Culture* 63, pp. 105–110.
- TYDEMAN, W. (1994) 'An introduction to medieval English theatre', in R. Beadle (ed.) *The Cambridge Companion to Medieval English Theatre* (Cambridge), pp. 1–36.
- UNWIN, K. (1939) 'The *Mystère d'Adam*: two problems', *Modern Language Review* 34, pp. 70–72.
- VAN DER WALT, A.G.P. (1986) 'Reflections of the Benedictine Rule in Bede's homiliary', *JEH* 37, pp. 367–386.
- VAN ENGEN, J. (1986) 'The "crisis of cenobitism" reconsidered: Benedictine monasticism in the years 1050–1150', *Speculum* 61, pp. 269–304.
- VERDON, T., and J. HENDERSON (eds.) (1990) *Christianity and Renaissance: Image and Religious Imagination in the Quattrocento* (Syracuse).

- WALLACE-HADRILL, J.M. (1988) *Bede's Ecclesiastical History of the English People: A Historical Commentary* (Oxford Medieval Texts) (Oxford).
- WALLIS, F. (2007) 'Cædmon's created word and the monastic encyclopedia', in A.J. Frantzen and J. Hines (eds.) *Cædmon's Hymn and Material Culture in the World of Bede* (Medieval European Studies 7) (Morgantown), pp. 80–110.
- WEIMANN, R. (1978) *Shakespeare and the Popular Tradition in the Theatre: Studies in the Social Dimension of Dramatic Form and Function* (Baltimore).
- WEIMANN, R. (2000) *Author's Pen and Actor's Voice: Playing and Writing in Shakespeare's Theatre* (Cambridge Studies in Renaissance Literature and Culture 39) (Cambridge).
- WEISER, F.X. (1958) *Handbook of Christian Feasts and Customs: The Year of the Lord in Liturgy and Folklore* (New York).
- WHITE, P.W. (2008) *Drama and Religion in English Provincial Society, 1485–1660* (Cambridge).
- WIORA, W. (1962) 'Jubilare sine verbis', in H. Angles et al. (eds.) *In memoriam Jacques Handschin* (Argentorati), pp. 39–65.
- WOOLF, R. (1963) 'The fall of man in Genesis B and in the *Mystère d'Adam*', in S.B. Greenfield (ed.) *Studies in Old English Literature in Honor of Arthur G. Brodeur* (Eugene, Oregon), pp. 187–199.
- WOOD, I.N. (2000) 'Some historical re-identifications and the Christianization of Kent', in G. Armstrong and I.N. Wood (eds.) *Christianizing Peoples and Converting Individuals* (International Medieval Research 7) (Turnhout), pp. 27–35.
- WOOD, I.N. (2008) 'The northern frontier: Christianity face to face with paganism', in *CHC* 3, pp. 230–246.
- WOOLF, R. (1972) *The English Mystery Plays* (Berkeley).
- WORMALD, P. (1976) *Bede and Benedict Bishop*, in G. Bonner (ed.) *Famulus Christi: Essays in Commemoration of the Thirteenth Centenary of the Birth of the Venerable Bede* (SPCK) (London), pp. 141–169.
- YATES, F. (1966) *The Art of Memory* (Chicago).
- YOUNG, K. (1933) *The Drama of the Medieval Church*, 2 vols. (Oxford).

Index

A

Abingdon, monastery 43, 44
Accarie, Maurice 185–187
Acts (4:32) 27
Acts of John (94–96) 152–153
Adoratio, see Cross
Aebischer, Paul 180
Ælfric of Eynsham 67, 79, 150
Ælfstan, monk 44
Aeschylus 146
– *Oresteia* 187–188
Æthelberht, king of Kent 36–38
Æthelred, abbot of Rievaulx 120–121
Æthelwold, bishop of Winchester 43–46, 67, 116, 150
Æthelwold Benedictional 96, 116
– for Candlemas (fol. 34v) 69, il. 3; for Palm Sunday (fol. 45v) 75, il. 4; for Easter (fol. 51v) 95, il. 5
Agathon, hermit 28
Aidan, monk of Iona 38
Alcuin, *Ep.* (137) 155
Albert the Great, on memory 115
albs
– Candlemas procession 68; Harrowing of Hell 126; Lent 63; Palm Sunday procession 76; Visitatio Sepulchri 92, 131
Alcuin, scholar 41
Alfred the Great, king of Wessex 18, 42
alms 54, 150, 152
Amalarius of Metz 52, 79, 157
Ambrosius, bishop of Milan 30
Ammonathas, hermit 29
Anne, prophetess 72

Anselm of Canterbury 164
Anthony the Great, hermit 28
Anub, hermit 29
Apophthegmata patrum 27
A porta inferi, antiphon 126
Aristophanes 146
Arles 31
ascetic 26–27, 30, 50–51, 134
asceticism 30, 34
Ash Wednesday 73, 177–178, 189
Athanasius, bishop of Alexandria 26
– *The Life of Anthony* 28
Augustine, first archbishop of Canterbury 36–37, 149
Augustine of Hippo 30
– *Confessions* 143; *De Genesi contra Manichaeos* 174; on singing 52; on Terence 60; on truth 55; *Praeceptum* 31; *Regula tertio* 31

B

Bale, John, *King Johan* 141
Bandinelli, Roland 163
Barking, monastery 41, 90, 122–135, 144
Basil, bishop of Caesarea 51
Bede 23, 35, 36, 39, 41–42
– *De temporum ratione* 38, 67; *Epistola ad Ecgbertum Episcopum* 42; *Historia abbatum* 39; *Historia ecclesiastica* 15–19 (il. 1), 21–24, 36–37, 41, 149
Bedingfield, M. Brandford 86, 111
Benedict Biscop (Baducin), founder of Wearmouth and Jarrow monastery 23, 38–39, 116
Benedict of Aniane, monk 149

219

Benedict of Nursia 25, 38
Benedictus, canticle 52
Benjamin, hermit 28
Berengar of Tours 161–163
Bertha, queen of Kent 37
Bessarion, hermit 29
Beverley 71–72, 121
Bevington, David 113
Book of Cerne 87–89
Boudicca 193
Boxley, monastery 140
bread 29, 70, 114
– in Eucharist 152, 154–156, 160, 162–163; monastic sign 57
Buber, Martin, *Elijah*, play 14–15
Burial, play 135–137

C
Cædmon, poet 13–24, 44, 191
– Hymn 15, 17–20
Cædmon Manuscript 175 (il. 12), 177
Caesarius of Arles, *Rule for Virgins* 31
Candlemas 67–72, 115
Candlemes Day and the Kyllyng of þe Children of Israelle, play 72
Canterbury 37, 44, 61, 70, 139, 151, 193
– catalogue of gestures 57–59
Canterbury Benedictional
– for Candlemas 68; for Palm Sunday 77
Caro mea requiescet in spe, antiphon 85
Cassian 51–52
Castle of Perseverance, play 186
celibacy 151, 156
cenobite 26
Chambers, Edmund Kerchever, on dialogue 111
Charles the Bald 161
chasuble 73

Chaucer 159
„cheironomic" notation 53, 100 (il. 6), 103–106 (il. 8, 9)
Chelmsford 72
Christina of Markyate, hermit 177
Christus resurgens, antiphon 128
Chrodegang, bishop of Metz 149
Cicero, *De oratore* (2.87.354) 115; (2.87.357) 116
circator 60
Clopper, Lawrence M. 120, 158–159
Cluny, monastery 56–57, 198
– dictionary of gestures 57–58
Cohen, Gustave 185
Coldingham, monastery 41
Compagnia delle Purificazione 72
compline 47, 50
Camulodunum (today's Colchester) 193
confession
– in art 94, 143, 164; in church 151; in monastery 54, 65
Constantinople 28
Contra Judaeos, Paganos et Arianos, sermon 168, 178, 185
Corpus Christi 78, 139, 155, 160
Cotton, Nancy 122
Cotton, Robert 45
Council of Tours 150
Cowthorpe 139
Cross
– Adoration of 82–86, 90, 94, 199; as allegory 158; as Jesus 78, 93–94, 115, 123–124, 126, 140, 199; from palm tree 77; „the real one" 27, 82
Crucem tuam adoramus Domine, antiphon 83
Crucifixion 84, 86, 114, 153
Cum inducerent Puerum, antiphon 70
Cum Rex glorie, hymn 127

Cuthbert, abbot at Wearmouth and Jarrow 41

D
Damian, Peter 163
Davidson, Clifford 137
Depositio Crucis 109, 111, 141
– in Barking 122–124; in Durham 140; in Winchester 86
Dioscorus, hermit 28
Divine Office 47–50, 57, 82, 97
Dodwell, Charles Reginald 58, 61
Domine abstraxisti, antiphon 127
Dream of the Rood 83–85
Duffy, Eamon 78
Dum ortus fuerit sol, antiphon 64
Dunstan, archbishop of Canterbury 43–44, 116
Durham 121, 140

E
Eadgar, king of England 43–44
Ecgberht, bishop of York 42
Eddius Stephanus, singing master 23
Elevatio Hostiae 139–140
– in Barking 127–128; in Durham 140; in Norwich 122
Elijah, prophet 14–15, 16
Enders, Joy 111
Eostre, goddess 38
Ephrem, hermit 29
Eriugena, John Scotus 161
Eucharist 29, 94, 148, **152–164**, 199–200
– Cædmon 24; Candlemas 70; *Regularis concordia* 54
Euphrenius, hermit 29
Eusebius, bishop 30
Eusebius, historian 26
Exodus 87
– (12:1–11) 82

Eynsham, monastery 133

F
fasting 55, 63, 73, 200
figurine of Christ 71, 77, 136, 140
Flanigan, Clifford 113–114
Fleury, monastery 43, 46, 57
Fleury plays 114

G
Gallese, Vittorio 119
Gaude et letare, antiphon 64
Gelasian Sacramentary 157
Genesis (1:1) 87; (3:1–5) 177
Genesis B 174
genuflection 64, 79, 81, 82, 88, 90, 190, 192, 199–200
Gerald of Wales 58, 61
gesture 56–60, 89, 117, 164, 194, 196, 198–199
– approval 59; beseeching 90; blessing 40; fear 59; grief 59; in early Church 156; in *Ordo representacionis Ade* 184, 187, 190–192; in Roman theatre 58–60, 118; pondering 59; puzzlement 59; stealing 82; supplication 59; see also genuflection, prostration
Ghent, monastery 44, 46
Glastonbury, monastery 43
Gloria in excelsis, song 87
Gloria laus, song 77
Gorham, Geoffrey de, abbot of St Albans 177
Gospels 66, 73, 150, 153
Gospel of John 65, 82, 96, 123
– (12:12–19) 76; (18:5–7) 97; (19:5) 114
Gospel of Luke 52, 72, 96
– (2:26) 70; (2:29–30, 32 and 52) 68; (22:19) 152
Gospel of Mark 76
Gospel of Matthew 72, 76

– (7:7) 110; (21:8–9) 77; (27:51–52) 125
Gospel of Nicodemus 87–88
Gospel of Thomas (16, 49 and 75) 26
Gratian, *Decretum* (Dist. 50, c. 64) 178–180, 188
Gregory I, the Great, Pope 23, 154
– evangelization of England 34, 37–38, 149; Gregorian chanting 22; *Liber responsalis* 177; on liturgy 157; on silent Word 57; *Regula pastoralist* 42
Gregory VII, Pope 150, 161
Grotowski, Jerzy
– *Action* 51; on Performer 197–200; vibrating songs 51

H

Habitabit, antiphon 85
Hardison, Osborne Bennett 101, 108, 111, 180
Harrowing of Hell 87, 90–91
– in Barking 125–127; in *The Book of Cerne* 88–90
Hatfield, monastery 123
Heidegger, Martin 80
Heitz, Carol 94
Helen, mother to Emperor Constantine 27
Henry VIII 140
hermit 28
Hesiod, *Theogony* 15
Hieronymus 30
Hild, prioress 13–14, 21, 23
Hinkmar, archbishop of Rheims 161
Holloway, Julia Bolton 85
Honorius of Autun, *Gemma animae* 157–159
Hooper, John, bishop of Gloucester 140
Hosea (6:1–6) 82

Host 78, 86, 134, 140, 156, 160
Hrotswith, canoness and dramatist 195
Hubert of Lavardin 163
Hugh of St. Victor 112
Hughes, Andrew 101

I

Ignorantia sacerdotum, catechetical manual 151
Innocent III, Pope 121
In pace in idipsum, antiphon 85
Ioly Walte and Malkyng, puppet show 137
Issac, hermit 29
Isaac, monk 26
Isidore of Seville
– on *dramaticum* 111; on *lectio* 50; on *theatrum* 112; on tragedians 159
Isidorus of Karanis 26
Iudea et Heirusalem, antiphon 64

J

Jarrow, monastery 23, 39
Jesus
– dancing 152–153; gender status of 71; in Candlemas 69 (il. 3), 70; in Easter rites 79–81; in Palm Sunday 75–77
John, arch-cantor 23, 39
John the Dwarf, hermit 28
Jonsson, Ritva 97
Johnston, Alexandra F. 138
Josephus, hermit 29
Junod, Eric 153
Justice, Steven 189

K

Kaestli, Jean-David 153
Katherine of Sutton, abbess of Barking 122–123, 129
Knowles, David 34

L

Lanfranc of Bec, grammarian 78, 162
Lambarde, William 138
Lambeth Conference 151
Lateran councils 151
Laurentius, prior of Durham 121
lectio 22, 48–49, 154, 168
Lent 48, 55, 63, **73–74**, 177, 180, 189, 198
Leofric, bishop of Exeter 64
Lérins, monastery 31
Lichfield 121
Life of St. Machutus 76
Lincoln 121, 139
Lindisfarne, monastery 38, 42
loci, locus 40, 115–116, 143–144, 181–184, 192, 194
Londinium (today's London) 193
Louis the Pious 149
Ludus Paschalis 129

M

Macarius of Alexandria, hermit 28
Magnificat, canticle 52
Malachi (3:20) 64
Maratonios, deacon 28
Mark, hermit 28
Mass 29, 33, 42, 47, 49, 54, 65–66, 113, 115, 151, **152–159**, 169, 189
– Candlemas 67, 70; Easter 93, 97–98, 101–102, 108, 125, 133–134; Lent 73; Palm Sunday 76
McGee, Timothy 101
Meditationes vitae Christi 136
Melania the Elder 30
melismas 53–54
Mios, hermit 28
Mirk, John, *Instructions for Parish Priests* 179
mirror neurons 117, 119

mnemotechnics 115–116, 192
monachós 26
Monkwearmouth, monastery 23, 39
Monte Cassino, monastery 34
Moore, Marie Delores 108
Moses, hermit 29
Moses, prophet 14
Moue, hermit 29

N

Nebuchadnezzar, king of Babylonia 168
Nehemiah 51
neume 52–53, 98–100 (il. 6)
Nitria 30
Noomen, Willem 169, 185
Northumbria 13, 23, 37–39, 42, 89, 139
Northumbrian Priests' Law 150
Norwich 121–122
Nunc dimittis, antiphon 72

O

Odon, abbot of Cluny 43, 57
O'Donnell, Daniel 18
Old Minster, monastery in Winchester 43, 103
Ordo representacionis Ade, play 113, 120, 144, 147, 159, **165–191**, 195
O rex gentium, antiphon 44
Orietur sicut sol, antiphon 64
Oswald, bishop of Worcester 43–45, 55
Oswald, king of Northumbria 38

P

Pachomius, founder of monasteries 27
Palestine 27
Paschasius Radbertus, abbot of Corbie 160–162

223

Paul, the Apostle
- I Corinthians (11:21) 155, (11:24–27) 152; Galatians (1:1) 15–16; Romans (12:1) 154
Paul, hermit 29
Pecham, John, archbishop of Canterbury 151
Placidus Varinus, abbot of Corvey 160
platea 110, 116, 143–144, 181–185, 192, 194
Pliny, *Ep.* (10.96.7) 155
Poitiers 31
polyphony 52–53
Popule meus, antiphon 82
prime 47, 49, 65, 80
procession 198
- Candlemas 67, 115; Easter 108; Elevatio 128; Lent 73; Harrowing of Hell 125, 127; Palm Sunday 75 (il. 4), 76–77, 115
prostration 54, 65, 80, 190, 199–200
Psalms
- (9) 110; (51) 48–50; (105) 110; (113 and 114) 51; (119) 47; (140) 82; in performance 50–51, 54, 64, 68, 79, 83, 92, 158
Pueri ebreorum, antiphon 76
puppets 137–138, 140–141
Putta, bishop of Rochester 23
Pythagoras 27

Q
Qolzum, mountain 28
Quinze signes du Jugement, prophecy 168

R
Rankin, Susan 101, 108
Rastall, Richard 136
Ratramnus, monk 161
Responsum accepit Symeon, antiphon 70

Resurrection, play 135–136
Rey-Flaud, Henri 181
Rhetorica ad Herennium (3.12.37) 116
Rizzolatti, Giacomo 117
Rozmital, Leon von 137–138
rubrics 88, 99, 107, 115
Rufinus of Aquileia 31
rules, monastic 13, 16, 21, 37, 58, 94, 144, 198
- of Augustine 31; of Benedictine 25, 31, **32–35** (il. 2), 41, 43–46, 50, 56, 149, 197, 199–200; of Caesarius 31; of Pachomius 27
Rupert of Deutz 164
Ruthwell Cross 85

S
Salisbury 121, 138
Salisbury Mass Book (*Missale Sarum*) 67, 76, 78
Sara, hermit 29
Schaseck 138
Seinte Resureccion, play 120
Sepulto Domino, antiphon 85
Serapion, hermit 29
sext 47, 49
Shrewsbury fragments 121–122
Sievers, Eduard 20
silence 56–57, 60–61, 79, 86, 137, 158
Simeon 68–71
Simon, hermit 29–30
Simonides of Keos 115
Sisoes, hermit 28–29
Song of Songs 112
- (3:1–2) 110
Southern, Richard 181–182
St Alban, martyr 193
St Alban's Psalter 164–165, 167 (il. 11), 176 (il. 13), 177
St Edith Convent in Wilton 133

St Gallen, monastery 53, 97, 99, 108–109
St Martial, monastery in Limoges 97–100, 108
Stoics 27
Stokoe, William 61
Super omnia ligna, antiphon 124
Surrexit Dominus, antiphon 93, 109
Symeon Stylites the Elder 27
Symons, Thomas 47, 55

T
Tacitus, Annales (14.32) 193
Taruskin, Richard 51
Te Deum, hymn 66, 93, 109, 133
Tenebrae **79–81**, 82, 87, 109, 199
Terence 59–61, 195
Theodore of Tarsus 23
Theodulf, bishop of Orléans 77
Thomas Aquinas
– on memory 115; on sight 116–117
thurible
– Candlemas 68; Mass 153; *Ordo representacionis Ade* 183; Visitatio Sepulchri 92–96 (il. 5), 110, 115, 199
Tithoes, hermit 29
Tollite portas, antiphon 126
tonsure 21–22
tonus peregrinus 51
tropes 97–109, 111
truth
– in charity 55; in liturgy 89, 93, 108, 160; in monastery 198–200; in performance 54, 119, 142–143, 145, 164; in *Tenebrae* 80
Tuotilo, monk 97

Twycross, Meg 136
Tydeman, William 122

V
Venite et uidete locum, antiphon 93
Verulamium (today's St. Albans) 193
Virgin Mary 67, 70–71, 136
virgins 30, 31, 41, 72
Visitatio Sepulchri 53, 92–96 (il. 5), 97, 108–110, 115, 116, 122, 195
– in Barking 128–133; in Braunschweig 129; in Cividale del Fiuri 129; in Dartmouth 135; in Dublin 133; in Origny-Sainte-Benoîte 129; in Taunton 135; in Wells 134–135

W
Waltham, monastery 123
Whitby, monastery 13, 18, 24, 41, 149
– Synod of 38, 63
William I, of Aquitaine 56
Winchester 25, 46, 70, 86, 116
– Synod of 52, 103, 150
Worcester, monastery 44
Wulfstan, archbishop of York 73, 79, 150

Y
York 121, 144
Young, Karl
– on Barking 127; on impersonation 111; on trope *Quem quaeritis* 101, 108

Interdisciplinary Studies in Performance

Edited by Mirosław Kocur

The series aims at presenting innovative cross disciplinary and intercultural research in performance practice and theory. Its mission is to expand and enrich performance studies with new research in theatre, film, dance, ritual, and art, as well as in queer and gender studies, anthropology, linguistics, archaeology, ethnography, sociology, history, media and political sciences, and even medicine and biology. The series focuses on promoting groundbreaking methodologies and new directions in studying performative culture by scrutinizing its transformative and transgressive aspects.

The series Interdisciplinary Studies in Performance publishes in English and German monographs and thematic collections of papers by scholars from Poland and from abroad.

Vol. 1   Paul Martin Langner / Agata Mirecka (Hrsg.): Tendenzen der zeitgenössischen Dramatik. 2015.

Vol. 2   Veronika Darian / Micha Braun / Jeanne Bindernagel / Mirosław Kocur (Hrsg.): Die Praxis der/des Echo. Zum Theater des Widerhalls. 2015.

Vol. 3   Magdalena Barbaruk: The Long Shadow of Don Quixote. Translated by Patrycja Poniatowska. 2015.

Vol. 4   Mirosław Kocur: On the Origins of Theater. Translated by David Malcolm. 2016.

Vol. 5   Matteo Bonfitto: The Kinetics of the Invisible. Acting Processes in Peter Brook's Theatre. 2016.

Vol. 6   Graziela Rodrigues: Dancer – Researcher – Performer: A Learning Process. 2016.

Vol. 7   Teresa Pękala (ed.): Witkacy. Logos and the Elements. Translated by Jerzy Adamko. 2017.

Vol. 8   Mirosław Kocur: The Second Birth of Theatre. Performances of Anglo-Saxon Monks. Translated by Grzegorz Czemiel. 2017.

www.peterlang.com